THE

YUKON

Life Between the Gold Rush
and the Alaska Highway

THE
YUKON

Life Between the Gold Rush
and the Alaska Highway

JOANN ROBERTSON

GRANVILLE ISLAND
PUBLISHING

Library and Archives Canada Cataloguing in Publication

Robertson, Joann, 1935–
     The Yukon : life between the gold rush and the Alaska highway / Joann Robertson.

Includes index.
ISBN 978-1-926991-09-2

     1. Robertson, Joann, 1935–. 2. Frontier and pioneer life—Yukon. 3. Yukon—Biography. I. Title.

FC4023.1.R618A3 2012   971.9'102092   C2012-901899-6

Copy Editor: Kyle Hawke
Cover and Text Designer: Alisha Whitley

Granville Island Publishing
212–1656 Duranleau St.
Vancouver, BC
Canada V6H 3S4
www.granvilleislandpublishing.com

Printed in Canada on recycled paper.

This book is dedicated to all those who share a common
Yukon history, whether they were there from its beginning
or came later, and especially to those whose families
arrived before the highways were built and the
Yukon changed forever.

When I began my research, I enlisted the
help of Alex Van Bibber. We had never met, but when I
mentioned my family name, he knew who I was instantly.
His warm reception and the discovery of a 100-year-old
connection between his wife's family and mine typified
the ties, person to person and family to family, that were
common when the Yukon Territory was large in size and
small in population. Those ties still exist today.

CONTENTS

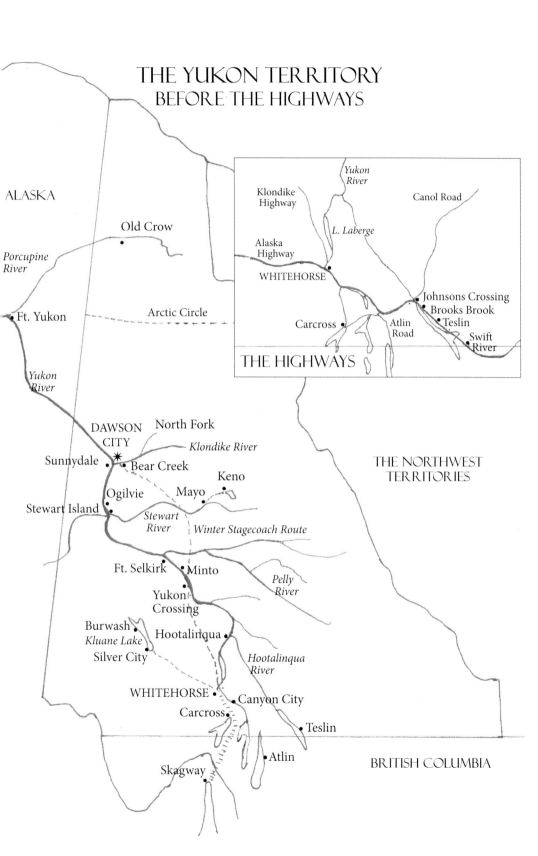

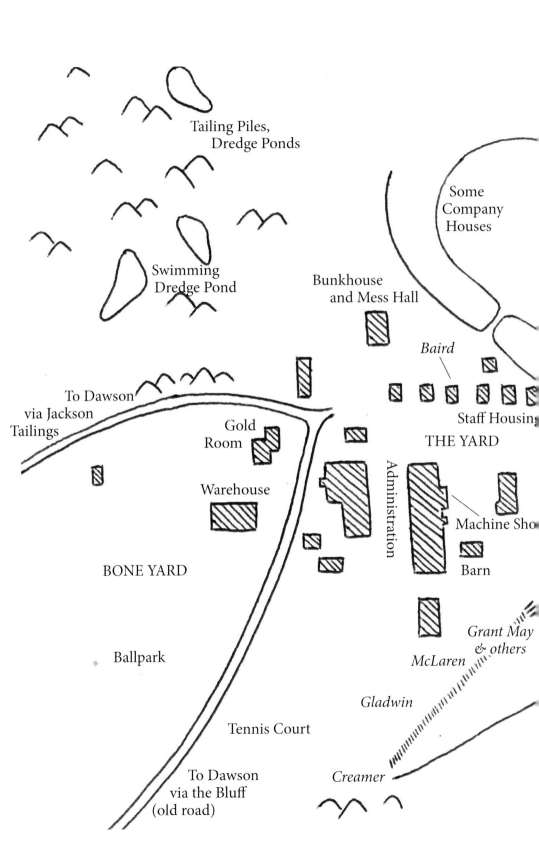

Tailing Piles,
Dredge Ponds

Some
Company
Houses

Swimming
Dredge Pond

Bunkhouse
and Mess Hall

Baird

To Dawson
via Jackson
Tailings

Gold
Room

Staff Housing

THE YARD

Warehouse

Administration

Machine Shop

BONE YARD

Barn

Ballpark

Grant May
& others

McLaren

Gladwin

Tennis Court

To Dawson
via the Bluff
(old road)

Creamer

BEAR CREEK 1935–1945

This map is Bear Creek as I remember it. There were more houses, more people, and more buildings in the camp than shown.

Dredging started in this area about 1942, eventually surrounding the island. Prior to that, besides the main slough, there were streams, sandbars with wildflowers, and a small island.

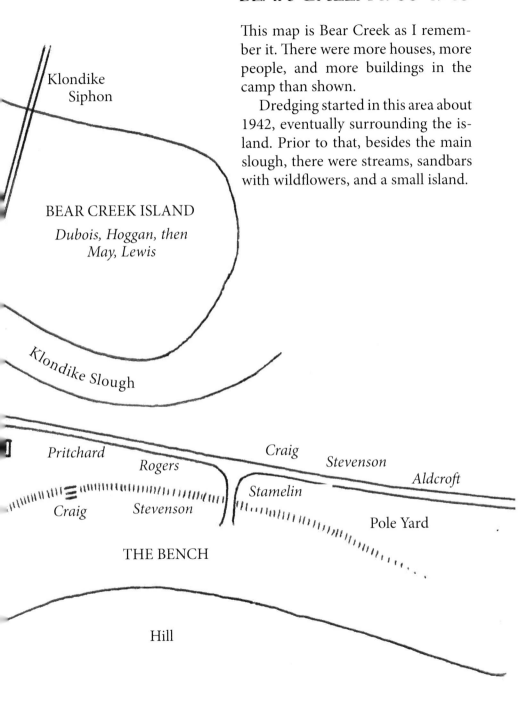

Klondike Siphon

BEAR CREEK ISLAND

Dubois, Hoggan, then May, Lewis

Klondike Slough

Pritchard

Rogers

Craig

Stevenson

Craig

Stevenson

Stamelin

Aldcroft

Pole Yard

THE BENCH

Hill

ACKNOWLEDGMENTS

This book would not have been possible without the writing of my mother, Marjorie Hoggan Stevenson. My friend Gillian Walker, Ph.D., was a tough critic and my thanks go to her for forcing me to do many revisions which made this a better book. My daughter Hillary Howlett provided an early critique. Thanks also to publisher Jo Blackmore, copyeditor Kyle Hawke, and designer Alisha Whitley.

I am fortunate to have had and am indebted to a number of people for their contributions to this book, principally Marion May Dore, her sister Doris May Chorney, Lorraine Craig Mackie, Anita Craig Mayhew, Nancy May Pope, my sister Roberta 'Bobbie' Cairns, my cousin Maribeth Tubman Mainer, Marilyn Nordale Stacy, and Betty Fournier St. Jean.

Michael Gates, retired Parks Canada employee, kindly gave me a transcript of an interview he did with my mother Marjorie and my uncle Greg in 1983. Trina Buhler of Parks Canada provided the map of the camp in Bear Creek. She also took me into the fenced camp in 2010. This was both a poignant and a happy experience.

My thanks to all of you.

INTRODUCTION

My family history in the Yukon began in 1897 when my grandfather John Edward Farnworth 'Ned' Hoggan joined the Klondike Gold Rush. Ned was born in Calcutta, India, the son and grandson of officers in the British Indian Army. At age 14, he went to Liverpool to train as a ships officer. There he qualified in both steam and sail. As a Master Mariner, he travelled all over the world, sailing out of Liverpool and Antwerp. Ned married Catherine 'Kate' Posetti in Brussels, where their first two children were born. Kate had been born in London. Her mother died when Kate was very small so her father, also a seaman, placed her in a convent to be cared for by the nuns.

Accounts differ but it is known that Ned formed a partnership with a man who was taking a large number of dogs to the Klondike. He left his ship in Boston and joined the Gold Rush. In 1897, when Ned went North, he was 33. When Kate joined him in 1899, she was 28. Their daughters, Lill and Helene, aged seven and three, were left in London. Ned and Kate spent the rest of their lives in the Yukon where they had six more children. Lill and Helene joined them as young adults.

This book was inspired by letters and news clippings sent to my grandfather's family in Scotland from 1896 to the 1930s. The material was passed along to my mother, Marjorie, their youngest daughter. She was writing memoirs and recording the stories of her elder siblings. When she went into a care facility, I kept all her papers. It seemed important to use what I had to write about a time in the history of the Yukon that is largely unknown, especially as I had access to the memoirs of other family and friends, as well as my own memories.

The book covers the time between the Gold Rush at the turn of the 20th Century, and the building of the highways in the middle of the century. It was a period of little change with a small and widely dispersed population. In 1928, the population of the Territory was only thirty-five hundred, 40 percent of whom were Native. The Territory is about the size of California or Great Britain.

The rivers were the highways. In summer, all the freight, mail, and people moved along them. In winter, there were roughly-made roads suitable for travel only when the ground was frozen and the ice-covered rivers could be crossed. Regular stagecoach service was carried out by the White Pass Company which carried mail and passengers between Whitehorse, the end of rail service from Skagway, Alaska, and other settlements. The primary one was Dawson City, the capital of the Territory. After 1921, when the coaches no longer carried mail, it was delivered by dog teams. There were freight sleighs, at first pulled by horses and later by Caterpillar tractors. People travelled via dog teams and walked, often long distances, as well. Air travel came to the Yukon in 1927 when Clyde Wann and others started carrying mail, freight, and passengers. This supplemented the other services but did not replace them. There was no regular air passenger service Outside—Outside being any place south of the 60th parallel—from Dawson City until 1937. There was no telephone service to Dawson until 1960.

The steamboats were the most used form of transportation. There were woodcutter's camps along the rivers to supply the boilers. All possible freight was shipped in summer on the boats which served the Yukon and the Alaska interior. The Canadian boats travelled down the Yukon river—which flows north, then west through Alaska emptying into the Bering Sea—to Dawson City and up the Stewart River to Mayo. American boats picked up freight and passengers in Whitehorse and went down the Yukon River into Alaska. They could stop only to take on wood, except at Dawson City where there was a customs office. The trip downstream to Dawson City took about two days; upstream to Whitehorse, four days. From Whitehorse, one took the train to Skagway, Alaska, then down the coast. Canadian Pacific Railway had ships that were on an eight or ten-day schedule. The trip down the coast to Vancouver (or Seattle on American ships) was about five days. Getting Outside could take up to ten days.

This isolation from the outside world formed the strong connections people had with each other. Their common backgrounds, experiences and knowledge of each other's families gave rise to the unique bonds and social fabric of the Territory. The question "What family are you from" might seem odd to Outsiders but it was important in establishing relationships and contacts in such a small and widely scattered population. The Vancouver Yukoners Association was formed in 1928 as a way for those Outside for the winter, or those who had moved Outside, to keep in touch. It is still an active organization. There are similar Alaskan groups on the west coast of the USA.

Recently, I met a woman at the annual Vancouver Yukoners Convention, Nancy Whitney Moulton, born in Mayo, who remembered visiting my grandfather Ned when she was a small child. He would feed them carroway seed cake he had baked and tell them stories about the old days. I never knew my grandfather as he died when I was a baby, but this illustrates the way in which we have snippets of each others history that enrich our lives and our ties. Those ties are a common theme in this book.

In 1951, the population of the Yukon Territory was still under ten thousand. The building of the Alaska Highway during World War II, and later other highways, opened the Territory to the world and changed it forever.

I have organized this book to take us from the early days of the 20th Century to the middle of the century. My hope is that the history of this in-between period, told through the lives of my family and others, will serve to bring that time alive before it is lost forever.

I have collected and collated the letters, memoirs and news clippings.

In most of the period covered by this book, Yukon was still the Yukon Territory, distances were in miles and Natives were called Indians.

.

1

OFF TO THE GOLD FIELDS

Like many men, my grandfather Ned Hoggan got caught up in the excitement engendered by news of the big gold strike in the Klondike and, like them, he was sure he would make his fortune. He had been at sea for almost 20 years and had been all over the world. Maybe he was ready for a new adventure. He was still a young man, only 33 when he left all that was familiar and set off. The environment he encountered was completely foreign to his previous life.

Much has been written about the Gold Rush and the harsh conditions faced by the men and women who went over the White Pass or Chilcoot Trail. I have edited Ned's letters because of the repetitive nature of the hardships: the up-and-down hills and gullies; the narrow trails; the danger of falling off the trail; the loads the dogs could carry; the necessity of moving one load, leaving it, and going back for the next one; the snow; the cold. The struggles that went on day after day have been written about many times. The excerpts serve to illustrate Ned's love of family and his indomitable spirit.

Ned was a prolific letter writer. Unfortunately there are periods where no letters survived, perhaps because they got passed around to various family members and were lost.

Stockyards Hotel
Hochelaga
Montreal, Canada   December 21, 1897

Dearest Mother,

    Having not quite got over the surprise of my last,
I will now endeavour to write you a full account of
my adventures as far as I have got.

    I left New York at 7.30 hours, 18th of Dec., with
a thermometer at 76 degrees. It fell to 40 degrees at
2.00 a.m. to 30 degrees. I then went to bed for they
have beds in the trains in this country. At 6.00
a.m., I got up, temperature at 10 degrees. At 9.30
a.m., arrived in Montreal, temperature 5 degrees. Not
bad in the way of changes?

    I am the second in command of this expedition
and part of my job is to move myself around
Montreal to visit all the principal wholesale houses,
harness makers, butchers, slaughter houses, flour
mills, etc. For we have 70 dogs, and they have to be
fed and exercised every day, and the beasts have a
strange desire to fight on the slightest provocation,
and they are quite a handful to look after and the
feeding and exercising with all the harness fittings,
clothing, and boot fitting, for they all have to be
provided with sleeping coats and boots to keep their
feet from freezing while working. They seem very
much surprised with their boots but I guess they will
appreciate them when the temperature falls below
50 or 60 degrees below zero.These working dogs are
exceedingly ferocious when out of harness, but whilst
working, they are quite amiable and work hard.

    The two sides of my life are very amusing. In
town, I am quite the business man and diplomat.
Down here at the stock yard, I am the roving gold

miner and dog herd. I have left my quarters at the
L.H. hotel, and I am now quartered at the Stock
Yard Hotel. My associates are drivers and cow herds,
etc. Here comes the advantage of my seafaring life,
am quite at home and get along famously with
them. The reason of my changing bids [hotels], I
found they were neglecting the dogs and so rushing
us into a lot of unnecessary expense, for 70 dogs
require a lot of looking after and the feed bills run
up very fast.

Down here, I am paying one pound per day bed
and food. The program is out at 6.00 a.m. and I am
cooking the dogs' food, then fed and exercised, then
off to town, back again to see them bedded down with
straw. Can't say I care much for the pitchfork work,
but it has to be done, so I go at it off coats as well as
my hired men have to work for shamesake when they
see me at it, but I guess they do not relish my way of
taking my money's worth out of them. I am paying
11/day per man, so I guess they have to sweat for
their money. After bedding down, off to town again
and make arrangements for next day's feed as the
menu has to be varied. One brute tried to vary the
diet by trying to eat me, but he got club sauce and is
quite content to eat the laid down bill of fare.

You will have the first nuggets, Mrs. Hoggan,
and if you please, I am not your sailor son any
longer, but the mining son. But until we move out
of this, love and kisses to all dear ones at home. I
thought of you all on Christmas Day.

Ever your dutiful and loving son,
Ned

P.S. From now on, write to Vancouver, c/o Post Office

Ned did send his first nuggets to his mother, Eleanor Hoggan. She had the gold made into a bar brooch with his name spelled out in seed pearls. He was her first-born son, born in India when she was only 17. Eleanor wore the brooch every day until she died in 1945.

Below Whitehorse Rapids   April 13

Dearest Kitty [Ned's pet name for Kate],

You must think your old man has gone out of the world. It being such a long time since you heard from him. Well, in the one sense, one is out of the world in this forsaken country but still manages to live in some way or another.

Since my last, we have travelled 150 miles and brought 2 tons of provisions along with us and it has been no small task either. Wind, snow, hail, and frost and Canadian police restrictions, all to fight against. The police instead of being here to protect the rights of people seem to be here to obstruct and hamper them in every way.

After leaving the last place I wrote from, we had to climb what they call the summit, it goes like this / and the path about 3 feet wide, one side hard rock and the other a steep precipice, in some places straight up and down, and others have a slight incline. The incline places being very dangerous for falling over, which many a poor devil did, but being so heavily covered with snow saves ones bones from being broken. The greatest danger being the sled or horse coming on top of one.

Out of all the numerous people passed up the summit, there has been no serious accident up to the time of our passing—but I am afraid that since we passed there have been one or two bad ones. But by great good fortune, we have been in good health and strength so far.

After getting to the summit, the North West Mounted Police [in 1920, the N.W.M.P. became the Royal Canadian Mounted Police (R.C.M.P.)] have tried to get all the duty they can out of one for goods bought in America or any country out of Canada and the reckon of your provisions to see if you have over 1000 lbs, or in other words, enough to last each man for one year. After all this, they put a stamp on your customs papers and tell you to go, and you go as quick as you can with a lighter pack and a great desire to get away from the N.W.M. Police.

Ned then goes on to describe the next stage of their journey in some detail giving the names of the lakes, and loads the dogs can carry according to the conditions. When he reached the end of Summit Lake, Ned wrote:

Then you come to what is called the canyon and that changes the state of affairs considerably, the trail being like a corkscrew up and down and around about each twist, rocks on one side and precipice on the other with 8 or 9 feet of snow. One poor devil fell over and we had to get ropes around his legs to get him out. At this beautiful place one can only get 150 or 200 lbs. along with 7 dogs. Well, we eventually got across with a few mild swear words and a few wallopings for the dogs.

From Hill Below the Log Cabin to Tushi Lake it was simply a horror, 100 lbs. on 7 dogs, over all sorts of ground, up hill, down hill through snow drifts. One minute you would be lying flat on your belly holding onto a rope attached to the back of the sled, to act as a brake, and next you would be at the front of the sled with a rope around your shoulder helping the dogs up the side of a hill. The next minute you would be under the sled and 2 or 3 feet of snowdrift, the sled having turned over on you, and this glorious state of affairs lasted for about 7 miles. We then struck what is called Lake Tushi and there we had a good run of 12 miles on ice with a good trail, and did we not appreciate it after the 7 miles of <u>bad</u>. I would like to use a bad word there in place of the underlined word, but since I am writing to you, I must not.

Then we had a splendid run and good weather, until the last day when we shifted camp and then we had another bad snowstorm and a devil of a struggle, we had to get our tent up. The wind is terrible in these snowstorms and you have to get under shelter as soon as possible and get the animals under shelter of trees or rocks or it will freeze them to death in a very short time. From Tushi Lake into what is called Windy Arm Lake, we had to make a portage of 3 miles and it was very good imitation of the other 7 miles we had passed over. At this point we had the satisfaction of knowing we were the farthest ahead of 600 who had landed with us. Then we started over Windy Arm, our first camp being 13 miles up the lake, a splendid sheet of fine clear ice. Dogs could draw 800 or 900 lbs. a load.

From first camp in the next shift, we made a place called Tagish House, 12 miles from our first camp. Here we had the N.W.M. Police to contend with once more. Captain being away on some duty, a sergeant was left in charge, and he was a man who liked to show his authority, so when I went and showed him my customs paper that had been passed at the summit he said that our weight of provisions was short of the government regulations. I explained that the nature of the goods we had were far and away above the required weight, but like all government officials, he was troubled with what the Americans call a "swelled head" and he would not let us pass. So the only thing left for me to do was to go back to the head of Lake Bennet and see Major Walsh, head of the N. W. M. Police. This meant a journey of 80 miles there and back. So we camped and next morning I started back at 5 a.m. with one team of dogs, 5 days food, sleeping bag and blanket and one kettle. Had a good run for 15 miles, that was at Cariboo Crossing and there it came on a snowstorm, well I kept going 'til the animals refused to face it any longer, then I made in for the shore and found a place where someone had sheltered a horse at some previous time. So that did for the dogs and myself. Made a cosy fire and boiled my kettle, had a feed, fed the dogs and then crawled into my sleeping bag and went to sleep about 7 p.m., snowing and blowing hard. Then to zero. Next morning awoke at dawn, found myself embedded in snow, the poor dogs all around me. Moved about and got the snow loosened and then crawled out of bed and lit my fire once more, boiled the kettle and made a cupful of Johnston's Fluid Beef, fed on that and a few biscuits rolled in my bag, harnessed the dogs and drove off, got into Bennet at 11 a.m. the same day. Went to see Major Walsh who gave me a pass without any trouble, but kept me waiting 3 or 4 hours for it. All the time, I wonder why government people have so little regard for time (something like you—no use for clocks). At 4 p.m., he gave me a written permit and wished me all success in my journey.

So off I started in the middle of a snowstorm and at 11 p.m., made in for the shore and found shelter

under a tree for the night for dogs and myself, cooked
some stuff to eat, what it was heaven only knows, but
it filled my belly. Fed the dogs and went to sleep.

Up at dawn next morning and off for camp where
I arrived at 4 p.m. and mighty glad I was of it, I
can tell you, for the dogs and myself were about
played out. On account of this delay, we lost 200
lbs. so that shows you how little things mount up
in this country. It costs one and a half £s. A day
to feed a dog and two and a half £s. to keep a horse,
everything is 25 £s. a hundred pounds above cost
price at Skagway and there everything is ten percent
dearer than anywhere else. For supper, bed (your own
blankets) and breakfast at Lake Bennet it costs
you 8 or 9. A meal at any place costs 11 and the
meal consists of pork and beans, bread and butter,
a cup of coffee or tea. I had to pay a £. the other day
for 6 feet of small rope. Now when we were stopped at
Bennet, it threw me out of all my reckoning of food
supplies for dogs and horse. We were making for the
head of Lake Laberge where the ice breaks up first
and one gets clear of the Whitehorse Rapids. Now the
4 days food for the animals that was consumed at
Tagish House would have just carried me to the head
of Lake Laberge whereas now I have only got clear of
the Whitehorse Rapids and there all the animal food
ran out, but hold on, I am going too fast.

We left Tagish House with a permit in our pockets
and a great hassle on ourselves. The first day we
did 14 miles over Lake Marsh and it was a tough
day I can tell you, there had been a slight snowfall
during the night and the snow had drifted over the
trail, which made it very heavy work pulling the
sleds, and at the lower end of Lake Marsh the ice
was giving out and we had the devils own job to get

the dogs to face the cold water and it was no fun for ourselves, but it had to be done and we did it. Then came that weary drag over the drifted trail. We got to camp ground at 7 or 8 p.m., pitched our tent, fed the dogs, had supper and went to sleep. I do not remember ever being so tired as I was that night. Next morning we went back to Tagish House for the remainder of our stuff (it takes us 2 days to shift from one place to another). You pile all your belongings on the trail side, take what you can and come back for it the next day. It is most amusing to see thousands of pounds worth of goods piled all along the roads in this country and nobody loses anything, for the penalty of stealing is death, hang a thief to the first tree is the law on the trail, and very closely it is observed.

Next morning our advance man returned and reported the road passable but that we would have to move right quick, so up we got and at it and from that time to the time we got across the river below the grand canyon [now called Myles Canyon] there was no rest for man or beast. It cost us our horse and 6 dogs and took all the life out of us—water, ice, snow. Axe and shovel at it we went, and we managed it. When we got to the foot of the canyon people advised us not to cross, but we were desperate and at it we went. 500 lbs. on a sled and 2 teams of dogs hitched on together and ourselves with ropes and up to our middles in a torrent of ice cold water and mighty little ice to support it all. Over we went and when we got across, we all shook hands with one another and were mighty pleased with ourselves. Camped, fed dogs, and slept at ease for the first time since we left Tagish House.

The last 3 miles of the road to the place where we made the desperate crossing is worth a better

description. As far as the southern end of the Grand
Canyon you come along the river bank which is
solid ice, 6 or 7 feet thick but the ice all shelves to the
river which is running in the centre at a very swift
pace, a wide opening and you have to keep a very
sharp lookout on your sleds or over you go into the
river, sled and all, and then they would draw your
club money in the morning. There would be no hope
of rescue as you would be swept under the ice at once.
After doing those miles of shelf work, you come to
the mouth of the Grand Canyon and here you would
have to stop and carry all your worldly belongings
on your back up a hill, for 300 yards the slope is at
this angle/and that knocks the stuffing out of you.
After all the stuff is at the top, you load your sleds
and proceed for 1 mile and then you lever the sleds
down a hill with a rope, the angle being about / then
you proceed for mile and again lower the sleds down
another hill, the worst brute of the lot, the angle
being straight up and down and 200 feet long.
Here one of our ropes broke and one sled had put a
soft bag of sugar on the load, and that bag of sugar
is there yet, much to our sorrow as sugar is one of
the most precious things with us, as we brought a
very small supply. This little uphill and downhill,
we had to make 5 times to get all the stuff over, so
you see, Kitty, Klondike is not all beer and skittles!
My advice to anyone who wants to start out for this
country is to stay at home, for it is simply hell on
temper and constitution. Get ahead is all that one
thinks of.

After getting over the river, we started again next
morning. We made 5 or 6 miles that just put us
clear of the rapids and all our dog food was finished.
We sent all the dogs to kingdom come, pitched our

tent, had a days rest and a wash, the first in 40 days. How is that for the height of cleanliness? Next day we started to build our saw pit to saw our planks for building a boat, and that we have been at for the last 4 days. This being Sunday, we stopped work and all indulged in a good sleep and wash. In fact, we all stripped off naked rubbing yourself with soap and spraying it off is no joke. But we were so beastly dirty it really had to be done. Washed and clean and clean clothes on is a fair treat. I often think of the days when I used to have clean clothes every other day at home and a clean shirt every day. When I come home again, will have 2 per day to make up for lost time. And I will eat beefsteak, pudding all the week round and black pudding every morning and salad every evening!

Now, there you are old girl, there you have all the news of the expedition as far as we have gone. Heaven only knows when you will get the next letter as we will be very busy for the next 14 days at least and then we will be busy getting down the river to the gold fields. There we will make our pile and then we will come home and spend it like fun. After you have read this letter send it to the General and mother and when they return it, send it to Mr. Hutchinson.

Your wandering and loving husband,
Ned

This unedited letter was published in *The Yukoner Magazine*, Issue 3, February 1997. The editor noted "Ned's spelling of place-names is often incorrect and thieves were not hanged on the trail although most stampeders thought so." The Canadian government were determined to make sure that the stampeders had enough provisions and that the laws of Canada be observed.

By the time the following letter was written, the partnership that was formed in Boston and Montreal had broken down. There were no supplies awaiting Ned in Dawson City as there should have been. Ned was on his own. He formed a new partnership with an old shipmate he met in Dawson City. They staked several claims in the Dawson area and seem to have made enough money to keep going, at least for a time. The hardships encountered on the way to Dawson continued as Ned kept trying to strike it rich, this time on Thistle Creek.

Dawson City   November 15, 1897

Dearest Mother and Dad,

My Thistle Creek claim is a fair bird, and will it need be! I will give you a description of how I got it. At 10.30, a man came to me and asked me if I felt alright for a long mush. (That is a long walk.) I said, "I am just fit for it!" Then he told me there had been a new strike 122 miles up the Yukon River, and only 35 claims staked. I said, "It is a tall order, but never venture, never win," so we put up grub for 3 weeks. Tramp on at 5.00 a.m. next morning, we put our blankets and feed in the canoe and started, thermometer at 10 above zero so we had hopes of making the Indian River.

The Yukon was running big ice floes. Seven hours after we started, we punched a hole in the canoe. Having nothing to patch it with, we pulled it out, cut off a thin slab of bacon and covered the hole and then lit a fire, melted some bacon grease, poured it over the slice and the frost froze it solid. Thermometer at zero by this time, but we had our canoe in good shape for proceeding so off we started up the river again—the way we go upstream here is one man sits in the canoe and the other pulls on a tow rope and this way we make from 10 to 15 miles a day.

After supper, we light our pipes, then get to work with the axes and chop enough wood for the night. Then get all the stuff out of the canoe and pull her out of the water. Then roll our blankets around us and sleep for the night. If you get cold, wake up, get the axe and have a little exercise in chopping wood for the fire. (You are liable to get cold once or twice during the night with the temperature at 10 or 15 below zero, for you can only afford to carry 2 blankets, weight is everything on these quick trips.) 4 a.m., up again, breakfast, and off again, ice very thick in the river but we held onto the canoe because as soon as we had to pull her out of the water, it meant only one blanket for the night as all had to be carried on your back for the rest of the trip.

Now commenced our hardship. All our worldly belongings on our backs and 87 miles of ice and snow to tramp over. Well, the first day we made 8 miles on the side ice. The next day, we made a good day—12 miles. This brought us up close to the Sixty Mile River post. The next day, we made 10 miles—next day we made up our minds to make the Stewart River. At 10 a.m., got in sight of a cabin, threw off our bundles and sat on them. Just then we saw a man outside the cabin and my partner said, "Go see if you can get any news." So off I went up to the man and said, "Good day partner, how are times?" "Oh so, and so," he said. My ear detected the old Dumphrieshire accent. "Well boy", I said. "What part of Dumphries do you come from?" "Thornhill," he replied. Before he had got the old place out of his mouth, our hands met. "Your name?" he said—and I said "Hoggan", and he said, "Ned!—by all that's holy!" We were at Dame's School together. And well I know him, Willie Johnson, they had a farm near

Ned, on right, in prospecting days

Durcester. Then out came the whiskey bottle and we drank to the old folks at home and he would not let us go until the next day. If ever I felt comfort, it was in that little log cabin at the mouth of the Stewart River.

He advised us not to start in the morning as the rest of the journey was a terror in the state of the river then, but, being Scotch, I suppose, I was stubborn and start I did, over the hardest bit of ground a man ever travelled. 3 hours after we left the cabin, it came on to snow and we went up like wild fire, and then it started to rain and all the side ice began to break away, then we had to start to climb up the hills as we could not get around the bluffs as all the ice was broken.

One hill we climbed, when we got on top of it, was the highest peak around and the snow was 3 feet thick and as cold as charity. We were wet through to the skin, all our clothes froze stiff, so as soon as we got down on the other side, we had to build a fire and dry out, and then it started to freeze again, so we camped for the night. Next morning the same thing again. Then the next day, we made the mouth of famous Thistle Creek, cold and hungry and on our last feed of chapattis. Next morning, we bought a few pounds of flour and bacon and started up the creek. Flour at 1/pound and bacon at 2/.

There were small trading posts or stores that would be built when a strike was on, close and move on when that strike ended. Entrepreneurs did much better financially that most gold-seekers.

Then we started down the river. We bought an old boat for 4 pounds, jammed her in the floe ice and drifted back to Dawson. The trip took us 17 days, and yesterday a man had the cheek to offer me 400 £s. for my claim. He heard that I was hard up and thought

he had a snap on! Instead of the claim, he nearly got
my fist in his eye! 3000 £s. is the lowest I would look
at for that claim, and then it would require a lot of
persuasion to get me to part with it at that.

Love to all,
Ever your loving and affectionate son,
Ned

My mother Marjorie notes that though there is no written record of any transaction, it is probable that Ned, having no funds with which to hire labourers, sold his claims on the creeks near Dawson, and perhaps the claim at Thistle Creek.

2

THE EARLY YEARS

Kate, an impetuous type, decided to join Ned in the Yukon, fully believing that Ned would make his fortune and they would come home rich from the gold fields. At that time in 1898, Ned was still optimistic that he would make the big strike.

There is some confusion about Kate's arrival. One account has it that Ned met her in Skagway, and another that he went to Victoria to meet her. My mother, Marjorie, said she had seen a picture of the ship on which they came north, covered with ice. It is uncertain if Kate arrived before the railway from Skagway was completed to Lake Bennett in 1899. If it was before that date, she would have had to climb the pass as Ned had done before her. If it was after that date, they could have travelled to Lake Bennett by rail and on to Whitehorse by ship or rail.

There is a gap in Ned's letters between the previous one, written November 1898, and the Boothy Creek letter, February 19, 1905. The time lines are therefore a little confusing. My mother, Marjorie, wrote the following based on what she had been told of the years between 1898 and 1905.

Marjorie—Ned gave up on prospecting, at least for a time and probably because he needed to make some money. He and Kate went to Canyon City at the head of Miles Canyon, where for a time Ned piloted loaded scows through the Canyon and Whitehorse Rapids to the town of Whitehorse for $25 per load. [The scows probably carried rail supplies to Whitehorse as the railway started construction at both ends, Skagway and Whitehorse, meeting in Carcross in July 1900.] Canyon City was about three miles above Whitehorse on what was then called the Lewes River but renamed the Yukon River in 1945. There was a wooden tramway used to carry freight around the canyon as well as the scows. Miles Canyon, now quite a tame part of the river, was very different and very treacherous until the dam above Whitehorse was built. Ned and Kate lived in a small log cabin where Dorothy Evelyn arrived in October 1900, the first of their six Yukon-born children.

In 1901, the family was living at Caribou Crossing (now Carcross) which by then was served by the railroad from Skagway to Whitehorse. Ned worked on the steamships which supplied settlements along the lakes.

In the winter of 1901/02, Ned and Kate owned, or managed, Takhini Roadhouse near Whitehorse on a winter-only road which crossed the frozen rivers. The stages could have stayed overnight and perhaps changed horses there, using four-horse teams. The drivers, or 'skinners' as they were called, were very hardy men, wore fur hats with ear flaps, and had heavy fur coats to keep out the cold. Some of them around Dawson in later years were often visitors at the Hoggan house. I remember my mother [Kate] telling how one of the skinners had, to his horror, found Dorothy in the barn, walking around under the bellies of the big draft horses, talking to them as if they were pets: "This child had no fear of anything on four legs and the horses seemed to know that they should not move or hurt her."

In and out of the kitchen, Kate helped the cook, Mrs. Ritchie, a woman who became a friend and later visited the family when they moved down the Yukon River. When the weather was not too cold, Kate and Mrs. Ritchie would take a horse and cutter to Whitehorse—Mrs. Ritchie probably drove because Kate was not very good at that sort of thing.

Ned, about 1902

Kate and Dorothy, about 1902

Ned found it hard to stay in one place so they sold the roadhouse and the family moved to Whitehorse for a time. John William was born there in 1903. The doctor in attendance for the births of Dorothy and John was Dr. Sugden, who in later years was drowned when he fell off a barge into the Yukon River.

Kate was a fun-loving woman who liked to dress well and she must have enjoyed their time in Whitehorse. The gown she wore to a ball (some references say it was North West Mounted Police Ball; others, the Commissioner's Ball) came from Paris. Ned wrote on the back of the picture "The boys said the dress 'took the biscuit'—and the bill took my breath."

Ned had been in the Yukon for seven years and was still hoping to make at least enough money to take a trip home to Scotland. He and Kate were adventurers and well-suited to the life they were leading. The hope of a big strike was still with them and when there was word of a strike in the Kluane country they moved there.

Boothy Creek   February 15, 1905

Dearest Mother,

I got yours and Bob's most welcome letters last week, also photos of you all and picture book for John. He calls it his "Violin Book", but is rather disappointed because there were no clock pictures in it. He is simply daft about clocks and his idea of a book that is great has clocks in it. Someone gave him a clock makers' catalogue and that is his most precious treasure and the little wretch tears all the advertisements of clocks out of all the magazines. He would be a good mate for young Bob out here. Dorothy and John have great times and are both looking well and some of their sayings would make a horse laugh. The little wretches never seem to feel the cold.

I have at last got my house built and a good hard job it has been. I am right on a summit and the snow is 5 and 6 feet deep all around me and it has been no joke to get the logs to build with. My house is 17 by 40 feet with a small 11 by 16 annex, and is only 16 miles from the diggings, which I hope the summer will turn out right. I have built the house at the instigation of the Bullion Creek Hydraulics who are backing me for the whole layout. [The house was probably meant to be used as a roadhouse or to house the men working the mine.]

It has cost in the neighbourhood of $700, and if all goes well, I should be clear by next June. They have also hired me to run a steamer on the lake this summer so Kate will look after the house and I will be earning money from the lake. I only hope it all pans out as it is set down and if it does, I will be able to take a run home next winter, at present my position in money matters consists of $3. But there is plenty of grub in the house and that is more than I have had for the last 2 years. Tomorrow morning, I am going out to see if I can get a mountain sheep or two to help out the expenses. I expect to be away 6 or 7 days. It is rather late in the season to go out, but I have not been able to go a mile from the house all winter and exercise and the pleasure attached and hunting will do me good. Nellie must be a beautiful girl by the photo. [Nellie is Ned's much younger sister.] Dorothy is the image of her at that age.

It was very kind of you to see the children when you were in London. [This refers to Lill and Helene, left in London when Kate joined Ned. They felt abandoned and often Ned had little money to send for their support]. I will forward some money to you as soon as I can get my hands on any, which I hope will not be long now.

Mother, I must close,
with all my love to your dear self,
from your loving and affectionate son,

Ned

Joann—Boothy Creek is not listed in *Yukon Places and Names* by R. Coutts but I assume it was in the Kluane area. There was a wagon road from Whitehorse to Burwash and Ned and Kate lived in the Kluane area at that time. My mother continues the story.

Marjorie—In the fall, they went to fish camp to hunt the winter's meat supply. While the men were hunting across the lake, Kate and the children were living in a tent. It was here that Kate faced a grizzly bear at the entrance to the tent when John cried, "Look at the big dog!" "That's not a dog," cried Dorothy, "that's a bear." Kate grabbed the only thing at hand which was a big metal bowl in which she made bread and the big sourdough spoon, and banging it fiercely did what she could to protect her children. The huge animal backed up and ambled up the beach. Kate said later, "My heart was in my mouth!" She then calmed the children and, gathering wood from the beach, built a big fire as close to the tent as she dared. She kept it going all night, but there was no more seen of the bear. Ned and Tom [Dickson] saw the fire from across the lake and, knowing something was wrong, came across to find out what it was.

After her experience facing the grizzly bear, Kate was not happy at fish camp when Ned was away, so they returned to Silver City at the head of Kluane Lake. Ned worked for a hydraulic mining company there. He had hoped for a job on a boat but since that didn't happen, he and a man named McKenzie bought two small boats. Ned, having spent three years on the training ship *Conway*, knew how to sew and mount sails made of flour sacks. He and McKenzie freighted supplies to miners and prospectors along the lake. It must have been hazardous for storms came up quickly on the lake. However, it could not have been worse than rounding Cape Horn in a storm. In the delirium of the malaria attacks that recurred throughout his life he would relive his past, shouting "Lower the top gallants" and other commands to his crew.

George Disraeli was born at Silver City in the Kluane country in 1906. Florence ('Florrie') was born in 1908, at either Jarvis Creek or Burwash, delivered by Louise Dickson, the Native wife of Tom Dickson, formerly of the North West Mounted Police (NWMP), who was Ned's hunting and prospecting partner at the time. Louise was from Carcross and was related to Skookum Jim who was a co-discoverer of the gold strike that led to the Klondike Gold Rush. [Louise was the mother of Alex Van Bibber's wife, Susan, which I learned when talking to Alex in 2010. It is in these ways that we learn bits of each other's history.]

Joann—Times were hard, and mining gave Ned and Kate no incentive to remain in the Kluane. In 1909, broke, with all their goods on a two-wheeled cart pulled by their horse, and, according to my uncle Johnny, who was then six years old," living off the land eating gophers, rice, and wild berries," they moved back to Whitehorse. Thus ended their gold-seeking days. Ned and Kate, like many, many others, had not succeeded in their dream of golden riches.

In June 1909, Ned signed on with the British Yukon Navigation company (BYN), taking a job as second mate. He was qualified to be a Captain but as captain he could not have year-round work which, with his large family, he needed. When the shipping season ended, the boats were winched ashore on logways to be kept away from the spring break-up, high water, and ice floes. Watchmen were required by the insurance companies to look after the boats and as second mate, Ned was able to work as a watchman during the winter. Ned was employed by the BYN for many years but as a watchman only in his later years. He was always referred to as Captain, probably as a mark of respect for his long years at sea and his skill as a river man.

3

HOOTALINQUA, STEWART ISLAND, AND FORT SELKIRK

The family moved to Hootalinqua in 1910. It was a small community comprising a telegraph operator, an RCMP post, and a few Indian families who might spend the summer there and move to their traplines in the winter. Robert 'Greg' MacGregor was born in 1911 in Whitehorse, Kate having taken a riverboat from Hootalinqua. He was the fifth of their six Yukon-born children.

Helene, their second daughter, who had been raised in London, England, was seventeen when she joined the family at Hootalinqua in the summer of 1913. When Lill, their other daughter, twenty-one, arrived in September of the same year, the family was together for the first time. Helene married Pete Peterson in Dawson City and they had a daughter, Doris. Helene and Doris were sent Outside to Pete's family in 1918. Pete was to join them when the last boat left in the fall. He was on the *Sophia* which went down off the Alaska coast in late October 1918. There were no survivors. The sinking of the *Sophia* was devastating to Alaskan and Yukon families and their friends. Many of the passengers had come up the Yukon River on the last steamboat of the season to Whitehorse, thence to Skagway and down the coast.

My mother Marjorie, like many youngest children in large families, believed she missed the best of times which her older siblings shared.

She, five years younger than Greg, was born in Sunnydale in 1916. She wrote these stories told to her by her brothers and sisters over the years.

Marjorie—Dorothy, who had an inquiring mind and was therefore interested in a variety of subjects, had sent Outside for instructions in taxidermy and had managed to stuff some animals which had been trapped. Lill told me of making a trip down the Thirty Mile River in a canoe in which they had 'hitched' a ride upstream on one of the steamboats to Lower Laberge. Coming back downstream in the canoe, they saw a duck with a number of ducklings and Dorothy quickly steered the canoe near them—"Oh, no!" cried Lill, thinking that her sister intended to catch some of the little ones to stuff and add to her collection. However that was not her intention—though it might have been before she heard Lill's horrified shout.

The Thirty Mile is a lovely clear stream with many small riffles and it would have been a lovely trip. There is a nice little bay at Hootalinqua and the youngsters must have had a great time swimming there during the hot summer days.

My oldest brother, Johnny, told me how he and Dorothy had crossed the Yukon River to the mouth of the Hootalinqua intending to hunt grouse on the mountains. Somehow they became lost and spent the night huddled up under a spruce tree. They must have built a fire for warmth and some protection, for it was August and the time of twenty-four-hour sunlight was long past so the night was black. They would have been aged about nine and twelve at the time. Meanwhile across the river, Mother must have wondered if she would ever see her children again. Indeed after raising such a lively brood, it's a wonder her hair did not turn grey at an early age, but remained dark to the end of her life. The lost ones arrived home in early afternoon carrying a dozen grouse and proceeded to pluck and clean them hastily in order to calm their irate mother.

Another time, Dorothy and John built a raft of dry logs and floated down to the island below, having worked mightily with the one-sweep (oar) to beach it on the island shore. George, Greg, Florrie, and Helene were with them on that trip. There was an old steamboat on the island

Johnny and George, about 1913

and they must have had a fine time climbing around the decks. The adventurers, in order to get home, had to cross the slough on the raft and walk home across the beach and over the big hill and across a small creek behind the settlement. This daring way of life was quite astounding to the sisters from England, Lillian and Helene, and they found it wonderful to be with the family of brothers and sisters they had just recently met. When Lill came downriver from Whitehorse, she was told by the captain, "There's your home!" She thought he was joking, but the boat pulled in at the island and there, in a small boat, were some of the family to meet her.

Joann—Lill, the elder of the sisters left in London, married soon after she arrived in the Yukon. Auntie, as she was called by my sister Bobbie and I and our children, was greatly loved by us all. Her upright stature and 'good' British accent belied her sense of fun and contemporary views. I had asked her about her early life and especially her feelings when she discovered the conditions under which her Yukon family lived, so different from her London home. She would not talk about it. So I was very pleased to find the following account of her Yukon life in my mother's papers. Her years at Hootalinqua were lonely ones as the rest of the family moved to Sunnydale shortly after Lill's arrival. She had written things down randomly as she remembered them. I have done my best to sort them into a coherent account without taking away her voice.

Lill—I left Liverpool, England on the *Empress of Britain* in 1912 to join my family in the Yukon. The trip took a week and then there was a long trip across Canada to Vancouver. I was met by Cousin Tom, or I should say Dr. T.R. Hoggan [Ned's cousin], who took me to his house on Harwood Street where I stayed for a week waiting for the *Princess Mary,* a C.P.R. ship which would take me to Skagway, Alaska. The trip was so exciting and as we put into different ports I was able to go ashore and look around. Alert Bay seemed to be mostly Indian people and I was very interested in their totem poles which I had never seen before, each gave a history of the family. We then went to Prince Rupert—the

Captain said it was always raining when they docked there, so he was very surprised as it was a beautiful sunny day and said it was especially for me. Our next stop was Juneau, where I saw the lovely Mendenhall Glacier. It was a very thrilling sight, I had never seen one before. Next we went to Skagway, where I disembarked. It was a strange little town and seemed to be only one street long with wooden sidewalks and a few people watching the people come off the boat. I got the train for Whitehorse there. It is one hundred miles through some of the finest scenery in the world. It was a very exciting trip over trestles and through rock tunnels. Looking down it was very awe-inspiring, and frightening too. We stopped for lunch at Lake Bennett, and had a choice of stew or baked beans, each costing a dollar. We went along Lake Bennett, just a lovely lake, and then on to Whitehorse where there were numbers of people waiting for the train to bring the mail which was eagerly waited for.

I was very disappointed to learn that my father had left earlier on the steamer *Canadian* on which he was first officer and of course couldn't wait for me. I felt lost and sat in the station wondering what I should do while waiting until evening when I could board the steamer *Casca* for the rest of the journey. Then a woman spoke to me and said she was the wife of Captain Williams, a friend of the family, and had been asked to look out for me. She was very friendly and took me to her home until I boarded the *Casca* at 3:00 am. We sailed down the river to Lake Laberge, 30 miles long and looking to me like a sea surrounded by mountains. It was late in September and the sides of the mountains were a blaze of colour. Then we entered the Thirty Mile River, such a clear blue water, full of rocks and difficult to navigate with a six-mile-an-hour current. A man had to have his wits about him to be able to steer a boat around the sharp turns of the river, especially in low water.

Turning into a bay, the Captain remarked, "That is where you are going to live." I laughed as we went by an island where there were two boats on the ways being repaired. I was told to get my suitcase and get into a launch. One of the crew carried off my trunk and I wondered where in the world I was being taken. I soon learned when the launch went back upstream and put me off at Hootalinqua. There seemed to be just four cabins. Was that the town? What a contrast to London! Some log cabins, a government telegraph office and something I noticed right away, a Union Jack flying from a long pole. For awhile I thought it was flying in my honour. I was soon informed that the flag was raised to signal there was mail to be picked up! Mother met me with the children that were born in the North, Dorothy, John, George, Florence, and Greg. Marjorie was not born until 1916. My dear sister Helene, who had come north before me because I was ill in hospital in London, was there too. How happy I was to see them all! But I had never dreamed there was a place like this. Well, I had come and there was no way I could return to England, so I made up my mind I would adjust to this strange country and try to be happy . . .

I met Jack Ward in 1913. He was the telegrapher at Hootalinqua and we were married at Lower Laberge by Reverend Blackwell from the little Anglican church in Whitehorse. We made the telegraph building very comfortable. In early June, we planted a garden. This was not very successful as the soil was mostly volcanic ash which was thrown from an eruption 1100 to 1800 years ago. It left a white deposit that can be seen on the cliffs along the Yukon river for many miles. My great joy was the fourteen-foot-tall sweet peas that I grew outside the screened porch. Passengers coming off the boats would stop and marvel at the size of the blossoms. How we cared for our gardens, covering the plants at night with newspapers so they would not be killed off with frost, which we had quite often, even in July.

In August, one could gather wild raspberries, gooseberries, black and red currants. These I would preserve for the winter. One year when the children were older, we were on a trip down the Thirty Mile when the engine of the launch stalled and we drifted onto a small island that was covered with blueberries. Needless to say, we returned many times to pick them, then we would freeze them in the icehouse my husband had built. We would have sufficient fruit to enjoy all winter.

My son Jack was born in January 1915. It was a bitter, cold winter. I was to go to the hospital in Whitehorse by dog team. But the baby refused to wait. I had one neighbour, she had no children. I had a doctor's book which we read, and after forty-eight hours of terrible labour, I had a ten-pound son. I will never forget Marie Thompson, how good and kind she was to me. I was so ill for a month, she bathed the baby and nursed me. I could not digest even soup. Marie would do everything possible to keep some food in me. I thought I was dying, but I lived to have three more children.

In June of 1917, William was born at St. Mary's Hospital in Dawson. I was afraid to go through another ordeal such as the last one so I went down in the first boat. My sister Helene was married to Pete Peterson and had a baby, Doris. Dr. Culbertson assured me I would not suffer as I had when John was born. I stayed in Dawson for three weeks, then with Helene, Doris, Jack, and William I sailed for Hootalinqua. The crew almost took over caring for the children. [This would be because Lill and Helene were Ned's daughters.] One day, I left Helene on deck with the three babies. When I returned, Helene, who was a very tiny person, was so indignant. A passenger had stopped and exclaimed, "You poor little thing. Are they all yours?" I laughed and said, "Why didn't you answer and say, 'Why, yes. I have them because it is a winter pastime here.'" My sister didn't always appreciate my humour. But over the years we have had some good chuckles over this and other Yukon memories.

In May 1918, my daughter Helene [who was always known as Babs] was born. We were still living in Hootalinqua so I was miles away from a hospital, the nearest one was in Whitehorse. I planned to go there and sent my clothes and the baby's to Whitehorse on the last boat. Mr. Cash, head of the White Pass mail service, was to come by car to Lower Laberge [this would have been a winter road over the ice in the lake], and my husband was to take me by dog team and meet him there. There was a sudden warm spell and the ice was needling in the lake. [Ice on a lake melts in such a way that the ice splinters vertically and resembles needles.] It was suggested we travel at night. I refused to go and made arrangements for my husband to deliver the baby. On the seventeenth, a small boat put in at Hootalinqua. There were two men and a woman aboard, and with the usual Yukon pleasure at having company, we invited them to stay. Mrs. Broughton was the bookkeeper at the Tantalus mine at Carmacks and was on her way there for the summer. During

Lill and son, about 1916

the night I became very sick and, as I had eaten a large tin of pineapple at one a.m., I received very little sympathy from my husband. I called Mrs. Broughton for breakfast, by that time I knew the baby was on the way. She told me she had been a nurse and she would look after me, which she did. She told me that she had her baby on the trail on the way to Fairbanks in forty-below weather. Four days later, her husband had been able to reach a trapper's cabin in which lived two men. They treated her royally, insisted in giving the baby a small poke of gold. They said the honour was theirs, and no doubt it was quite an experience for them to suddenly have a four-day-old baby arrive! This would be a topic for many an old trapper to relate and enliven the few people who would pass by on their way to a fur-trading post.

During the long winter evenings, I would make up stories to tell my children and Babs never tired of hearing of her birth. She wanted to know what she wore if all her clothes were in Whitehorse. I would tell her I wrapped her in a shawl until the first boat came from Whitehorse, bringing her clothes and mine. One day she came to me and said, "Mummy, I'm just like the baby Jesus, no clothes and born in a manger."

In 1921, we went Outside to Vancouver. We thought it would be good to get away from the cold weather. This was a wonderfully exciting experience for the children. When we left the ship, Billy looked up Granville Street and said, "What a big trail!" We lived in a hotel while we looked for a house.

We could not find a house to rent, but we found a suitable house in Burnaby and bought it. Then came the job of putting the children in school. I was so pleased to find they were all advanced and ahead of the children in their age group, [Jack was seven, William five, and Babs three] so I felt rewarded for all the time I had spent teaching them.

In April, my husband decided to return north so the plan was that I would sell the house and return to Hootalinqua while the river was still open.

The time was going quickly but money was very scarce, so it was difficult to sell the house. Many came to look at the house, but it seemed all were lookers until Mrs. O'Grady came along. She bought the house,

I sold the furniture, and two weeks later we were on our way north much to the delight of the children who made plans about what they would do when they got back. I was concerned about the schooling they should have, but I put that aside and made up my mind to enjoy the lovely trip up the coast and rest after the hectic time just passed.

Going up the coast was enjoyable and the children had fun until we got to the Queen Charlotte Sound. It was very rough and they were all sick but soon recovered until we came to Dixon Entrance, when they all got sick again. I was glad to arrive in Skagway and get on the train to Whitehorse.

The children were very tired but the steamer *Dawson* was at the dock and we were able to board it and go to bed. The crew were very happy to see the children and filled them with goodies out of the galley. The children were well-liked by all crews on the river, and when boats stopped at Hootalinqua to wood up, the men would invite them aboard for dinner. I was very proud of my family, more so when I would hear comments on how well-mannered they were, as I believe one wears good manners like a garment.

Hootalinqua looked dreary and alone after the Coast [a common term for Vancouver at the time], but it was my husband's job and where he had to be. It was such a change from Outside, the children seemed lost for awhile but, after a day or so, they settled down to lessons and the old way of living. The days were very short by then so the children played outdoors while it was light and we had lessons later. We would have lessons at odd times of the day when I was free of chores, or I would set some lessons such as reading. If it was nice out, I would omit the lessons. The children would spend hours along the river fishing, building rafts, and watching the pike in the slough and muskrats swimming under an old barge. In winter, they would put snares out to catch the rabbits we fed to the dog team.

The Eaton's catalogue is no more now but how we looked forward to its arrival in the spring and the fall! The orders went out in July when we would make our order for the winter: heavy underwear, overalls, jackets to keep out the wind which would be very bitter, especially at thirty below. There would be one toy for each child to be put under the Christmas tree. What a disappointment it would be when Eaton's substituted an article because there was no way it could be returned as the parcel usually arrived on the last boat to Dawson.

There was no school within a hundred miles of Hootalinqua, so all the school supplies came from the catalogue: blackboard, scribblers, and some readers. The children would spend hours pouring over it and learned much of their spelling by reading it. By the time the new one came, the old one was ready to be sent to the outhouse where it served a purpose too.

There was little in the way of entertainment, not even a radio. We did have a wind-up gramophone and Gilbert and Sullivan operas which we played so often we knew them by heart. I learned to telegraph and was able to read what came over the wire—some of it was not meant for a woman to hear! During World War I, I was able to read all the press reports going through to Dawson. After hours, I would 'talk' to the operator at Little Salmon. He was very young and I felt so sorry for him coming from British Columbia and not realizing how isolated he would be. I got in a lot of practice as we would discuss books and any other things we would find to talk about.

Mail came once a month by dog team. George Scott was the mail carrier then and it was a great day when he arrived with the mail and a month's supply of the *Daily Province* from Vancouver. I would read every line of each paper, found politics fascinating reading, and I very much admired Grace Lockhart, a columnist. The CCF [Co-operative Commonwealth Federation, later the New Democratic Party, was composed of democratic socialists who united to become a formal political party in 1932] were beginning to be heard and Mrs. Steeves, I think, was a member of the House in Victoria. She could really hold her own in the BC legislature. I think Harold Winch was the leader of the party.

Although we saw few people, especially in the winter, I did meet some very interesting ones. I remember one man who pulled into Hootalinqua on his way upriver to Teslin Lake to hunt moose. He came into the office to send a wire. Lying on the desk was a volume of *David Harum*, a book of mine. The man said he was the son of the author, Edward Noyes

Westcott. He said it was an original copy and signed it, saying he was living on the royalties. The first winter I was at Hootalinqua, the mail carrier was an interesting person, a graduate of Cambridge University. He looked so much like King George V, rumours were that he was the son of Madam Melba, an Australian opera singer who at one time had been the mistress of King Edward.

The odd Indian would pass on his way to his traplines. The winters were very cold. Sometimes, the temperature went as low as sixty degrees below Fahrenheit, which meant we could not stay outdoors for very long. If the weather was warm enough, we would hitch the dogs up and go for a picnic up the Hootalinqua River. We'd make a big fire and cook a steak pegged on the end of a willow stick over it and bake some potatoes. We washed it down with coffee. In 1917, the temperature registered twenty below Fahrenheit and the last boats had a hard time getting through to Dawson. The water was very low and one boat was wrecked at Five Finger Rapids. This caused great strain on the crews and the Dawson people who were waiting for their winter supplies which had to come by boat before freeze-up.

One winter Mr. and Mrs. Waller, with their daughter Doreen, came. Frank had been hired as watchman in charge of the boats, one of which was the *Canadian*. Nothing could have happened to the boats but the insurance companies needed someone to watch over them. Babs had never had a girl to play with. She was so happy to have some one other than her brothers to play with and it was good for Doreen who was an only child. She and Doreen would play house and with dolls although Babs much preferred to play out of doors where they would do things like using a pie plate to slide down the police barrack hill.

Myra Waller and I became great friends. We hiked together, played cards and at Christmas, Frank made Doreen a beautiful cookstove where the girls would bake and cook just as well as with a large stove. Myra and I made doll clothes and bedding all to be hidden away until Christmas. I did not like sewing but I carried on and felt quite virtuous. Sewing was not a talent I had, but I did knit all the socks, sweaters, and mittens.

That spring, Myra and I were fishing off the shore ice when it suddenly gave way and Myra went into the river. I grabbed her hair and yelled to

Steamboat running through an early freezing of Lake Laberge—the last boats of the season carried necessary winter supplies and were very important

my husband who was working on his boat. Myra was very tall and we had a hard time pulling her up on the ice. We finally got her out and into the house, where we wrapped her in a blanket. Frank fixed her a large glass of overproof rum which she downed, fell asleep, and woke up the next day no worse for the dunking. Of course, she took a lot of ribbing, the men saying that the rum was for 'medical purposes' and they did not consider that event as calling for a drink of their precious rum! But our adventures were not over. A few days later, we were walking on shore ice on the Thirty Mile when suddenly the ice gave way under me and I had the presence of mind to throw out my arms which caused me to dangle over the hole. Myra pulled me out or I would have drowned in the swift water running below. It was a frightening experience. I could only lie on the ice shaking before starting home. I did not get a drink of rum, but I owed my life to Myra. Alone, I would not have been able to get off the ice shelf.

Spring was always welcome and usually in May, the ice started to melt in the rivers. We would hear the water running in the creeks, find the first crocus blooming on a side hill. I would sit in the sun and enjoy the children fishing with a bent pin on a willow stick and catching greyling in the pothole below the old cabin, their excited cries when they hooked a large one. The fish were such a treat after a winter of moose and caribou meat. When they tired of that, they would make little boats out of bark and race them. They made their own fun and were never at a loss for something to do. I was a bit lax with their lessons those spring days, it meant so much to them to be free of indoor living. They would even take their lunch out and sit on a large packing case in the sun and really enjoy themselves.

Then crews would arrive in a launch from Lower Laberge to prepare the two ships that were on the ways a mile below the island. How good it was to hear news of the Outside and have someone to talk to. One spring before the Wallers came, I told Kid Marion, one of the pilots, how I wished there was a woman to talk to. He said there was a woman at Laberge who was waiting for the river to open and the boats to start running. He said he would bring her down on his next trip, just for the day. I was delighted to have a woman to talk to. I got out my nice lace tablecloth and my few nice tea cups and of course made some goodies. Kid brought her to the office, she was all smiles as I asked her to the house. I must admit my tongue was really going. She touched the tablecloth and I asked if she liked it. She just kept smiling but never said a word. Next day, Kid asked if I enjoyed the visit and I said I did, but she did not say a word the whole time. Kid laughed and said she was a mail-order bride from Poland and could not speak a word of English. Kid was well-known for his jokes and this little episode became the talk of the crews on the river. Once, a tourist asked him what the holes along the river bank were. He replied that they were where the N.W.M.P was shooting at a desperado. [They were probably cliff swallow nests.]

Joann—The Wards, Lill, Jack, and the children, Jack Jr., Bill, and Babs were at Hootalinqua until 1925, when they moved to Stewart Island. The Hoggans, Ned, Kate, George, Florrie, Greg, and Marjorie had moved to Stewart Island from Dawson in 1923. By 1923, Dorothy had been Outside to take teacher training and after teaching in Mayo, Yukon was teaching Outside. Johnny had been on his own for some time. Helene was living in Washington State, married to Jim Jones. Lill writes of their time at Stewart and Fort Selkirk.

Lill—We moved to Stewart Island in 1925 so that, with my children and my young brothers and sisters, there would be enough children for a school. Stewart, an island, was only two miles long and we lived at the mouth of the Stewart River, where it joined the Yukon in what had been the Mining Recorder Office. The school was a mile away in a large room at my parent's house. It was a bitterly cold winter and all the children got frostbitten feet and ears. This is very painful when in the process of thawing out.

When the NWMP made their patrol from Dawson, they found many tragedies, old prospectors who had been sick and without help had died. Some were found frozen on the trail, possibly on their way to Stewart.

In April, there was a break in the telegraph line between Stewart and Dawson. My husband and my young brother George went on snowshoes to find the break and repair it as there was no communication south. I had learned to telegraph and asked Bruce Watson in Whitehorse to let me receive the business going north. This he agreed to. I was petrified and sat and looked at the instrument, hardly moving. But I did the job and got less and less frightened. Although I learned telegraphy at Hootalinqua and 'talked' to others, this was the first time I was actually authorized to do so.

George and my husband were away for over a week and there was no way to get in touch with them. Suddenly the weather turned warm as a Chinook wind began to blow, there was the terrifying sound of ice in the river breaking up. At the mouth of the Stewart there were huge cakes of ice, some four feet thick and all going downriver like icebergs. The water rose over the island and almost to the door. Our house and the Mining Recorder's were the only places not under water. So my parents, with Greg, Florrie, and Marjorie, all came to us. I lifted the cellar door to get some cans to feed all the people. The water was up to the top of the cans, the labels off, and the cans floating around. With the labels off, we never knew if we would get fruit or vegetables! When the water receded some, my father and I went to the folks' home to see how it had fared. It was a terrible mess, the water had been almost up to the piano keys, and the carpets were sodden and full of silt. We dragged them to the river and got rid of as much mud as possible. All this time, we had no word of the men downriver and we all wondered where they were and if they were safe, as the water had come up so fast. Some days later, our two very tired men turned up. The water at Ogilvie had risen so high, they got on the roof of the cabin and stayed there until it receded.

There were a couple of horses and I had always been very nervous around them. One day, I opened the door and there was one right there. I gave it a carrot, thinking it would go away. I soon found I was mistaken. The outhouse was some distance from the house and on my way there, I heard something behind me, looked around and there was the horse trotting behind me! I took to my heels and ran into the outhouse. To my dismay, the horse stuck his head through the so-called window which was a cheesecloth cover nailed over the star-shaped hole in the door. I started to yell as his nose was right in my face. All I could hear was the men laughing at my predicament.

We did not stay at Stewart long as Mother and Father planned to move back to Dawson and we would not have a school, so my husband then applied for the posting at Fort Selkirk. There were other children there so we asked for a teacher and school. There were no teachers available but Pauline White, a young high-school graduate got the job. Polly, as we called her, was full of the joy of living and was so good to have around. She lived with us for the two years we were there.

Selkirk was a bigger settlement than Hootalinqua or Stewart Island and there were twelve children in the school. There were community dances, with someone to play the violin. Pauline and I made a tennis court and sent away to Eaton's for a tennis net and racquets and anxiously awaited their arrival. When they arrived, we set the net up and had a game. We left the net up and the next morning it was in holes! The dogs from the Indian Village had come down and chewed it beyond use. What to do? Then I got the idea to send to Whitehorse for some chicken wire which we strung across. The court was a huge source of amusement to the passengers on the boats when they called for mail or to send a telegraph. With nearly twenty hours of daylight, the court was well-used by everyone!

In 1927, we all went to Bill Schofield's house at midnight to hear, very faintly, a whisper from Los Angeles on his crystal set. It was talked about for days.

Pauline and I did a lot of hiking and, in winter, took the dog team out or went on snowshoes. That Easter, with school out, we decided we would take the team and go to Minto. It was about thirty miles away and they had fresh eggs, delivered by the stage. My husband tried to put a damper on our plans telling us that we would not be able to break trail ahead of the dogs. I was, and am, a very stubborn person so I decided that I was going on the trip and show that a woman could do it. We set out at six a.m. in twenty-below weather, full of vim and vigour. The team was in fine shape and raring to go. We crossed the river, the ice was about four feet thick. We started our trip in fine spirits, we sang, or at least made noises. At first, the trail wasn't too bad as we took turns riding in the sleigh and breaking trail in front of the lead dog. We rested and admired the scenery too, it was very beautiful, miles of deep snow. We were trying to get to Minto before dark as we did not want to meet a wolf or other animal on the trail. Pauline was a Yukoner and used to being in town but not the huge outdoors along the river. She was only eighteen and I loved her like a sister. It is said if you really want to find a person's disposition, travel the trail with them and see how they react to a hard trip, they will either keep their good humour or complain all the time, which neither of us did. We got very tired of snowshoeing as the snow was deep, but we finally made it to the roadhouse and were happy to have a good stew of moose meat. We rather surprised the men there who were stopping on their way to Dawson.

During the night a wind came up and when we woke, we were dismayed to see water running off the roof of the roadhouse. It was a Chinook. There was no communication to Selkirk and so no way to let anyone know we were on our way home. The dogs would sink into the deep snow and we would have to pull and push them along. With the snow melting it was very hard going and we had a big load—a large sack of mail and thirty dozen eggs. We were pleased that not one egg broke! We finally got to the river bank across from Selkirk and shouted and waved to attract attention. The ice on the river was soft and we did not have the strength to pull the heavy load and dogs across. Finally my husband and Bill Schofield, the storekeeper, came over. Pauline and I picked our way over the river, water running over our feet. Though we knew about the four feet of ice under our feet, it was still rather frightening. The men looked after the dogs and the sleigh. We were very tired and wet, had a hot rum, and went to bed. Everyone was happy to get the eggs and mail and, being young, we soon got over the rugged trail aches in our legs.

Another time, Pauline and I went to Coffee Creek twenty-five miles away on snowshoes to meet my brother George who was on his way to Stewart.

Joann—Babs, Lill's daughter and my cousin, born in 1918, adds these memories of her Yukon childhood to those of her mother.

Babs—My older brother and I were born one hundred miles from any settlement. My second brother was born in Dawson. The three of us had fun times setting snares to catch rabbits under fallen birch trees, learning to shoot a .22 rifle as soon as we could hold a gun, learning to skate when the river froze and fishing through the ice. In the summer, we floated on red five-gallon gas cans in the slough, we fished with a bent pin and string attached to a willow branch while Chum, my St. Bernard stayed close by to rescue me if necessary. My brothers and I climbed the hill behind our house to look into the eagle's nest which was a no-no as the wing span of a northern eagle is fifteen feet and a small child could have been picked up and taken away. Our special treats were the trips we took up the river in our launch to an island where we picked blueberries and, as this was near the Thirty Mile River, where it narrowed into a gorge, the grizzly bears frequented the spot to fish so we had to be alert at all times. In winter, we would hitch up our four dogs and at perhaps 20 degrees below Farenheit, travel over the ice to a favourite spot. There we would build a huge fire and bake potatoes, cook a piece of moose meat over the fire, and have a happy picnic.

I recall a time when there was a forest fire behind our cabin and the boat was made ready with food and other supplies so we could get away if any sparks fell on our cabin. Fortunately that did not happen. Another incident was when we were alone and mother brought the dogs into the house as a bear was rolling in the dust beside the window. [Sled dogs were not pets and were usually kept chained near their dog houses. The dogs were a mixed breed known as 'Indian dogs'; they may have had Husky or Malemute blood, but were not bred to be sled dogs.]

There were no medical or dentistry services of course. My father had forceps for pulling teeth and once when my mother was having a tooth removed, we three children ran to the river so we wouldn't hear her crying in pain. Another memorable time was when I was about four years old and decided to catch Monarch butterflies. I had been told not to take a glass jar to do so. Being a Taurus and strong-willed, I did not obey, fell over a rock, and ran the broken bottle into my arm. My father telegraphed to Whitehorse for directions from a doctor. He was told that the ragged flesh must be cut away to prevent it from becoming gangrenous. My mother held me while my father cut my flesh away. I was fortunate, with the clean northern air, my arm healed quite quickly and I was left with just a four-inch scar.

My mother taught us until we moved to Stewart where my school chums were my mother's siblings. My memories include walks through the bush to the slough where we were not supposed to go because of the wild animals. We watched porcupines walking the fences. We had experienced many of our dog's encounters with porcupines and having to have the quills pulled out with pliers, which is painful for them but dogs never seemed to learn to leave porcupines alone. From Stewart, we went to Selkirk where there were three other families with children so we had playmates.

We would knock down the wood piles at the mission and ring the church bell at Halloween. The bell was used to call the Indians from the upper area for church, so of course they came down and proceeded to the church. We suffered the consequences as we had to pile the wood again the next day and be reprimanded by the missionary. However, these mischievous adventures were worthwhile under the Northern Lights. We left Selkirk and moved Outside to Victoria in 1927.

Joann—Bab's brothers, William and Jack returned to the North as young men. Bill lived in Whitehorse for the rest of his life. Jack lived in Atlin, BC which was accessible by water or air only from Whitehorse until 1950 when a road was built connecting Atlin to the Alaska Highway and Carcross. Jack mined on Gold Run, Otter, Spruce, and other creeks. His five children were born there, or in Whitehorse. The family moved Outside in the mid-1950s.

4

SUNNYDALE AND DAWSON CITY

The Hoggans—Ned, Kate, Dorothy, John, George, Florrie, and Greg—who had been at Hootalinqua when Lill and Helene arrived, moved to Sunnydale, probably in 1914. It was across the Yukon River from Dawson City. Lill, married to Jack Ward, remained at Hootalinqua. Helene was married and living in Dawson.

A number of boats and barges wintered over at Sunnydale Slough. The family probably moved so that the children could attend school in Dawson City. They had not been in school since leaving Whitehorse in 1910. Ned was winter caretaker at Sunnydale as he had been at Hootalinqua and would later be at Stewart Island, working on the steamboats in the summer.

My mother Marjorie, born at Sunnydale in 1916, wrote the following. The early years at Sunnydale and Dawson were told to her by her siblings. For later years, she adds her memories.

Marjorie—We moved to Sunnydale, across the Yukon River from Dawson City when Dad became winter watchman for the British Yukon Navigation, the Company that owned the steamboats. The paddlewheel steamboats and barges were over-wintered at different locations along the Yukon River. It was there I was born on March 12, 1916, delivered

Boat steward, Johnny, Dorothy, George, Florrie, and Greg

by Dr. Culbertson who walked across the river to help Kate through her last delivery. Helene, Kate's second daughter arrived in time to give me my first bath. When I was born, I was already an aunt to Lillian's son Jack and Helene's daughter Doris. Helene told me many years later that when Greg, then five years old, was told he had a baby sister he said, "That's what mother was yelling about last night!"

There were six of us at home: Dorothy, John, George, Florence, Greg, and me, named by Helene after her friend Marjorie Hall. I did not like the name which I thought didn't fit me. I did have a number of pet names—Pup, Muggins-babe, and others. We lived in a cabin at the base of a big hill that faced the river. We lived there for two years. Next to our cabin was a long narrow cabin where Mr. and Mrs. Pinska lived in the summer. They had no children and were quite fond of the young Hoggans. I loved the water and whenever I could escape I would run down to the slough. The muddy shore was great for what we called 'pig pie', a spot we would jump up and down in and create a lovely mud hole. When I was missing, someone would be sent to find me because of course I was not to go there without a brother or sister. I would be brought home wet and muddy. Mr. Pinska told my mother he had a cure for my penchant for water. He picked me up by the heels and dunked me head first into the rainwater barrel. Rather than cure me, I liked it and begged him to do it again. So he decided the only way to keep me safe was to tie me to a tree or assign me a guard. [The Pinskas went down on the *Sophia*.]

In the spring when the ice went out, those in school were rowed across the river by Dorothy and John. One summer, the government supplied a motor launch but there were times when they had to walk up and over the big hill and catch the cable ferry across the river. On one of these walks, George, who had quarreled with his siblings, lingered far behind and was confronted by a big bear. It's hard to say who was more surprised, the animal or the boy. George ran off the path and wandered around the hill for hours. When Mother became alarmed, the whole camp went to search for him. He was found unharmed but Mother decided the direct water route was much safer. In the spring and fall when the river was thick with broken ice and could not be walked or rowed over, the children would stay with friends in Dawson.

In the North, babies were put out to 'air', winter or summer. In winter, they would be wrapped up after their bath and set out in a sleigh or buggy in summer. One sunny summer day, Mother and Mrs. Pinska were having tea and heard birds making a great outcry. Mother looked out the door and saw a lynx with its paws on the rim of my wicker buggy, looking at me. Mother grabbed the nearest thing at hand, a chair, and rushed at the lynx which quickly retreated. After that we were always told to listen to the birds, which could warn us of danger, something we always remembered.

Joann—The following account explains the family's move from Sunnydale:

Dawson Daily News	Monday November 12, 1917

Fire at Sunnydale. Mrs. Hoggan and Daughter Victims of a Lame Explosion. Both are in Hospital. Dorothy, Fourteen-year-old Girl Proves Genuine Heroine.

Mrs. Hoggan and daughter Dorothy, of Sunnydale, had a narrow escape from death Saturday evening as the result of the explosion of a kerosene lamp when near another lighted lamp. Others of the family also had a fortunate escape. The mother, Mrs. Hoggan, wife of Capt. Hoggan, well-known Yukon Steamboat man, was burned about the head and hands. Dorothy was burned about the hands. Both are in the Good Samaritan Hospital, but are doing well, and will be out within a few days.

Dorothy's case is aggravated somewhat by the exposure she suffered through her heroic efforts to save the mother and Verdun [Marjorie] the baby of the family and in her plucky work in crossing the Yukon river on the ice during a blizzard, nearly a mile distant, to obtain relief. The explosion occurred about 8 o'clock in the evening. The family was moving that day from Sunnydale to the West Dawson ship yards, where the captain is to be the watchman for the winter. Most of the goods were packed, and Mrs. Hoggan was in the act of attempting to eject some kerosene from an unlighted lamp which had a pump device attached to the side. Another lamp was burning nearby. The lamp she was working on suddenly exploded from the pressure, and threw the oil so that it ignited the clothing of Mrs. Hoggan. Little Flora 6 [Florrie was actually 10] years of age, and Verdun [Marjorie], 2 years of age, and Dorothy, were there. Mr. Hoggan and the boys were at the new home at West Dawson. The moment the flames burst out, Flora seized the baby and rushed out of doors. Dorothy picked up her mother and regardless of the flaming garments, rushed out of doors with her and rolled her in the snow, and threw a blanket over her. That quickly checked the flames. Dorothy then ran in and got a blanket, and took it out and covered the baby, to prevent her from freezing in the Northerly gale then sweeping up the river in the bleak night. This done, Dorothy helped her mother to her feet, and together they ran back to stop the flames in the house. Fortunately the walls and ceilings were lined with asbestos, and there was not much opportunity for the flames to get much of a start in the meantime, so that quick action by Mrs. Hoggan and Dorothy saved the building. They threw blankets into a tub of water and spread them over the flames, and also threw water on the flames with buckets. As soon as the flames were extinguished both mother and daughter were badly exhausted and damp, but Dorothy remained perfectly calm through the ordeal, and when the excitement was over immediately applied first aid in restoring the mother. Dorothy at every step encouraged the little mother, to divert her mind from the painful blisters about the head, and then quickly secured some olive oil and flour and made a preparation which was smeared on the burns, and it was a great relief.

Then Dorothy got the mother and the two little girls into the adjoining summer cabin, owned by A.D. Pinska.

Immediately thereafter the brave girl set out for relief, and with no wrap but a mans ordinary cloth coat over the clothing she was accustomed to wear at home she struggled the whole distance through the dark in the blinding snow and the poorly marked trail across the river to Klondike City, the nearest point to Dawson. Only the lights of town were her beacon, and the road was so heavily drifted with snow she frequently was struggling knee deep across the drifts. The temperature was near zero, and the gale piercing and the falling snow blinding.

Fortunately reaching Klondike City Dorothy got Mr. Duggan to telephone to the Greenfield & Pickering barn for a rig. She then told what had happened, and immediately Dr. Culbertson was called. George Billings took a rig and drove across to Sunnydale with the rig with Dr. Culbertson, who temporarily dressed the burns of both victims and escorted them to Good Samaritan hospital, where they are resting easily. Dorothy insisted on going back to Sunnydale with the rig after having given the alarm, and although still chattering with cold she returned to be with her mother. Another rig driven by Mr. Dillon went after Mr. Hoggan and brought him to town at once.

Dorothy learned her first aid in the Girl Guides, of which she has been a faithful member for years. She is a Native daughter of Kluane, Yukon, and one of the pluckiest and most heroic girls the Yukon has produced.

In the work of the Girl Guides Dorothy is a patrol leader, in the second class division, and has passed proficiency tests of electrician, laundress and house woman, and is recommended for the swimmer test. She is a student in the Dawson high school. Mrs. Frank Osborn, captain of the Guides, says that Dorothy rendered all first aid tests in the trying ordeal at the fire exactly according to the Baden-Powell rules. D.W.

Ballentine attempted to rush to the aid of Mrs. Hoggan with his car, but the trail across the river was too soft, and the car stalled. D.C. Upp met the returning rig with a car at Klondike City.

Joann—Dorothy was in fact seventeen when the fire occurred. When she finished high school she went Outside and took teacher training which cost $500 according to a letter Ned wrote his mother. By all accounts, Dorothy was quite a remarkable person and well thought of in Mayo, Yukon where she taught for a number of years. In a later letter to his mother, Ned reports that she was teaching in Wasa, BC and earning $125 a month. Later, she married and lived in Wardner, BC.

After the fire at Sunnydale, Ned, Kate, and the children still at home— Dorothy, John, George, Florrie, Greg, and Marjorie—moved first to West Dawson where there was another shipyard where boats wintered over, then to Dawson so the children could go to school. From there, Ned could continue his winter job as watchman for the steamboats and scows wintering at West Dawson.

Marjorie—We did not live in West Dawson and the new shipyard for long. It was downriver from Dawson and a longer walk over the river ice in winter and to the ferry landing in the summer for those going to school. I do have one memory of my brother Greg and me running around with one of my dolls. We were passing the low wood heater and my doll got tossed on it. I don't know what happened after that, perhaps the doll began to burn and remembering the fire that had burned my mother so badly the incident got firmly fixed in my mind. Years later, I asked Greg if he remembered it, but he didn't. He was 5 years older than me but always had time to play with me. Some of the happiest memories of my growing up were the things we did together. He was a wonderful brother.

Probably Dad bought the Dawson house so my siblings could go to school more easily. It was registered in my mother's name so that if anything happened to him we would at least have a home. He was subject to times of ill health. I have a picture of him and two other men

Potato pickers, Sunnydale, 1918—Dorothy on right,
cabbages in foreground and background

in quarantine for some reason in a little house on the hospital grounds. Greg remembered taking him clean clothes and some food, passing it over the fence.

Our house was a big two-storey house in town on the north end of Second Avenue. I remember that there was a newel post on the stairway. It was the joy of my life, how exciting, to start at the top and slide down, coming to a halt with a bump at the round ball at the bottom. The kitchen was in a flat-roofed addition to the house and off the kitchen there was another room, not heated. That is where the toilet was, walled off for privacy. It had a metal bucket which was emptied by the garbage man who drove what was known as the 'honey wagon'.

There was an outside stair leading to the roof which was a great place for my playmate, Edie Low, and I to play. She had come down from Hunker Creek, where their father was mining, with her two brothers and mother so the children could go to school.

Many years later, in Vancouver, Mrs. Low told me that when they arrived in Dawson, my mother called with a big pot of stew, knowing what it was like to have hungry children to feed on arrival. She had made many such moves herself and knew settling in was easier with a hot meal at hand. My memories of living in Dawson are those of a small child and somewhat fragmented. I remember that wherever we lived, we always had quantities of hot water because Dad would install pipes in the fire box of the kitchen range, and run it to a barrel on a stand behind the stove. There was a barrel for cold water or snow attached to the pipes in the stove too. A lot of snow was needed because it melts down into a disappointingly small amount of water.

Laundry was done in round tin washtubs. Dad had made a stand for the tubs with a round holder where the wringer between the wash and rinse tubs was located. The wringer had to be hand-operated, which was hard work. Sometimes laundry was dried in the house but most often it was hung out to freeze and dry. It would be brought in, stiff as boards, especially the long underwear which had been dancing in the wind, a common sight on wash lines in the winter. The thawing laundry filled the house with a lovely fresh scent which is well remembered by Yukoners. It was as if the outdoors had been brought in to clear our heads and minds of winter stuffiness. Water was either melted snow for washing or bought from the water man for twenty-five cents for a four-gallon bucket. Outside in the street was a water hydrant, a metal affair where water was piped from the power station, but not in winter as the lines would freeze. The fires were all wood and, as it was a big house, it must have cost a lot to heat.

I remember dressing by the heater in the living room each morning. The older ones would be up earlier so I had no need to jostle for a place as they did. Greg told me that he had to hurry to get to the heater before George or he would take all the socks. The woolen socks were left by the heater overnight and each boy was allowed two pairs—but George apparently liked three or four and he would simply appropriate whatever was available. Mornings must have been somewhat hectic.

Sunday dinner usually meant potatoes cooked around a roast of beef or moose, or mashed with plenty of gravy and other vegetables. Dessert would be a plum duff of some sort steamed in a five-pound lard pail and served with a sweet sauce. Ours was a hospitable home and my mother was never sure how many would be at the dinner table. Dad would invite men he met on the street to Sunday dinner and, as they appreciated a good home-cooked meal and my mother was known as a good cook, they often came. Fred Caley was a frequent diner—my parents felt sorry for the young Englishman and he was glad to join the family whenever invited. Pat Penny was often at the house and no doubt others I no longer remember. There was always plenty of 'grub' in the house winter and summer—my sister Florrie's friends and the boy's companions were always welcome. One of her friends was Gladys Sauer, whose parents had a baby. I remember seeing their house on fire and that the baby died. Mother sent Florrie to bring Gladys to our house to stay.

In Dawson, there was a bathtub on the other side of the kitchen wall. The tub stood on four legs and had a band of wood around the top. This would be filled with water on Saturday nights, the family entering the tub in descending order, the eldest to the youngest. But for some reason I was bathed in a small washtub. This led to my introduction to profanity . . .

The 'Pioneers at Home' was held each March in the A.B. Hall. It was a family gathering and there may have been entertainment, but what I remember most clearly was the long supper table piled high with food. Northern women were proud of their culinary expertise and with good reason. Some prided themselves on their baking, others on different aspects of cooking. I don't remember what my mother's specialty was but I do remember Mrs. Beaupre, a Belgian woman who was famous for her baked beans which were always there in great quantities.

I remember one dinner when I was about three or four years old, for I remember being tucked into blankets in an ice cream box nailed to a small sleigh which my father pulled. The usual Saturday scrubbing had taken place earlier. How my brothers yelled when Mother tucked each head firmly under her arm and washed their ears! I had, as usual, been washed in the small round tub. On coming back from the dinner, my father had fumbled with the door latch, gained entry, and while seeking the light switch, fell into the washtub! "Who left that #*&^%#@ tub right in front of the door. Any fool should know better than that!" Then realizing the extent of his bad language, and my mother's abhorrence of cursing, he rather shamefacedly apologized. My father was a seafaring man so had quite a large repertoire of profanity, though he never used it—except in time of total surprise such as this. I remember this as it was the only time I heard my father curse!

Joann—I have included a letter from Kate to Eleanor, Ned's mother. Kate adds an adult perspective to my mother's memories. She refers to a recurring illness Ned suffers from. We know he had malaria attacks and I suspect, from what few details we have, that he may have had hepatitis as well. Both could have been contracted when he was sailing in the Far East. Kate writes of the struggle to keep the family healthy and her pride in her children, a pride both she and Ned shared.

Dawson   May 22, 1922

Dearest Mother,

Your letter to hand today, as Ned is over at the shipyards, I thought I would answer it, as he will be two or three weeks over there. It is about 3 miles from here, down the river and seeing that the river is not safe also, or else I always send George or McGregor to him every evening. I must tell you he is regaining strength gradually of which I am very thankful indeed, for he has not been himself since last September, but I do hope by the time he has to go navigating that he will be thoroughly well. Well, one blessing, there are no idle men here. This has been a very strenuous winter for us as we have been behind in our bills. It takes all summer to pay up our bills. I just got our grocery bill today and it is $85 for the month of April. Wood is $20 per cord, we certainly burn some too, the winters are very severe. Sometimes I get disheartened, then again I stop to think of you all over there. Flour is a little cheaper now, it is only $12 per 100 lbs. My neighbours think I am a wonderful manager. Of course, we have the general routine of 3 meals a day, sometimes 4. The children have oatmeal porridge every day of their lives with canned milk and stewed fruit, which is very good for children. The midday meal consists of soup or broth and meat and potatoes and a pudding of some sort. I find it is better to feed them well. It keeps the doctors bill down. There are a lot of people here in the hospital, it is full of patients.

I am glad that I have my husband near me always. I do not expect to leave this for the outside world. Ned has been here for 24 years and I have been here for 22 so you can see we are both pioneers of the Yukon. Did you ever get that souvenir book I sent you last summer? Let me know if you did or not for things seem to go astray out here in the mails. I am pleased to hear you are all well, also all your family, as we are at present. Dorothy is making good as a school teacher, and John at his work, I expect him down from Mayo at the opening of navigation, he is such a dear, good boy, just like his old dad. Lena [Helene] is very happy living in Tacoma, Washington in the great and only United States, as they call it. Her husband is a man named Jimmy Jones. I am glad for her sake she has a good husband, and she has only one child too, as a family now is quite an expense, but still I love them all, my darlings. Florence is growing into a woman too, she is thoughtful and unselfish and is indeed a great help in the house, for here we have nine rooms and do all the washing and baking.

I wish I was near you so that I could let you taste some of my bread and tea cakes. I will be glad when we can have some shortbread, as the butter is cheaper, for that is my long suit—shortbread. Butter is only $1.50, that is 6 shillings in your money. I fear my letter is getting very monotonous but you know there is not much to write about. I hope you will keep in good health.

Yours sincerely,
Kate Hoggan

Marjorie—I remember that there was always a masked ball on New Year's Eve to which my older brothers and sister went. There were prizes for the costumes, one of which was, strangely enough, a spider about three inches long with legs made of small springs. He became, also for some strange reason, a part of our Christmas decorations. My grandmother would send parcels from Scotland to her grandchildren. I remember in one package there was a petticoat for me. I was probably about five years old at the time. I had to wear this hated garment under my school skirt. It was a long walk from our house to the school and we had to be warmly dressed. One day, when I had just stepped out of the school on my way home, the drawstring around the waist broke. To my red-faced embarrassment, down it came. I hastily bundled it up and took off at a run. I took a shortcut behind the *Dawson News* building in order to avoid the street. Arriving home, I burst into the kitchen, hurled the offending garment to the floor, shouted, "I'm never going to wear that thing again!", and rushed up the stairs in tears. My mother, patient with me as with her other fiery offspring was most sympathetic. And I never did wear that thing again.

Another parcel held a pair of black patent slippers with pointed toes and were tied with black grosgrain ribbon. I had never seen shoes like that and seized on them with cries of joy—soon to be replaced by tears for though my toes fitted in, my heels would not, try as I might. My mother said it was too bad and maybe the shoes would fit my friend Edie. "No, no, no, they are my shoes and she's not going to have them." Later when Edie came up the street from her house, my mother said, "Marge, get the shoes for Edie to try on." This was not a request, it was a direct order and in our house, Mother was to be obeyed forthwith. This was my father's way of discipline and she agreed with him. So, reluctantly, I brought the treasured shoes and Edie tried them on. They fit perfectly and I was filled with envy as she paraded up and down the living room. Of course she took them home, and I recall walking beside her down the wooden sidewalk looking longingly at my shoes twinkling along on her small feet. Strangely though, when I talked to her about this when we were middle-aged, she had no memory of it.

Years later, I was sent to Bear Creek to my brother Johnny and his wife Gladys (and two small children) so that I could take the school bus into Dawson for school. There was a girl, May, whose birthday party I was invited to. I had never been to a birthday party and looked forward to the occasion. So in my blue rayon dress from Eaton's catalogue, carrying my brown lace-up house shoes in a bag so I could change out of my felt boots, I arrived at the party. There I beheld the other four girls in party dresses, ribbons in their specially done-up hair. I had a plain Dutch cut and felt somewhat out of place. Then there was a game in which we had to sit on the floor, legs thrust out in front. Me in my brown stockings and serviceable shoes, them in white stockings and black patent Mary Janes.

When I got home, very upset, I told Gladys what had happened. Gladys had no idea how to deal with a woods child like me suddenly thrust into her home but she immediately sent to her sister in Vancouver and got Mary Janes for me. I was delighted and, after each wearing, I wiped them gently with Vaseline and wrapped them in tissue paper and put them back in their box until the next wearing.

5

LIFE ON STEWART ISLAND

I have included this news clipping because it shows the importance of the rivers in the life of the Yukon. Stewart Island, at the confluence of the Yukon and Stewart rivers, was the junction where goods and passengers transferred from one river to the other. There were a number of tiny settlements along the Stewart River. Many existed for only a short period of time, with Mayo probably the only one still in existence. The family's move to Stewart Island is also included in the clipping.

Dawson Daily News   October 1, 1923

Last Boat of the Year Goes up Stewart. Hazel B. sails for Mayo where she will go into Winter Quarters. Nasutlin off for South. List of passengers on final trip to Mayo and some for outside.

What is expected to be the last boat of the year to go up the Stewart River to Mayo got away from Stewart City at 9 o'clock this morning, when the gasoline launch Hazel B. sailed from that point. She took a little freight and a number of passengers who left at 10 o'clock yesterday morning on the steamer Nasutlin, which is on her way to

Whitehorse. The Nasutlin is not expected back here this year. The Hazel B will winter at Mayo and likely be the first boat down to Dawson in the spring. The passengers who left on the Nasutlin were:

For Mayo: J.H. Carpenter, C. Cameron, John Smaker, Louis Bowden, Fred Bishop, A. E. Lamb, Frank McNeil, V.O. Seguin, Eli Verreau

For Scroggie: Robert Patton

For Maizie May: Joe Roy

For Reindeer: G Farrer

For Indian: George Becker, J. Lennon, L. Legorio

For Stewart: Mrs. Hoggan, Florence, George, Marjorie, and McGregor Hoggan go to Stewart City to Spend Winter Captain J.E.F. Hoggan of the White Pass Service and Mrs Hoggan will spend the winter at Stewart City where Mr. Hoggan will have charge of the steamer Julia B. and several barges of the White Pass which will be in winter quarters there. Mrs. Hoggan and daughters Florence and Marjorie, sons George and McGregor left here yesterday on the Nasutlin for Stewart. Mr. Hoggan has been there for some time. Mrs. Hoggan was active in various social circles and the children were attending school and took part in the juvenile games. The boys were in the junior hockey teams. All will be missed by their Dawson friends this winter.

Joann—My mother was only seven when the family moved to Stewart Island and writes the following as she imagined it would have been.

Marjorie—I do not remember much of our move to the island at the mouth of the Stewart River where it joins the Yukon. I can imagine the packing up that must have taken place. By this time, my mother would have, of necessity, become a seasoned mover for, during her life in the Yukon, she had lived in many temporary homes and managed to make each one a happy home for her family.

There would have been the usual assortment of trunks, boxes, and various containers crammed with the household pots, pans, and the accumulation of odds and ends of her large family. I remember there were big heavy canvas bags into which blankets, sheets, and any extra clothing would be stuffed. They were very sturdy, closed with a rope drawstring, and probably some gunny sacks too. The medicine chest would certainly accompany us.

Wherever the family lived, this important item was always at hand. It was a wooden box with a hinged lid which held what would later be called a first aid kit. In this were rolled bandages, probably made from white sheets which had become thin and soft from years of use and the constant scrubbing on a washboard. In later years, how I'd wished my mother had known the joy of using an automatic washer and dryer, but looking back on her life and mine, when I too used a washboard, I know I will always be grateful for modern conveniences and hot water that gushes from a tap and does not have to be heated in a big copper boiler on the woodstove.

In the medicine chest, there would always be two bottles of Friar's Balsam, one for the family and one to be used on the dog's paws in early spring when their pads might be cut by ice on the trail, or on other cuts caused by fighting. When any of the family had a chest cold, they would be given a few drops of balsam on a teaspoon of sugar as well as a mustard plaster on the chest. Zam-Buck ointment, liniments, eucalyptus (a handkerchief well-soaked with this was used, too)—perhaps the reason that all my life I have disliked that scent! However, my brother George when he was over 80, used a few drops of eucalyptus in a humidifier, saying it eased his breathing. Perhaps it did. In the medicine chest, there would be a piece of oiled cloth, for at that time it was believed that burns healed better when covered, at least until scabs had formed. There was always a bottle of ginger extract in the kitchen, for a hot drink for a cold or stomach ache. My father used to bring us ginger in syrup, which we loved. It was in an Oriental ginger jar and though I have often looked, I have not been able to find any. Another remedy was Scott's Emulsion, which was really cod liver oil in an easier form to swallow. My brother Greg was constantly dosed with this, Mother being afraid of lung damage with him being out on the trail with his dog team in cold windy weather.

Dad, in his days at sea, had often been called upon to render first aid for injuries that had befallen crew members, for those were in the days of sailing ships, tall masts to be climbed, and sails to be let out or furled according to the weather so wherever the family lived, he was available for help in time of injury. There were many long miles to a doctor or hospital in those days, by river travel in summer, dog team in winter.

Kate would have made sure we were well-scrubbed and dressed in clean clothes, however much the boys may have protested. There were just George, Greg, Florrie, and myself home at that time. Our two older sisters were married with their own children. Johnny may have been working on the steamboats the summer of 1923 and Dorothy was in Mayo where she was teaching school.

The reason for this relocation was that Ned had been offered the position of winter watchman at Stewart where barges were wintered in the slough. So off we went to our last family home. We were leaving a comfortable two-storey house in Dawson where we had lots of room and had made many friends. We had lunch, then later dinner, in the dining room of the *Nasutlin* and were on our best behaviour. Table manners had been strictly enforced by Ned when he was home in the winter and in his absence during the summers we were not allowed any slackness. Of course, 'Cap's kids' had the run of the ship and we were quite at home with the entire crew. It was fascinating to watch firemen heaving four-foot-long spruce wood into the firebox to create the steam to move the paddlewheel. Sweat would be rolling off their muscular arms. Each member of the crew was a special person to us, but we stood somewhat in awe of the firemen. The engineer too was a friend and we watched with interest the shining pistons which turned the red paddlewheel. The engine room I remember as being so clean and the engineer was always wiping something. Of course, the biggest thrill was climb the ladder into the pilot house and be allowed to touch the shining spoked wheel which steered the ship.

In 1926, when my mother and I made a trip on the *Whitehorse* with my Dad, I received my first lesson in 'reading water'. He would say, "Pup, see that shining water over there and the dark water on the other side, now where do you think we should go?" Of course it was to the darker, deeper channel. At that time the first class fare, Dawson to Whitehorse, was $55.

My school days began in Dawson City. The large grey building erected in 1902 was quite an imposing place which might have frightened me but for the fact that older members of my family also went there. Probably, when I started, there would have been two brothers and one sister still walking each day from the north of town where we lived so I would not have had to walk alone. I have a vague recollection of some kindergarten attendance—I remember the small green chairs and little else.

At any rate, I had only one year in school when my family moved out of town and up the Yukon River to Stewart Island, at the junction of the Stewart and Yukon rivers, seventy-five miles from Dawson. There my sister, two brothers, and I were free from school, at least for a few years, until my sister Lillian with her two boys and one girl came to live at Stewart. Her husband was a government telegraph operator and had bid for the opening at Stewart. There would then be seven of school age and Stewart would be eligible for a school. This unhappy task was assigned to Hattie Stone, a recent graduate from Dawson school.

So there we were in 1925 with classes consisting of seven aunts, uncles, nieces, and nephews in grades from one to ten. It could not have been easy for Hattie. George, who was seventeen, was not very happy to be back in school, but he was needed to make up the numbers. He may not have attended school every day but that was the year George learned telegraphy, taught him by Lill who had become very adept. The desks had been sent up from Dawson on one of the steamboats. Our desks were much more comfortable than those provided now. They had seats, hinged, attached to a shaped back and bolted to the floor. The desks had a drawer to hold pens, papers, etc.

Joann—For a number of years the family lived in Smythe's Hotel which they had bought. It was a large building constructed to house a store, warehouse, sleeping quarters for any men who might be working there in the summer, private living quarters, and it also housed the school the

Wreck of old steamer, *Dawson* on left; the *Casca* pushing barge of oil barrels on right

Natsulin being launched

Riverboat under full steam

The *Whitehorse*

year there was one. There was a barn and out buildings, dog kennels and a large garden. Stewart Island is where my mother Marjorie grew up and is the subject of much of her writing.

Marjorie—When Lill and her family moved to Fort Selkirk, we were freed from school again and I had many happy years with my dog, my horse, and all the island and sloughs to explore. At age eleven, I had a small trapline where I caught weasel and one coyote. My mother and I were partners as she had bought the traps and we shared the small profit when we sold the furs. I did the skinning out and stretching of the pelts.

For one winter, my brother Greg and I went up to the telegraph cabin and were taught arithmetic. I do not recall other subjects but I do remember being drilled in the multiplication tables 'til I felt I could recite them in my sleep! I have never had any difficulty with figures. Dick Gooding, who taught us, was by belief a communist and somewhat of a free thinker, and my mother was always afraid we would be indoctrinated with his beliefs. He was also an atheist, but we didn't absorb that either. We did take some books on evolution home, to my mother's horror, but my father just shrugged his broad shoulders and laughed and said, "Don't worry Kate, they will make up their own minds later." We always had good books at home, accumulated by the older brothers and sisters, so we had a broad range of subjects to sharpen our seeking minds. As a small girl in Dawson, I had attended Sunday school and my brothers and sisters were sent to church regularly, so we all had some basic religious training. My brother George told me in later years how he and Greg used to shoot rabbits and sell them for 25 cents for pocket money, but the profits must have been small. One Sunday on their way to church, clutching the donation they were supposed to give, they passed the hardware store and saw in the window boxes of .22 calibre shells priced at 50 cents. The temptation was too strong so they bought the shells, intending to put their future profits into the collection plate. They did not count on the minister meeting my mother and commenting that the boys had not contributed as usual. So that led to what my mother called "a good dressing down." Probably what Dad

Smythe's Hotel—Marjorie and Kate on right

would call part of a well-rounded education—do not cheat the church, you may get caught.

At Stewart, however, there was no Sunday school to attend except for the occasional service held by Bishop Stringer while waiting for the steamer *Keno* to arrive. It would take him to Mayo, where the silver miners were and my mother thought the miners were more in need of prayers than us.

Early mornings at Stewart, I woke to the sound of kindling snapping in the kitchen range, my Dad having risen to start the fire. Wood was our only fuel and the heater would be banked with green logs at night, but it was still chilly in the morning. The Smyth house was a big barn of a place and seldom warm in the winter. Dad would be slicing bacon from a big slab and perhaps making hotcake batter as the griddle warmed on the stove. He was home in winter, navigation having ceased in October. When the kitchen was warm, he would call, "Kate, the kitchen's warm." Then, to the rest of us, "Rise and shine! Hit the deck!" which meant it was breakfast time and when Dad spoke, we obeyed.

After breakfast, a large granite pot was placed on the stove. This was for the dog feed. Rice or cracked wheat, grown on the Pelly farm, went into the pot with chunks of caribou meat from the frozen carcasses and some water. The dogs were fed once a day, in the evening. The pups, when old enough, were put into harness and broken to run in a team. Of course, they were dragged along until they discovered it was easier to run than be dragged. In the spring, my dad, and later me, would make the moccasins for the team because when the sun warmed the trail during the day it would freeze at night and the dogs feet would be cut. They would be treated with Friar's Balsam. Dogs were always well cared for because they were important.

A common cry was "Wood pile," which meant that the wood boxes near the kitchen stove and heater needed filling. This job was my brother's responsibility—I was the doorkeeper, and would, at the cry of "Open up," open the door. If I was not fast enough in closing it, I would be accused of heating all of the outdoors. Before someone made up a gas-engine saw to cut the wood, it was all done by hand. My job then was to sit on the log on the sawhorse while Dad or a brother used the big hand saw. I would fidget and squirm and they would say, not unkindly, "Sit still, you little beast!" An expression which we accepted and never realized how it would sound to a stranger. To us, it was almost an expression of affection as well as exasperation. It has always been my belief that where there is a lot of love, there can be a lot of discipline with no hard feelings. When Dad was away in the summer, Mother took over the discipline. On his brief overnight stays, he would demand an accounting of our behaviour in his absence. Being the youngest and no doubt somewhat spoiled, I was to a certain extent pardoned for my transgressions, though I received many a swift smack on my bottom when my mother's patience was at an end.

The washing machine we had at Stewart was a wooden tub with a dasher in the middle and a big handle to turn it. I was too small to take a turn at the handle. My brothers had that chore. The most popular machine in the house was no doubt the ice cream maker which consisted of a wooden bucket with a metal dasher in the middle and a cap which fastened down on the top. There was space around the outside of the centre metal container which was packed with ice. A custard mix made by mother went into the container. The handle was not unlike the washing machine handle. There was no problem getting someone to turn the handle, the job would be taken in turns. It was a fair arrangement and, though there may have been arguments as to whose turn it was, no doubt my mother kept track of the rotation. The person who churned the ice cream got to lick the dasher.

We had a White treadle sewing machine with which my mother sewed the heavy canvas parkas we wore over our woollen sweaters and jackets, the canvas serving as some protection from the wind. These garments had large pockets where we would put our mitts when they had to be removed. Dog booties were made on it too.

We were a vociferous lot and encouraged to have definite opinions. When Dad was home, he would instigate discussions on many subjects. When prohibition came in in the US, I remember him holding a vote, "Wet or dry?" We would each raise a hand and take turns in speaking. I didn't always understand then what it was all about but voted anyway. There was also a lot of talk when elections came around. My father was a staunch Conservative and so were we when we reached voting age. These discussions no doubt made up for our lack of regular formal education.

Ours was a lively household, to say the least for we were all quick to anger and, fortunately, just as quick to get over it—most of the time. My sisters Lill and Helene were married and had their own families. Lill, the eldest, was twenty-five years older than I and I don't remember Dorothy and John being at home at all. So my siblings were George, Florrie, and Greg.

One Sunday when I was about eight years old, Florrie had offered to get up and make breakfast so that Mother and Dad could sleep in, an unlikely situation as they were both early risers. Florrie got up early and, as the first one up, got the heater stoked and the fire lit in the big kitchen range. She put bacon on to fry, mixed batter for the hotcakes and made a big pot of coffee. Then she called upstairs where George and Greg were sleeping in the bunkhouse, an upper floor where longshoremen or other travellers stayed in the summer. At this time, though, there were only family there. "Hurry up and wash," she told them as they came stumbling downstairs.

I was awake so I came out into the dining room in my blue wrapper, as we called our bathrobes. "Get back in there and get dressed!" she ordered but I was already seated at the table and had no intention of moving. She grabbed me by one shoulder and dragged me off the chair. "Leave me alone, you're not my boss." "I am this morning," she answered, slapping me on the side of my head. This only added to my rage and I kicked out at her shins. By this time both of our voices had risen considerably, so out of the bedroom came Dad. "What's going on?" he asked in his no-nonsense tone of voice. Florrie was in tears by this time, something she was prone to do when provoked. "She won't get dressed, and she knows we are not allowed at the table in our wrappers." I continued kicking and screeching. This was not Dad's idea of how to start on Sunday morning, so he picked me up, sat down and taking off one slipper gave me what was referred to as 'slipper sauce'. This was an outrage I was to remember all my life, my one and only heartbreaking spanking from my adored Dad. By this time, Mother came out also.

"Whatever's the noise all about?" "Oh," cried Florrie, "This little beast wouldn't get dressed, and she knows very well she is not allowed to sit at the table in her wrapper!" Mother reached for me. I escaped her grasp and dashed into the bedroom adjoining the dining room. There, I threw myself onto the bed in paroxysms of rage and hurt feelings, as well as having a sore bottom. No one came near me. So I got dressed and climbed out the window—this was possible because there was no storm window where mother slept, she believing in fresh air at all times. Then I harnessed my dog and took off into the woods on my sleigh, thinking "Nobody loves me, nobody loves me." Which was of course was not true at all. Going through the woods had, as always, a calming effect—it was to be that way all my life, for there I felt at one with the universe. When I got home, breakfast was over and the only evidence of cooking was the big pot of dog food bubbling away on the stove. So I fixed myself some bread and jam. "Wood box needs filling," said Mother. Knowing that was part of my punishment for causing the morning's uproar, out I went into the yard where Greg was busy sawing wood. I staggered into the kitchen several times with armloads of wood. Suddenly George appeared and filled the wood box. Later that day, Dad picked me up and, hugging me, cried, "Oh my Pup, my Pup." Then my world returned to normal and my hurt feeling were somewhat healed.

Probably most people would think of a hayride taking place in summer warmth and sun, children bouncing along on a high load of hay on a wagon pulled by a tractor or there might be a team of horses straining at the traces. However, the story I am about to tell originated in mid-winter on a snowy trail by the Yukon River. My two older brothers had, that fall, bought a team of horses from the estate of a woodcutter who had been drowned with two others on a canoe trip on the river. Husky was a bay, hammer-headed and ornery. He and I didn't like each other and in summer I took him down to the slough and tried to make him buck. (I was reading Western stories at the time). He wouldn't, of course, so I soon gave up on that idea. He had at one time stepped on my foot with a big hoof. This did not make me feel any kinder towards him. Ben, his mate, was black with wide blaze on his nose and had quite a different temperament from Husky. He had been used at the firehall in Dawson, and must have been well-treated there. Two large horses required a good deal of hay during the long winter, and we also had a smaller horse, Casey, to feed. So my brothers decided to go about seven miles up the river to a meadow where wild hay had been cut, cured, and piled during the summer.

One morning, they harnessed the team to a big sled and took off upriver. Though I begged to go along, they refused to take me—a real disappointment as they usually let me tag along, whatever they were doing. However, I was not to be left out so, as soon as they were out of sight around a bend, I saddled Casey, telling my parents I was going for a ride. Then making sure they were not watching, I started along the river trail. It was not easy travelling. Casey stumbled in the loose snow, but kept on. I was not afraid, though I hoped no wolves would appear. But there was no sign of life along the river, just the wide expanse of snow. I was accustomed to being out alone either with Casey or a dog team—though with the dogs, I could carry a rifle on the toboggan. I don't remember just how long it took us to reach the meadow where the hay was being loaded. My brothers were not at all pleased to see us! "What are you doing here?" cried George, and Greg echoed his words. I answered, "You wouldn't take me with you, so I came anyway!" Then: "Do Mum and Dad know about this?" asked Greg. When I didn't answer, he muttered, "There'll be hell to pay about this when you get home!" They had a fire burning and water boiling in a billy can so he threw in some tea and we ate the lunch Mum had prepared. George said later, and still does, that I ate most of the lunch and gave the rest to Casey, but I don't believe that happened. It was getting dark when we left for home. George said, "Poor little Casey looks exhausted. I hope he can make it home." "Of course he can," I insisted. "He made it up here!" So off we went, Casey on a rope behind the sleigh.

We were warmly dressed. Our hats had ear flaps lined with wolverine fur which does not frost up as badly as other fur does. These tied under the chin. Our canvas outer jackets had big pockets in front large enough that moosehide mitts could be tucked in when one needed to attend the harness with bare hands. Greg and George were huddled up on the front of the sleigh, occasionally stopping to give Casey and the big team

Kate, Greg, and Scotty Hever

Florrie, about 1924

Unknown man, Kate, and George playing the fool in Kate's dress—note the high-top boots and Kate's moccasins

a rest. I was told to "get out and run ahead for awhile to keep your feet warm." I didn't argue. I was wise in the ways of winter travel and knew it was necessary.

It was dark when we reached home. Mother and Dad were relieved to see me for I had not stayed out after dark before and I knew I was in for a good scolding. Before that could happen, I was told in no uncertain terms to "Get Casey into the barn, give him a good rub-down and some oats!" The cayuse was obviously weary and I was concerned for he was very dear to me, so I quickly carried out those orders. Meanwhile my brothers had to unhitch the team and get them into the barn before they could go into the house for some soup and a hot meal. Our mother always had a big pot of soup on the stove for as she said, "There's nothing like a good bowl of hot soup to put life into one." "Don't give that little weasel any!" said George. "She ate most of our lunch and gave the rest to Casey."

It is often said that animals take on the personality of their owners. This was certainly not the case with old Mike, for while he tolerated people, he hated other dogs. He belonged to my eldest brother, Johnny, who was a peaceful person. In later years, we agreed that he had the nicest disposition, was slow to anger, whereas the rest of us were quick-tempered. Old Mike had been returned to my father to spend his last days in comfort, free from all team duties. He had been lead dog in John's team and when my brother no longer had room in his working environment for sleigh dogs, Mike was retired. To be a leader, he must have been intelligent, though he showed no signs of this in his old age. He was an inveterate fighter and would attack any dog in sight. He was only spared being bested by the dogs of our home team because they, unlike the privileged old-timer, were chained by their log houses. Due to his fighting nature, Mike's ears hung in scallops and his body carried many battle scars. He would always attack any porcupine that he could find and would return home with his mouth and muzzle full of quills. My father would shake his head and say, "Mike, you old fool! Will you never learn to leave porkies alone?" Then, out would come the pliers and scissors. The quill tips would be trimmed to let out the air and the painful pulling would begin. Old Mike never objected to this treatment, probably because it was so often necessary. He was also rather jealous when he did not get what he felt was his share of attention.

This characteristic was to bring about an incident which made him an object of loathing for some time. A traveller coming down the Stewart River in a small boat noticed a moose calf, apparently abandoned on a sandbar. Thinking the mother had been killed by wolves or met death in some way, he picked up the calf, tied its legs and brought it to us. It seems our family was known for accepting strays of many kinds. My brother and I were delighted to have this new pet and he was put into a large barn with a comfortable bed of hay. My mother devised a feeding bottle and with some difficulty we managed to get some warm milk into him. We would tie a rope around his neck and gently lead him around. Old Mike would eye this procession with obvious dislike and jealousy. However, we felt the calf was quite safe as the heavy door was made with double thickness. However, this turned out to be no barrier to Mike, for one morning when we went out to feed our pet, there was a hole chewed through the door. We rushed in and, to our horror, there beside the body of our pet was Mike, looking rather proud of himself. His age and special position was no protection to him however—never had I seen my brother in such a rage. This disgraceful act resulted in a beating for Mike. I ran into the house with the dreadful news, and it was some time before any of us could look at Mike with anything but loathing. Only the fact that John had left his old leader in our care to live out his time in comfort saved Old Mike from taking a one-way trip into the woods with a rifle.

Joann—In 1928, when she was twelve, Marjorie had to leave her home on Stewart Island to attend school in Dawson City. She went to live with her brother Johnny, sister-in-law Gladys, Peggy, her niece who was three, and Frank, who was a baby. They lived in Bear Creek, six miles from Dawson City. The log cabin they all lived in on the island was very small, as were most cabins. It was still standing in 2010 but slowly disintegrating, one of only two houses left on the island. She went to school in Dawson in the same school bus that my sister and I took years later.

It must have been difficult for all of them. I know it was hard for my mother who had almost no memories of Johnny as he left home when she was quite a young child. In effect, she was living with two strangers and two young children in a settlement much larger than she was used to. She was going to school, something she had done only previously for brief periods in Dawson City when she was 6 and for one year on Stewart Island, the latter with her neice, nephews and brothers George and Greg. Now, she missed having them around, as well as her parents, especially her father. Going home was eagerly awaited in the holidays. In later years, she recognized and appreciated what Johnny and Gladys had done for her. At the time, she was not always grateful.

Since Marjorie had little formal schooling, she was placed in grade one, then quickly moved through it and all the grades until she reached grade six. There, she was assigned a desk at which she felt quite welcome because her brother Greg had carved his initials, R.M.H., on it. She quickly advanced to grade seven, and skipped grade eight. Her spotty formal education did her no harm and she was awarded the "Mrs. George Black Award, Dawson Public School 1929–30 for General Proficiency". It is a sterling silver plate, suitably engraved.

By 1927, the family had moved out of Smythe's Hotel and lived in a much smaller cabin. That is where they were living in 1928 when Marjorie writes about her trip home for Christmas, her happiness to be home, and the typical Christmas dinner celebration. In the account, Marjorie refers to Greg sleeping on the floor in his robe at the woodcutters' cabin at Indian River. A robe, like a large down-filled blanket, was essential equipment for anyone travelling, especially by dog team, and sleeping rough.

Marjorie—Christmas in the Yukon was like a scene on a card. Spruce trees laden with snow, willow bushes bending with their burden, and the cold crisp air of a northern winter, it was a time of outdoor fun for children. We were lucky in that we had dogs to hitch to a sled and pull us around, or skis on which to travel the trails through the woods. This was an exhilarating experience with a fast dog pulling one on. Slower, but giving one time to enjoy the calm of winter woods, was tramping through deep snow on snowshoes. Sometimes a startled squirrel would dash up a tree and, high on a branch, would sit scolding whoever had dared to invade his space. Tracks in the snow were fascinating. There might be the round prints of a lynx or the tiny lines of mouse travel. Ptarmigan were scarce but occasionally there might be a flock on a willow clump, so lovely with their white breasts and black on their wings. When my Dad or brothers brought some home for my mother to cook, I felt sad to see blood on those white feathers but we ate whatever was available during the long winter months.

Although I didn't know it at the time, my last Christmas with my parents and my two brothers at Stewart began when I came down from Bear Creek to Dawson City on the school bus. I was to meet my brother Greg who had a contract to carry and deliver mail, in front of the administration building in Dawson where he was waiting for me. He had already picked up the mail from the Post Office and was ready to load me on top of the mailbag and whatever small freight there was room for on the toboggan. His team of six dogs were leaping at the traces and eager to be off. This enthusiasm would not last long, for once on the river and hitting the trail, they would settle down and go at a steady pace. It was not cold that morning, probably not more than ten degrees below zero, fortunately, for we had three days travel ahead, going south to the mouth of the Stewart River where it joined the Yukon.

Our first day's travel was about 29 miles to Indian River, this being the longest day. There we stayed overnight with a woodcutter in his small one-room cabin. How well I remember the foul-smelling tobacco which he smoked in his blackened pipe! I slept in my clothes on one of the pole bunks, while my brother lay in his down robe on the floor. We were up early and, after a breakfast of hotcakes and coffee, left on the next leg of our journey, about 25 miles to Ogilvie Island where our brother George was telegraph operator, sharing the island with an old Scot who had a farm there.

We arrived there in the late afternoon, to be greeted with the lovely odour of a moose stew simmering on the kitchen range and the sight of a lemon pie on the cupboard—George was rather proud of his reputation as a good cook, and rightly so. After the dogs had been unharnessed and fed and my brothers had finished their hot rums—"to take the chill off their bones," they said—we sat down to this welcome feast. Next morning, we were off again, 25 miles to travel, me with rising excitement at the thought of reaching home. I had not seen my parents since leaving in August to go to Johnny and Gladys' where I stayed while going to school. We were fortunate in that the weather remained calm, for it is bitter cold when windy and if a snowstorm should blow up, difficult to say the least.

One stop at Rosebud slough to leave a bottle of 'Christmas cheer' with Belgium Joe who cut wood and trapped there. Then we were off with no more stops, except for the sometimes necessary ones, 'til we saw the island miles ahead. How very welcoming was the sight of smoke wafting up from the log cabins! With harness jingling, we drew up beside the home cabin. My dad rushed out, pulling me out of the toboggan with cries of "My Pup, My Pup!" As the youngest of eight, he always called me that. My mother stood there waiting to give me a hug. "Oh Margie," she said, "how nice to have you home, even for such a short time!"

This was the 17th of December. There was time in the week ahead to hitch up my dog and, on skis, travel the narrow toboggan trails that were so familiar. Time also to saddle my cayuse and ride. I missed these things so much while away. I had a short trapline when living at home but there was no time for that now.

On December 24th, we threw the harness on the horse, cut down a small spruce tree to decorate, and dragged it home. This was set up in a corner of the small front room, well-anchored, and out came the box of ornaments, somewhat battered and lacking brilliance, having been used down through the years by the older children, now all away with their own families. How familiar was the angel we placed on the tree. Her hair was a bit scraggly and her face had often been repainted, but to us she was as lovely as ever. Small candles were clamped on the branches, for we had no electricity. These were never lit because of the danger of fire—but, oh, the lovely smell of the wax. Even now, that scent takes me back to those days. Complete with ropes of tinsel, there was our Christmas tree.

From the small kitchen came the lovely odour of spices from the plum duff steaming in a ten-pound lard pail. A long table had been set up, brought from the Smythe house, now closed for the winter. This was covered in an Irish linen cloth, with matching napkins, all laundered by hand and carefully pressed with irons heated on the stove. At each place was a Christmas cracker. They had been ordered from the Eaton's catalogue during the summer when the steamboats were running. The table was loaded with vegetables, dishes of wild cranberry sauce, relishes, and pickles. At one end was a large roast of beef, at the other there was a ham, decorated with cloves and smelling delicious. There were mounds of red, green, and yellow jellies, more for decoration than dessert. We had, when smaller, referred to these as 'staggering dick', for how they wobbled when we shook the table. That is until my dad would peer over his glasses and firmly say, "NOW THEN!" and we knew enough to stop. The huge plum duff was brought in and placed in front of Dad who would pour brandy over it and light it. How pretty were the blue flickering flames from the pudding which finished the meal! The crackers were quite a novelty and it was fun to all join hands and pull 'til they snapped, disgorging paper hats and small novelties.

The annual dinner was attended by all miners and trappers within walking distance, 25 miles being the average traversed either by horse-drawn sleigh, dog team, or on foot. We sometimes had as many as thirty arrive for dinner. George had permission to leave his station and had walked the 25 miles the day before. After dinner, cigars having been passed around by my father, most present would contribute a joke, a story, or a recitation. Everybody contributed something—no matter if we had heard the same jokes before, we still enjoyed them. And each year, Arthur Davidson would sing "Biddy, McGee, McGaw" and sometimes mother would play the piano. Christmas presents were few and not expected, but Greg and I each got a can of Eagle Brand condensed milk.

Andy was a Laplander who, with his son, had years before come across from Europe bringing a herd of reindeer to the Yukon with the object of introducing them to the Alaskan and Canadian Arctic. The son had returned home, but Andy had remained and later lived in a tiny cabin at Stewart. He was a wizened gnome-like figure with deep-set dark eyes that sparkled. At an earlier Christmas, of all the prizes from the crackers, Andy's was the nicest—for it was a shiny gold ring which I would have liked to have. His little face lit up with joy. It was probably the only ring he ever had. Years later, when I was given a diamond ring, I was of course delighted but I'm sure my joy was no greater than Andy's. After dinner, everyone contributed to the entertainment—songs, recitations, and the same old stories retold. Old Andy sang songs of his homeland in a thin, reedy voice. He really appreciated an audience.

Shorty Donar was another Christmas visitor, described as looking like a little owl. He mined on Henderson Creek and sometimes cooked for other mining crews. He was noted for cheating at casino and always wore a white cloth at the back of his neck to keep the snow from going down his back.

6

OTHER STEWART ISLAND RESIDENTS

Northerners pride themselves on their independence and are not inclined to ask for anything. In their later years, many old-timers refused to apply for their old age pension, regarding it as charity. It was not a princely sum, about twenty dollars a month. Most were content with very little: bacon, beans, flour, some canned milk, tea, coffee, and tobacco. Their meals were rounded out with what game was available.

It was the custom for the IODE (Imperial Order, Daughters of the Empire) to make up Christmas hampers for the old men on the creeks around Dawson City. Mrs. Harriet Osborn, who was Regent of the IODE at the time, knew them all as her son Franklin constantly travelled the route known as 'over the hill'. This was over the summits to Granville, Quartz, and other mining areas. The hampers consisted of a pair of woollen socks, a can of tobacco, or a plug of chewing tobacco, some hard candy and a fruitcake. The fruitcake was baked in one-pound Nabob coffee cans. One old fellow returned his with indignation each year. He "didn't need charity from anyone!"

Marjorie wrote about the men she knew at Stewart Island, single men like Andy, Scotty, Arthur, and Walter, men who came north in the early days and stayed on because they no longer had ties to the Outside, didn't have the money to leave, or had become so accustomed to their way of life that it was all they knew. These men led lives unremarked and largely unknown. Many are lost to history. They were important in the development of the territory as miners, trappers, woodcutters, and labourers. My mother left a list of names. Presumably she planned to write something about them too: B. Dawson DeWitt and Bill Hayes who were telegraph operators, Albert 'Shorty' Donar, Alec Sundeen, Jack Iversen, John Laurence from England who mined at Henderson Creek, Charlie Gage, Belgium Joe from the Winnipeg area who had worked for the Guggenheims on the hydraulic system, Frank Agnew from Duluth, and Hugh Charters from Michigan, for whom my cousin Hugh, Greg's son, was named. Hugh was still living there in 1953. Andy, Scotty, Arthur, and Walter serve to represent all of them.

Marjorie—Andy Kries lived at the small slough which entered into the big slough behind Stewart Island through a narrow entrance. In winter, my brother and I would harness three dogs to the toboggan and taking a lunch, we would go to visit Andy where he was cutting spruce trees for firewood on the left bank of the slough. He would limb the trees after falling and I remember how wonderful the green branches smelled in the frosty air. The old Laplander would have come on his skis with his axe in one hand. No one really knew his age for he was truly ageless and never seemed to change through the years. His little wizened face always looked happy. He would light a fire, hang a lard pail of water on a stick to boil, and we would join him with a cup of tea. There perhaps would be some rabbit droppings floating in it, but they could be scooped out. Maybe they even added to the flavour!

Andy had a few traps set along the banks of the slough and these he would have checked on the way to his woodlot, hoping to have caught a mink or weasel. Money was scarce and, though his needs were few, he still had to buy his meagre groceries. He would haul one log at a time on a sleigh behind his skis which would not have been an easy task even for a much younger man. We had a set of bobsleds which were sometimes used with the dogs for hauling. Greg, after seeing Old Andy struggling to get his logs home, decided to help him. He went up with his dog team and, by making several trips, saw that the old man had a considerable pile of wood beside his cabin. The logs would be green and heavy but Andy would have some of last year's cutting which had dried out during the summer so he would have enough to see him through the winter.

I am afraid that, looking back through the years, we must have teased him, as children will do. We would ask him to sing in his Native language which he loved to do. His national anthem sounded to us as "Yovioska Nevelanda" though I never did know if the pronunciation we used was correct. His high squeaky voice we found very entertaining and he obviously liked the attention.

In summer, Andy's slough was a place of enchantment. The water was crystal clear and the bottom a virtual fairyland with all the small greenery. For some reason there were no tall reeds to dwarf the growth. I used to hang over the side of the rowboat and marvel at the perfection of that underwater garden.

Sometimes a pike would dart by, glistening and darting away. I remember being up the slough with my brother George when he shot a pike. I grabbed an overhanging willow and tried to keep the boat steady while he scooped up the fish. However, his movement caused the boat to shift and there I was, feet in the boat, hanging on to the willow with one hand with my rear end in the water. My brother was in no great hurry to help me and sat there laughing as I screeched at him in great rage. Many years later we laugh about this, but at the time I could see no humour in the situation. Sometimes we would hang a net at the entrance of the slough but only caught a few whitefish which were not especially good eating. There was very little current in the slough as the entrance below the big bluff on the Stewart River had been almost completely blocked by driftwood brought down by high water each spring. I learned to swim in the slough by watching the frogs. One place I remember well was a narrow shallow spot which in summer was fragrant with the scent of pale mauve flowers, bravely blooming from shore to shore. It was a lovely thing to come round the bend and suddenly find this, another fairy garden.

Years later, I went back with my daughters who had often heard of the beauty of Andy's slough and found that the magic had gone, for channels change and through the years the spring ice break-up had gouged out the entrance to the big slough so that muddy water now covered my underwater fairy garden. Forty-five years does bring changes, though the memories of childhood stay on and one can still remember things as they were. Andy's slough is still very real in that it was so very memorable.

Scotty Haver was another of the men who came to dinner every year. He had been a seaman which was apparent in his rolling gait. He was of average height, had a mildly Scottish accent, and a ready laugh and smile. His face was somewhat reddened and blotchy due to his weakness for liquor, for he could not resist imbibing whenever the opportunity arose. My mother, who was a born reformer, would in her own words "rake him over the coals" after each fall from grace. Scotty would hang his head, not really listening or answering—he probably could not have gotten a word in edgewise anyhow as my mother was not one to be easily silenced when on a tirade about the "evils of drink!"

He, like other men on the island, worked as a longshoreman. At that time, silver ore was brought down the Stewart River by the steamer *Keno*. The ore came from the mines at Keno and Elsa and was taken to Mayo on long sleighs, a train, pulled by Caterpillar tractors (commonly known as 'Cats') in winter, stacked there until it could be shipped down the Stewart River to the island on riverboats in the summer. All summer, there were long stacks waiting at Stewart Island to be reloaded on the barges and transported upriver on the Yukon to Whitehorse, thence by rail to Skagway and down the coast. The steamers *Whitehorse*, *Aksala*, *Klondike*, and *Dawson* (until it sank) pushed the barges upriver.

Longshoring was not a steady job, only being available when there was ore to be loaded. It was not an easy one either for these men were all past middle age but they had to make a dollar whenever possible. The ore sacks weighed about 125 pounds and it was my ambition to be able to lift one—this I accomplished when I was twelve. My brother Greg, who was five years older, started the job at a young age. I remember him telling me of an old Norwegian who always whistled when pushing his handtruck up the gangplank. Greg once asked him why, to which the old fellow replied, "It's like this. I am an old man and this is hard work—I whistle to to keep my courage up." This must have made a lasting impression on Greg for he resolved right then that, when old, he would never be in that situation. Greg became a successful man and retired comfortably when he was in his fifties.

Arthur Davidson was a kindly man with white hair and a well-trimmed neat beard, he resembled a member of the royal family and indeed was rumoured to be the son of a somewhat dissolute prince. He had been an actor in earlier years, having been on stage in Montreal playing what were known as 'Heavy Parts'.

We found him to be a great entertainer at the end of our Christmas dinners when, with few exceptions, everyone contributed to the programme. He would sing "Three old crows sat on a limb—Biddy, McGee, McGaw." We heard this every year but always enjoyed it. I remember his log cabin on Stewart Island as being very clean, the logs having been peeled and well-dried. Where most cabins had one—or at most two—windows, his had three windows on the sunny side with shelves built across. On these, he always had plants, for he had once been a gardener. How he kept them from freezing in winter was a mystery to us, for even with storm windows added in the fall, frost would still form. In spring, he would supply my mother with bedding plants for the beds in front of the Smythe house where we lived. Although we had bought the house from Mrs. Smythe, and perhaps because her name was on the sign, it was always the 'Smythe house'. He planted them in a somewhat formal pattern on each side of the gravel walk. There was a circular bed in the centre of the path, corners were marked off, with a path around the middle bed. The main flowers were always pansies which grew to very large sizes in the long daylight hours. One of the riverboat captains had taken seeds from them to Victoria and later boasted of the prize they had taken at a flower show.

Arthur Davidson had a large and productive garden. The cabbages we grew were no doubt from his seedlings. My mother was not fond of gardening, so it is quite likely that he did our planting.

Among his many talents, he was also an excellent brewmaster. This was a sideline and he sold beer for 50 cents a quart. This was not considered bootlegging in our small community, simply a way to support himself with whatever skills he had. He was also official skinner

Scotty Hever on the Yukon River

Cat train hauling ore from Keno to Mayo, *photo by W.S. Hare*

of whatever animals were trapped in winter. He charged 25 cents for a small animal and 50 cents for a larger one—a fox or a lynx. There were animals hanging and thawing out indoors before they could be skinned out and the fur put on stretchers. Consequently, his front yard became the depository for many carcasses that accumulated over a winter. In spring, they would be taken down to the river to float away when the ice went out. There was no thought of pollution then and the river served many purposes, garbage disposal being only one of them

In later years he went, as did many 'old-timers', to St. Mary's Hospital in Dawson, for there was no old folks home and those who needed care went there and were looked after by the Sisters of St. Anne. He lost his memory and one of my brothers who went to see him was not recognized. I remember walking up the hospital hill to visit my mother who had had surgery and seeing the hearse passing, black horses in harness. It was a cold and windy day in November. I was saddened to hear later that it was my old friend Mr. Davidson, who had loved all living things, going to his grave.

Joann—Arthur Davidson is buried in the Pioneer Cemetery in Dawson City. I was pleased to see his Yukon Order of Pioneers (YOOP) headboard when I was there in 2010. The YOOP maintains the wooden headboards that were commonly used to mark the graves of its members. My mother would be pleased too, as the last time we were there the graveyard was badly neglected.

Marjorie—Walter Mittlehauser was a diminutive man, barely five feet in height. What he lacked in size, he more than made up for in volume of expression. When aroused or vexed about something, he would cry "Mein Gott! Mein Gott!" And his walrus mustache would twitch and curl with great abandon. As children, we found this to be most entertaining and would at times try to provoke him so as to see his vibrant reaction.

Walter had once, after great persuasion, appeared with a faded and somewhat tattered bundle of music and, sitting down at the piano, had astounded my parents with his expertise, especially as it was unlikely he had touched a piano for years. However, he would never play for a larger audience and would not contribute to the Christmas entertainment the few times he was there for dinner.

He was missing half a thumb and, when we asked how it happened, he told us he had been in the Boxer Rebellion in China and when he leapt over a wall to escape his pursuers, had landed with his thumb in the mouth of a dying Chinese, who bit it off. True or not, to us it was a fascinating story and, being blessed with vivid imaginations, we could almost picture that happening!

Along with two other trappers, Walter built a boat of a size and shape suitable for river travel and large enough to hold his winter outfit of trapping gear and dog team. This trio were known as 'The Mosquito Fleet'. In late August, they would leave for the long trip up to the head of the White River where their traplines were, and all the residents of our small community gathered on the riverbank to see them off. They would not return 'til after the spring break-up, following the last ice flowing down the Yukon River. What a wild appearance when they appeared after a winter in the bush! Shoulder-length hair, bearded, clothes badly in need of laundering.

One summer, Walter's dog Nellie had pups, two of which he left with me, supposedly for a short time. Little did I suspect that he would leave for his trapline without them. He thought it was a great joke when he returned in the spring. My father did not think it as funny as he did not like feeding two more dogs all winter. But the next fall I sold one pup to a friend for $40, though it was only partly broken to harness. Probably if Walter had known of this, he would have claimed the money. Fortunately he did not or, if he did, perhaps thought it best to keep quiet.

Joann—The population of Stewart Island fluctuated according to mining activity in the area. At one time, it had an RCMP post, mining recorder office, stores, and two hotels. By the 1920s, the population was much smaller and was to decline even more. Now, what is left of the island, as most of it has washed into the Yukon River, has only one occupant, Robin Burian. Robin is a descendent of Alfred Woodburn who moved to Stewart Island about 1922. Alfred was a Master Baggage Handler on the riverboats.

My mother did not write about the Woodburns, maybe because Yvonne and Joan Woodburn were children and she did not see them in the same way as the old men. Yvonne was just enough younger that she was not a playmate. As a confirmed tomboy, Mum would not have been interested in younger children. Still, they knew each other all their lives. I remember Joan telling us about the time she came to Dawson City as a child and was picked up by my mother and taken to Bear Creek. It was Joan's first car ride and she was terrified at the speed. Years later, when Joan lived in Vancouver, my sister Bobbie (Roberta) and her husband Roy Cairns housesat for Joan and her husband Chuck McKenzie when they went north one summer. Bobbie remembers visiting Mrs. Woodburn in North Vancouver with our uncle Greg in the 1950s. The ties between the families were maintained over the years.

I have included the family because, to me, they are part of Stewart Island and I wanted that fact and their family to be recognized. I am indebted to Margaret Burian Underwood for the following. I got her contact information from my cousin Maribeth. She met Margaret in 1953 when she and her mother Peggy stopped at Stewart Island on their way to Henderson Creek where my uncle Johnny, her grandfather, was mining. They became pen-pals and have kept in touch ever since.

Alfred Woodburn took part in the Chisana gold strike on the White River just over the Alaskan border in 1913. Like many others he did not strike it rich. He had a fiancée who went down on the *Sophia*, but on a trip Outside, he met and married Victoria and they moved to Stewart Island. They had two children—Yvonne, born in 1921, and Joan, born in 1926. Their schooling was mostly by correspondence courses but they did spend at least one year Outside.

Rudy Burian and his brother Renny went to the Yukon in the early 1930s. Renny settled in Mayo and raised a family there. Rudy moved to Stewart Island in the mid 1930s where he met, and later married, Yvonne Woodburn. Rudy worked at many trades: he was a longshoreman loading ore coming down to Stewart from Mayo, a rancher at Maisie May on the Stewart river for a time, a trapper, a miner, and hotel owner. He and Yvonne had five children: Alfred who was nicknamed 'Spike' by my uncle George who was the telegrapher at Stewart when Spike was young, Robin who still lives there and barges supplies to miners working Thistle Creek and other mines in the area in the summer, Margaret, who lives in California but goes home every summer, and Linda and Ivan who still live in the Yukon. Margaret (born in 1944) was delivered by their father at Shand's Hotel, which Rudy then owned. Margaret remembers that Walter Mittlehauser died at Shand's Hotel. She also remembers Hugh Charters who was still alive in the 1950s. Margaret and her siblings schooling was by correspondence courses, but Margaret went to Whitehorse for high school. They spent some time Outside too and had some schooling there as well.

Robin Burian is the last lone occupant of what is left of Stewart Island.

7

LEAVING STEWART ISLAND

Marjorie did not go home from Bear Creek for Christmas in 1930 as her mother Kate had been ill in St. Mary's Hospital in Dawson. Greg had room for only one passenger on his mail run and took Kate home from the hospital. Ned wrote my mother a letter thanking her for the poem she had written him and thanking her for the Christmas cards she sent to the old men she was accustomed to seeing at Christmas.

There were no telephones into Dawson City from the Outside until the 1960s but there was a line from Dawson City to Bear Creek and the other mining sites. The telephone message Marjorie received calling her home to care for her mother would have been telegraphed to Dawson and telephoned to Bear Creek.

When Bobbie, my sister, and I were in our early teens and exhibiting anti-mother behaviour typical of early adolescence, my mother would say, "You don't know how lucky you are! At least you have a mother. I had to care for my mother when she was dying…" and so on. Reading the account of Kate's death many years later gave me a much greater appreciation of my mother who had her 15th birthday a week before her mother died. My mother begins the account with having to decide which dress to bury Kate in.

Marjorie—Which dress was I to choose? It was March in the Yukon and the season required warm clothing, not that the cold would be felt by my mother who was about to be placed in her last, final resting place. The black silk dress with the lace sleeves and low wide belt with a big silver buckle seemed out of place in the middle of a northern winter. The dress had been bought for her from the Eaton's catalogue by Greg, her youngest son and she had been proud of his gift. She had told us many times, as had our father, of the lovely hand-sewn clothes she had worn as a young woman in Belgium, France, and later in England. In later years, fine clothes were of the past and life was different. The choice was left to me, her youngest daughter and the only one of five who was still in the North. The rose flannel with a rayon bodice and flannel bolero had been made for her by Gladys, wife of her eldest son, John. It seemed to me to be the most suitable and, as Dad agreed, that was the garment I got out of her trunk. Others have had to decide on final attire for a loved one but the circumstances for me were somewhat different.

My mother had, in the fall, been taken to St. Mary's Hospital in Dawson where she had an operation for a stomach ailment which had been bothering her for two years. After a stay in the hospital and a brief time in the Principal Hotel, she was to come home. While at the hotel, a daughter of the Boutillier family brought her fresh milk and other tempting foods. The families had been friends since the early days in the Yukon. I was with her at the hotel when Dr. Rogers said to her, "It was not cancer." She answered, "Oh, I know that," and proceeded to ask him about his family. I was to remember their brief conversation and marvel at how a doctor could look a patient in the eye and calmly lie about her condition. Was it training or compassion? I still wonder.

On December 1st, Greg arrived with his team of six dogs to take Kate home to spend what were to be her final months at Stewart Island. Their first night was spent in a trapper's cabin at Indian River, about 29 miles from Dawson. Fortunately, the weather was mild with no wind. Next morning, they set out for Ogilvie where George, my brother, was the telegraph operator. That was a shorter run. The next day, they would travel the remaining 25 miles to Stewart where Dad awaited them.

At that time, I was living at Bear Creek in order to attend school in Dawson eight miles away. In February, I was told in a phone call from Dawson to come home with Greg who would be leaving on his mail run and would return to Stewart in two days. I wondered why but I was soon to find out.

So I made the trip upriver as my mother had done two months before. I remember between Indian River and Ogilvie, we saw a dog team coming down the trail. Greg pulled his team aside, stopped, and pushing his fur hat back, a habit when he was about to make a statement, said, "Marge, you know, Ma is not going to get better." I said "I guess that's why I'm going home." The other team approached. It was Sgt. Kronkite of the RCMP out on patrol. I realized then that Greg had thought the approaching traveller might be bringing bad news so he had warned me by telling me of our mother's condition. "How are things at home?" he asked the sergeant. "Probably the same as when you left." So we continued our journey and he hit the trail too.

Travel on the river in winter can be cold and the miles seem so very long and the rock bluffs when sighted take longer to reach than one would expect. We were lucky there was no wind as it can be biting, though we wore over our sweaters canvas parkas our mother had made. However, the time passed and we reached Ogilvie in late afternoon. Brother George had a moose stew ready with layer cake for dessert. After Greg had unharnessed the dogs and chained them, each to their own log dog houses, he came in and we took off our outdoor clothes. Then George opened the bottle of overproof rum Greg had brought and they had a hot drink before dinner. George also hit the telegraph keys to inform the operator Dick Gooding, at Stewart, that we had arrived and would reach home the next day. So in the morning, after a hearty breakfast, Greg hitched the team and we were off on the last leg of our journey.

We passed Louis Cruikshank's farm on the upper end of Ogilvie Island and then took the river trail again. Once again the miles stretched ahead, but now I began to feel the excitement of seeing the familiar hills of home looming ahead. The big bluff around the bend of the Stewart River appeared in the distance almost like an old friend and across the river from our island, there was the bluff with the eddy at its base where we put the salmon net Dad had made when the fish were running in July. Then the home cabins came in sight. Anyone who has been away knows the feeling of returning home—mine was a bit apprehensive as I did not know just what the situation would be, with my mother so ill. Dad came out when he heard the jingle of the dog harness. I leapt off the toboggan and was enfolded in his arms as he cried out, "Oh my Pup, my Pup, my Pup," his pet name for me. Then, into the house to my mother's bedside. I tried not to show how shocked I was at her wasted appearance. "Margie," she cried, "I'm so glad you're home." Then, "Ned they must be hungry—get them something to eat!" This was her first reaction to someone coming in, always to feed people as she had been doing that all her life and I was heartened to find that at least was not changed.

So I was home and realized how much I was needed. Though I was the least domesticated of her daughters, I did know that my help in the house was greatly needed, so proceeded to do whatever I could to help Dad take care of my mother. I began each morning giving her a sponge bath, brushing her hair, and applying a bit of powder to her face, knowing these little touches were important to her. She had always been careful of her appearance, though indeed had little in the way of cosmetics. I remember a woman who had a store in Mayo and was short of cash while waiting at Stewart for the steamer *Keno*—having stayed at our place, gave my mother a lipstick in lieu of money. It was Mary Garden brand and was rarely used. Sometimes I would put a few curlers in her black and still-abundant hair. We moved her from the big bed to a cot in the front room each day to give us a chance to freshen the bed she usually occupied. Sheets had to be washed and rinsed in a washtub and hung on lines in the back room to dry. Fortunately, we had plenty of water as there was a pump in the kitchen.

One morning shortly before her death, Dad and I were washing a sweater she wore as an alternate bedjacket when out of the pocket fell her rosary. "My God," cried Dad, "we've just given Jesus Christ a bath!" We both gave way to our tiredness and tension, sat back on our heels, and gave way to paroxysms of laughter. Suddenly, we heard a drawer open in the kitchen and leapt up to see what was happening. There stood

Mother, having somehow gotten out of bed. She was leaning against the cupboard and clutched in her trembling hand was a big knife! "You are making fun of me," she cried. "You're laughing at me!" "No Kitty," said Dad, "we're not—we were just washing your sweater and this fell out of the pocket." "Give it to me!" she shouted. I took the knife from her while Dad gently led her back to bed. Later, Dad said to me, "Margie, you must realize that the pain and her basic helplessness does affect her mind at times. She would not really hurt either of us."

My grandmother died when Kate, her only child, was quite young so her father, who was a seaman and away a great deal, had entered her in a convent, as both parents were Roman Catholic. Though Mother had not followed her religion in later years, she had during her hospitalization in Dawson been influenced by nuns, the Sisters of St. Ann, and had been visited by the priest who "welcomed her back to the flock." He also informed her that, as she and my father had not been married by a priest, they were not really married! "Well," said Kate, "if I am not really married, then nothing you could say would make any difference." Nothing more was said on the subject, but she did feel better after attending the lovely little chapel the nuns had on the ground floor of the hospital. And found some heart's ease with her rosary.

The episode with the knife in the kitchen had been quite the shock to me but I tried to realize that she was not really responsible for her reaction. In later years, I was to find that patients at times turn on their caregivers.

Sometimes in the evening when Kate felt like talking, I would curl up on the foot of the bed and she would tell me about her younger years— how her mother, Therese, had died when Kate was quite young and her father, Giovanni, had housed her in the convent. The young Kate, being of independent nature and of fiery temperament, found it quite difficult to adapt to the convent rules as laid down by the nuns. She told me of one occasion when, having 'talked back' to the Mother Superior, she was put on a diet of bread and water, and not much of either. She was made to sleep at the foot of a stairway with only a thin blanket for a cover. This, added to the other disciplines to which she was subjected, fuelled her anger. By some devious means, she was able to get paper and write a note for the butcher's boy to mail to her aunt Martha. Martha, though she had a family of five and was well aware of her niece's volatile nature nevertheless, and not without some misgivings, offered Kate a home. On Giovanni's next visit, this was arranged. Her cousins in the Colwell house did not make her welcome, but their father, a photographer, was a kindly man and treated her well, as did her aunt. The same aunt and uncle took Lill and Helene into their home when Kate left to join Ned in the Yukon.

Kate remained with them until she was sixteen when she got a job as a maid to a Jewish woman and went to Belgium with her. This arrangement did not last long, for one day her employer, shouting that Kate had been to too rough doing her hair, threw a heavy jewelled bag at her. This ended her employment.

I wish that I had heard more of her adventures in Belgium and France, but there was little time left now and she was sometimes too weak for conversation. I do know that she met Ned (Captain John Edward Farnsworth Hoggan) through a friend, Henri Mousse in Brussels. The story is, true or not, that he, a ship's doctor, and Ned sailed for South America and that the first one back was to marry Kate. The losing suitor would be best man at the wedding. Ned's ship was first in port and that is how my parents were wed. Apparently there was an agreement that the first-born child was to be named for the loser in the matrimonial stakes. So when the first baby arrived, a girl, she was named Lillian because my mother liked it, and Henrietta as per agreement. I suppose every family has some kind of romantic history, true or not, but that could very well have happened.

Sometimes, in the afternoon, I would harness my dog Paddy and with him pulling me on skis, we would cross the slough at the top of the island, go to another nearby island, and travel a trapper's trail through the spruce trees laden with snow. There was a good stand of timber and it was here that my brothers, a few years earlier, had cut the logs with which they built the cabin after we left Smythe's Hotel.

These brief outings brought my spirits up and enabled me to go home with renewed energy and assumed cheerfulness. It was a very difficult time for my father and to see him so thin and old really hurt. We were very close and looking back now, I can see it was more of a grandparental relationship as he was over fifty when I was born. I remember saying once to my mother that she could not have been very pleased to find another baby was coming at the age of forty-six. She drew herself up and answered, almost angrily, that "none of my children were unwelcome!" Now here was the 'Last of the Mohicans', as she sometimes called me, to care for her during her last illness. I have always felt we are each born for a purpose in life and this was mine, or so I believed.

Sometimes Mother would rally and tell me of her plans and what we would do in the summer. Of course, I knew there was no possibility of us having that time together and it was hard not to show my feelings. It was not easy. We tried to feed her some of the barley soup which always simmered on the stove (somewhat of a family tradition—always to have the soup pot on) but, even strained to clear broth, she was unable to swallow any. Unable to take any nourishment and ravaged by cancer, her body became nothing, literally, but skin and bone. Difficult to imagine and hard to believe until one sees such a condition.

It was the middle of March, one week after my fifteenth birthday, when we realized the end was approaching. A message was sent to George at Ogilvie and the next day he walked the 25 miles. Greg was back early from his mail run, so we were together to give strength to each other and to help Dad face the loss of his dear Kate.

On March 18th, it was obvious that mother's time had run out and her valiant spirit could fight no more. I was exhausted and went to bed about midnight. I actually slept a bit, but awakened at 4 a.m. as Mother drew her last long, long, sighing breath. I leapt up and saw George beside her bed where he had sat all night with his big hands under her frail back, trying to ease her pain. Then we stood there, Dad, Greg, George, and I in tears. But there was much to do and I have found that keeping busy helps one through many difficult times. Greg went with Hugh Charters to dig a grave in the small cemetery, no easy task in winter when the ground is frozen. It was made more difficult by the fact that after clearing away the snow and picking the frozen earth, they struck a coffin and had to start all over again. George went with Louis Locke, who ran the Taylor and Drury store, to find lumber and build the coffin.

Meanwhile, I took the rose flannel dress from Mother's trunk and with Dad's help readied our dear one for her last and final resting place. Mrs. Woodburn was weeping copiously and cried out, "But she told me once that when her time came she wanted to be buried in the black dress Greg had bought her." But it was too late for me to hear that as I could not change her now. The two women had never gotten along, though when Mrs. Woodburn first came to Stewart with two small children to join her husband, my mother had been kind to her. In later years, I was to realize that the island just wasn't big enough for the two women with their different temperaments.

When George and Louis brought the coffin, Dad and I padded it with excelsior from egg crates and then lined it with a sheet. George lifted the tiny body in and then took me with him to the telegraph office, for other members of our scattered family had to be notified. While we were away the coffin and its sad contents had been taken over to the roadhouse (closed for the winter), there to stay until the funeral. Dick Gooding, the telegraph operator, was away on a line-repair trip, so Dad thought we should not hold the ceremony 'til he returned. Meanwhile, not wanting the coffin to be bare, I cut some spruce branches and, wiring them in a circle, made a wreath. I remember my mother, in Dawson, doing this for Frank Osborn's grandfather. I also made white flowers from tissue paper and fastened them among the branches. There again, keeping busy was a help in controlling my grief. When Dick returned two days later, we proceeded to hold the funeral. Before the coffin lid was closed, I placed her rosary in those cold hands, the last thing I was able to do for her. The coffin was placed on a sleigh and pulled by my two brothers, with Dad and I, followed by all the members of our small community, walking along behind. I can still see my dear old Dad in his heavy black overcoat with the beaver collar, his eyes moist as he said goodbye to the partner who had shared his life through good times and bad. I do not remember who read the service, but on a bright sunny day with snow on the ground and wind soughing through the treetops that scene comes back to me very clearly. As well as my father pointing to a spot beside that grave and saying, "When my time comes, put me right there, boys, and if you don't, I'll come back to haunt you!" In later years, he lived in Mayo so he never got his wish to lie beside his dear Kate. It has been my lifelong regret that I was not even able to attend his funeral. It was in February and I had no means of traveling to Mayo and I had two small girls less than two years of age. So there was not the closeness to share with my brothers that had been there when my mother died.

After my mother's death, I stayed at Stewart for nearly a month and then had to return to Bear Creek and school. It was not a good year for me. I had skipped grade eight which was a great disadvantage to me as grade eight grammar would have made a big difference in learning both French and Latin. Consequently, I did not do well in high school though I had been a top student until then. The difficult time I had been through with my mother's illness and death had more of an effect than I had expected. It had been so hard to leave my dear old dad there alone at Stewart. I wanted to stay but had to leave and not see him until the summer holidays. We had only three short summers together.

Joann—Kate died on March 19, 1931. The previous September, Dorothy, the eldest of their Yukon-born children, who was living in Wardner, British Columbia, near Cranbrook, was murdered by her husband who then committed suicide. Helene, her older sister, and Helene's husband, Jim Jones, drove to Wardner to rescue the children. Paul was about two years old and baby Dorothy was under a year. It seems that Helene and Lill, who was living in Victoria, decided that Helene and Jim would take Dorothy and raise her with their girls. Lill, whose youngest son Douglas, born in Victoria, was close to Paul's age would take Paul. The 1930/31 winter was a most difficult one for the family. At the time of Dorothy's death, Ned wrote to his eldest daugher Lill.

Stewart River   Sept.29 1930

My Dear Lill,
    Just had a letter from Helene, about the state of affairs at Cranbrook. It is simply beyond my conception how such a thing could happen. Unbalanced mind after all the horrors of war is

about the only thing I can say for him. And I love my Dorothy & the dear children have one of the finest mothers on earth. I would dearly love to have Paul, but it is impossible, as things stand now. & the last boat leaves tonight.

But I am glad you have him & it sure is very fine of you to take the little fellow to your heart, with the big family you already have on your hands. Now remember this is a joint burden on us all. You have the hardest part of it, but the brothers & ourselves are going to shoulder our monetary share of it. It is for you to decide what the amount is to be. Let us know as soon as you can & we will be found ready to respond.

Having a hard time with mother. She was not at all well before this happened & now she is in a state of collapse.

We will be able to close this B.H. [I have no idea what this means] shortly and I will have more time to attend to her. Thank God George and Gegs [Greg] are at home.

My dear, I cannot write just now, my heart is full of sorrow. After awhile I will be better & will write again then. I am just writing this to thank you for your kindness to the little fellow. Give him a big hug from his grandfather, I so wish I could do it myself.

Love to all the children & your dear self,
Your loving Dad,
J.E.F. Hoggan

As Stewart Island washed away in the spring floods, Kate's grave, along with the others in that small graveyard, went into the river. Kate's headboard was still in place and had been well-maintained by the YOOP when we saw it in 1978. It was found in Eagle, Alaska when it washed ashore many years later. The good people of Eagle sent it to the museum in Dawson City where it remains. Now, there is little left of the island.

After Dorothy's death in late 1930 and Kate's death the following March, Ned spent some of his time with George at Ogilvie but was at Stewart Island in the summer when my mother could be at home.

Stewart River   July 21, 1932

Dearest Lill,

Tomorrow is your birthday, if I remember rightly, you are getting to be quite an old lady now, but as long as health holds out, old age does not matter. I am keeping fairly well, in fact better than I have been for a long time, get an attack once in awhile but by being careful I get along O.K.

I have Marjorie and two of her school chums here just now and it is good to hear laughter again in the old home. They just laugh and play all the time but they have me scared to death they will catch colds, the little devils will not wear any warm clothes.

Marjorie is getting more like Dorothy every day and her voice is an exact replica of Dorothy's and she has her jolly laugh. George takes them around in his launch every evening...

Yes, I bet you have your hands full with the kids. It is great to hear of Paul getting out of that quiet shy way, and being about the same age [as Douglas] they will think a lot alike. Ah, well, the less Paul knows of his father the better, live in hopes he develops his mother's character and happy disposition. Last letter from Helene was great, she seems to be in good health and very happy. Her husband, Jim, must be a fine man, every once in awhile I meet someone who knows him and they all say he is a prince of a man.

Florrie seems to be happy with Bob. Although he is not getting much work these days, he keeps a stiff upper lip and takes what work he can get. The Casca is just coming in so I must close this up.

Love to all, many happy returns of the day,
Your loving old Dad,
J.E.F. Hoggan

In 1934, Ned moved to Mayo to live with George and Greg who were working at nearby Elsa. He died there in 1937. As a mark of respect for him the stores and businesses closed for his funeral.

The *Mayo Miner*, Friday February 19, 1937, published the following obituary:

Captain J.E.F. Hoggan, Illustrious World Mariner and Yukon Pioneer, Called by Death in Mayo General Hospital. Large Funeral Held Thursday.

Veteran of the Yukon Waterways Was Widely Known and Esteemed In Northland for His Hale, Hearty Bluff Good Nature and Kindliness. Survived by His Mother and 7 Children.

Death on Monday evening, February 15, brought to a peaceful close to the end of an illustrious life and took from the ranks of early-day pioneers a beloved father, a loyal friend, and a true and courageous citizen of the Northland, when Captain John Edward Farnworth Hoggan passed away quietly in Mayo General Hospital.

Funeral services were held from St. Mary's Church Thursday afternoon, Rev. Wm. Valentine officiating. The church was packed to the doors with sorrowing friends from all parts of Mayo silver district who came to pay their last respects to the memory of the grand old sea captain. Dozens of beautiful wreaths and floral sprays were placed on the

Ned, about 1933

Marjorie, same year

casket by sorrowing friends of the late Captain Hoggan and his bereaved family. Burial was made in Pioneer Cemetery and the burial service of the Order was read at the grave by Chaplain D.A. Matheson.

The late Yukon Sourdough leaves to mourn his passing, his mother, now in the 90's and 3 retired brothers, Mrs. J. Ward of Victoria, Mrs. J.D. Jones of Tacoma, Mrs. R.E. Crow, Seattle and Mrs. J. Stephenson of Bear Creek. Of his 3 sons who mourn the death of a devoted father, John the eldest, is located at Bear Creek, Y.T. and George and Greg at the Elsa, Mayo district. All are married except them.

Born in Calcutta, India 73 years ago, the late Yukoner took to the sea when he was 14. He was, perhaps among the last of the old sailing skippers and had sailed the 7 seas. Prior to coming north he had seen many years of service in the India Marine. His father, General Hoggan, was an officer with the Imperial Army of India.

Coming to the Yukon during the gold rush days in '97, the late sea-faring adventurer soon became noted for his exploits in piloting steamboats and other craft through the treacherous Whitehorse Rapids. He eventually went to Dawson but only remained a short time before venturing into the Kluane country in southern Yukon where he mined for 6 years.

Following his mining ventures, he then joined the service of the British Yukon Navigation Co. and for over a quarter of a century was a familiar and colourful figure on the White Pass Steamers plying up and down the Yukon river.

About 1914 Captain Hoggan, his wife and family moved to Dawson where they made their home for many years. In 1923 they moved to Stewart City where they conducted a hotel for 2 years. Mrs.Hoggan passed away several years ago. Captain Hoggan retired from the White Pass Co. in 1929 and spent the evening of his years at Stewart until he came to Mayo 16 months ago to be with his unmarried sons.

Since last fall he had made his home with his two sons in the house which Greg built near the Elsa during the summer.

The late Mayoite was hale and hearty and spry right up until a few weeks ago when his fatal illness overtook him. He was brought to the hospital Saturday, passing away on Monday evening.

With the death of Captain Hoggan the Yukon has lost a highly esteemed and deeply loved citizen and father. His genuine kindness of heart, jovial disposition and other sterling qualities had won him friends in legions in all parts of the Northland. His only trip outside was in '98 when he went out to bring his wife back to the Yukon. The late veteran was a member of the Orange Lodge and also a long-time member of the Order of Pioneers. In the passing of their devoted father, sons George and Greg and other surviving relatives have the deepest sympathy of all Mayo.

Joann—While I remember little of the 1940 trip that my mother Marjorie writes of below, I do remember that Bobbie and I seemed to have the run of the ship as Captain Hoggan's granddaughters, and I remember going to the wheelhouse and being allowed to 'steer' the boat.

Marjorie—In 1940, the girls and I were returning north to Dawson City after spending the winter in Langley, near Vancouver BC, with Curly's mother. We had all been there since October, having left on the last steamboat from Dawson. We stayed in Langley until navigation on the Yukon River opened up in May. After taking a ship from Vancouver up the coast to Skagway and from there to Whitehorse on the narrow gauge railway, we boarded the first paddlewheel steamboat to go downriver after break-up.

The first boat downriver that spring was the *Yukon*, an American ship which had wintered over in Whitehorse. In summer, it travelled the river between Dawson and Alaskan points. We were in the largest stateroom and were treated royally. As an American ship, it was not allowed to stop at ports between Whitehorse and Dawson [except to take on wood for the boilers], but to my surprise when we neared Stewart, at the confluence of the Yukon and Stewart rivers, the ship pulled near shore and the captain, with his megaphone, called out, "George Hoggan, would you like to come aboard? Your sister is here." The front plank was hastily put out to shore and my brother, who was the telegraph operator at Stewart, came aboard and we had a few minutes together. The girls were thrilled to see their uncle and later I took them to the wheelhouse to thank the Captain, saying, "I didn't think you knew who I was." He replied, "Of course I know you! You're Captain Hoggan's daughter!" In later years, the girls remembered being allowed to touch the wheel as they were Captain Hoggan's granddaughters.

I was gratified to know that my father's twenty-two years of life as a steamboat man was still remembered and honoured. There was a great feeling of comradeship among the rivermen and I was pleased my young children were made aware of the family ties to the past.

+ ✦ +

On June 7th, 2011, John Edward Farnworth 'Ned' Hoggan, was inducted into the Yukon Transportation Hall of Fame in the Transportation Museum in Whitehorse in recognition of his long service on the steamboats on the Yukon River.

Ned and Kate were Yukon pioneers who suffered hardships and often had little money, especially in the early years when Ned continued to prospect off and on between work on the steamboats. Although they never realized their dreams of golden fortune, they appeared to have had few regrets and no bitterness about the way their lives turned out.

Ned and Kate were proud of all their children. Ned wrote his mother that he looked back on his younger days with pleasure:

> I have done my best to make home a happy place for my kids. In fact that is about all I have accomplished in my life...the kids will always be able to say that they had a good time at home. Although the going was rough at times

we have always pulled it out some way and had
a good laugh at it afterwards.

Ned was right. All his children spoke of their parents, especially Ned, with love and affection.

The children of Ned and Kate, from Lill, the eldest, to Marjorie, twenty-five years younger, had strong ties to each other. Lill and Helene did not join the Yukon family until they were young adults but the fact that they had spent enough time in the North to become part of it, gave them a common connection with their Yukon-born siblings. That connection held over the years. Eventually, all the siblings lived in the Lower Mainland of British Columbia and in Washington State. They got together often.

Greg, Lill, George, Helene, Johnny, and Marjorie, about 1973

8

DOGS, TELEGRAPHY, AND DREDGES

All my uncles were very family-oriented and especially enjoyed children. In one case, I remember Johnny and Greg arguing about whose turn it was to hold Richard, George's grandson, some three months old and the current baby in the family. I think they must have had many of Ned's qualities.

The schooling my uncles had and the work they did was typical in the Yukon. They rarely lived near a school but all were well-read and able to succeed at any job they took on.

I begin their stories with Greg, the youngest, as he was the first to leave the Yukon.

Robert McGregor 'Greg' Hoggan, as Ned noted in his letters to his mother, worked hard and saved money from an early age. He trapped, hunted, and worked on the boats, as a woodcutter, in the mines, and on the dredges. One year, he bought a railway pass and travelled all over the US. As a young man, he spent several winters on the mail run with his dog team. When he started working the mail run, Greg was only eighteen years old. George also worked the mail run for a time.

George wrote the following article about Greg. The original article did not reproduce well enough to be used, but the picture of the dog team is from it.

Johnny, Greg, and George, about 1968

Family Herald   January 11, 1933

Mail Service in the North
By G.D. Hoggan

Mush, dogs, mush! Is the cry that rings out in the cold frosty
air in the front of the Dawson Post Office on the morning
of November the fifteenth, when Greg Hoggan, veteran mail
carrier and his team of seven husky dogs start their first
mail of the winter season—a service between Dawson and
Coffee Creek. It is a distance of one hundred and twenty
miles south along the Yukon river over a vast and bleak lonely
territory, with scarcely a sign of other humans marking the
winters' eternal snows.

Carrying on through the winter months 'til the fifteenth
of April, leaving Dawson the first and fifteenth of each
month regardless of weather conditions, be it fifty below
zero or ten above, the mail moves on to bring a word of cheer
to the lonely trappers and woodcutters scattered along the
Yukon valley.

There are few places in the world today which have
not yielded to the changes of the twentieth century and
accepted the rapid mode of travel provided by airplanes and
motor tractors. One can accurately say that this service is
the hardest and one of the last mail services in existence
operated by means of the sleigh and husky dogs. Other
routes which were formerly handled in this manner having
given way to air and motor transport.

Greg Hoggan, the contractor on this service, is twenty-
two years of age, born and raised in the North and a hardy
veteran of many winter trails, having carried the mail for
the past four years over this route. In all kinds of weather
and heavy weather conditions he has always won through. A
man of the happy-go-lucky type always having a smile and
a cheery word no matter how hard or bleak the trips may

be, having been tried in every manner by the Arctic's cold treacherous storms and not found wanting in any of the requests necessary to combat the Northern elements.

The team of dogs which Greg drives on this route is one of the finest in the country as he says "not much to look at but all real dogs." When he says this it is a lot, as he knows his dogs as well as if they could talk. A team which have in them the necessary fighting spirit to stand the hard knocks handed out to them by old man winter. "Whiskey," the lead dog is a wonder dog, short coupled and built from the ground up, knowing every trick in the game of hard trails, having been on the mail run the last four years, wise to river travel and river ice.

Travel conditions over this route are of the very worst kind owing to the closing of the river in the fall when it jams and ice is piled twenty feet in the air in places. For one not accustomed to seeing ice piled high in this manner it is unbelievable to imagine that a river could have such power to place ice in such a manner.

A stranger to river travel would turn back but not Greg Hoggan, he just takes it in his day's work and makes the best of it by finding a way around it or over the top. This mail route is the only one of its kind where there is no overland route, it being entirely on the Yukon river. Much danger is encountered on the route by cold temperatures causing the water in the Yukon river to drop away from the ice, making what is known as shell ice. When the mail team comes along weight of team and sleigh sometimes cause the ice to break through, wetting Hoggan, dogs, mail. Were the carrier not an experienced man at his business this would prove disastrous for him and team. When a mishap like this occurs he immediately makes for a spot where dry wood can be found and builds a fire and proceeds to dry his outfit out. In many cases, men have been known to perish through getting wet in the extreme cold and not knowing how to take care of themselves.

Published in *Family Herald* with article written by George (p. 123)

At Bear Creek with the Klondike siphon in the background—we
had a sled much like this one, and a very similar dog named Tony

Open water is often encountered in places where the mighty Yukon river runs too quickly to freeze over, this means added danger to the mailman, for in sixty below weather sometimes a thin crust of ice forms over the fast running water, then a small fall of snow conceals the danger. Were the carrier of His Majesty's mail not always on the lookout for such hidden dangers his time would be short on this route.

When the heavy snowstorms come and the snow becomes too deep to make progress anything but a slow crawl, the sleigh is abandoned and a toboggan is used in its stead. This time generally comes about the fifteenth of December and from this time on the real heavy work commences, drifting snow and heavy storms making it impossible to keep any kind of a trail on the river. This forces the carrier to snowshoe ahead of his dogs from daylight to dark.

After a heavy snowstorm all semblance of a trail is lost and at this time is where "Whiskey" the lead dog is used to advantage. He is turned loose and worked as a loose leader to find the old trail. A dog who has had experience at this kind of work is a wonder in action. It is marvellous to see him follow an old trail that is ten inches under the snow, and from all appearance to the human eye just a vast blank field of endless white, but it appears to the old lead dog a mere trifle in a day's work.

Weather conditions during the winter months on the river are of a varied kind. Out on the open river the wind never ceases to blow and snowstorms of the blinding kind are encountered daily with extremely low temperatures. Regardless of weather conditions a hardy man of the North never fails to keep going, making his regular run of twenty-five miles a day. Often though when condition get too heavy he has to 'siwash'. This means make a brush camp along the river in some spot where there is plenty of dry wood and spend the night in the open, a thing which is not greeted with much relish by man or dog.

In early winter months, caribou are often encountered along the river migrating from one feeding ground to another. Of these a few are killed by the mail carrier to use for dog feed. With corn meal and grease cooked in a heavy kettle, it makes a strong feed for heavy working dogs.

In early spring, moose are often seen along the river feeding on the willow islands that dot the mighty Yukon Valley. They come down to these islands after the snow becomes too deep in the higher parts of the country to permit them to feed with ease.

In these days of rapid travel a thought is scarcely given the lone men of the North who carry mail to outlying districts at the risk of their lives, who are out in all kinds of weather and during the short days of December and January on the trail from daylight to 'til dark asking no odds from anyone and greeting the hard knocks handed out to them by nature with a ready smile and a cheery word. It is a thing which brings back the old days of long ago when the old-timers of ninety-eight shouldered their packs and crossed the divide into the North, using dog teams and other convenient means of travel to reach the gold fields. The feeling still remains that the North has not altogether changed as it was in early days, when we see and hear of such men and carry on as they of days gone by were wont to do.

The first day south from Dawson Greg Hoggan and his team with their load of mail stop at the old Indian River post, which in early days was a post of the Royal Canadian Mounted Police. This is some thirty miles south of Dawson.

The next day his stop is at Ogilvie the mouth of the Sixty Mile river where in early days old-timers used all to congregate for the winter after their summers prospecting. Ogilvie was named after the Ogilvie survey party who erected buildings at this point and wintered there in 1897.

The third day south his stopping place is Stewart. At this point the Stewart river joins the Yukon river. During summer months the White Pass and Yukon route transfer some ten thousand tons of silver lead ore which is brought down the Stewart by flat-bottomed boats and shipped to Whitehorse and thence by rail to the coast.

The fourth day is spent reaching Thistle Creek which is extensively mined by hand miners and which was stampeded in early days.

The fifth day south brings him to Coffee Creek the end of his route. At this point the old Wellesley Lake trail joins the Yukon. It was formerly used in 1913 and 1914 to reach the old Sushana [Chisana] diggings located at the head of the White River Valley. Freight rates are high along the river during the winter months, as high as twenty-five cents a pound is charged.

George and Greg both worked in the mines at Keno in the 1930s. Later in Dawson, Greg had a business cutting wood for sale, then went to work on the gold dredge at Upper Dominion. He worked on the dredges for several years but quit when it seemed he would have to leave the cabin he built and furnished on Sulphur Creek. The ground there wasn't going to be worked so he would have to move or leave. Greg moved Outside to Vancouver in 1942. Like many others, he sold what little he could and simply walked away.

Outside, he soon joined the army and was sent overseas. While on leave in 1945, he looked up his Scottish family. At that time his cousins, Bob and Ellie, were living on the family estate, Waterside. He was the first of Ned's Yukon-born children to meet Ned's family. Bob's boots were worn out and, because of rationing, it was impossible for him to get new ones. Fortunately, Bob wore the same size as Greg so they exchanged boots as Greg could easily get his replaced. Unfortunately, Ned's mother Eleanor had died the previous January in her 99th year, so she never met any of Ned's Yukon children of whom she had read so much.

Following his service in the army, Greg fished out of Vancouver for awhile, then went to Colombia in South America where gold was mined using dredges. Many experienced dredge men from the Yukon

George leaving Dawson post office with mail, about 1928

Dog team

found work in Colombia. He started as a winchman, then became Dredge Master and was Superintendent when he retired and returned to BC in 1968 with his wife Romana, whom he had met on a holiday trip to Vancouver in the 1950s. Their three children, Hugh, Jean, and Catherine were born in Colombia.

After Greg and Romana moved back to BC, they spent many summers travelling in the Yukon. In the early 1980s, Greg was hired, along with George Ball and John Bergstrand, other Yukon and Columbian dredge men, to set up and get a dredge named the 'Johnny Hoggan', up and running on Henderson Creek for Queenstake Resources. Marjorie spent the summer there too. This was the same ground that Johnny Hoggan and Pete Foth had worked with the dredge in the 1950s.

When Greg died in Maple Ridge, BC in 1999, there was a memorial at his daughter Jeanne's house. Family came from Alberta and Washington State. Marjorie told the group about Greg's days on the mail run. I pointed out that it was by dog team which astonished the younger American relatives, Florrie's children and grandchildren, who know very little about the family history and assumed it was simply a rural mail route covered by car.

✦ ✦ ✦

George Disraeli Hoggan, was trained as a telegrapher by his sister Lill, who taught herself telegraphy while living at Hootalinqua. George was only about 18 years old when he started working as telegrapher at Ogilvie. This was lonely work for a young man as the telegraph stations were often isolated. He worked on the dog team mail run for a time and in the mines at Keno in the mid-1930s, but his major career was as a telegraph operator, a career which later took him to Dawson City, Stewart Island, and possibly Fort Selkirk in the Yukon and Atlin, Telegraph Creek, and Brackendale in British Columbia. He moved to Brackendale in 1946 with his wife Margaret and daughter Georgina, who was born in Whitehorse.

For the last twenty years of his working life, he was an engineer on tugboats up and down the BC coast.

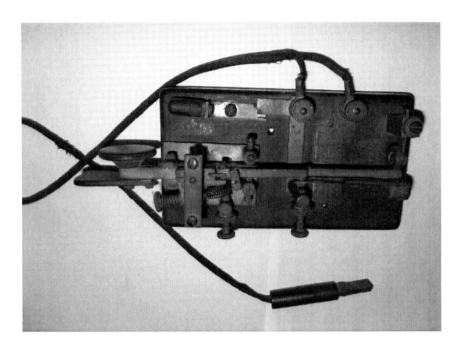

George's telegraph key, *photo courtesy of
Jeanne Swanson & Hugh Hoggan*

George died in 1995 and we had a memorial gathering of friends and family. Hillary, my daughter, who was living in Ontario at the time, sent this letter to Marjorie, her grandmother. Hillary captures my uncle George's personality very well. Her letter also reflects the pull the Yukon can have on those whose roots are there and have heard the stories, even though they weren't born there. Hillary had been to the Yukon twice before George died. George's son-in-law, David Hales, read the letter at the memorial:

Dear Gramma,
One of the first memories I have of Uncle George is at a family gathering at his house in Langley. I don't remember how old I was, probably about four or five. We were all sitting around and I remember feeling very happy, although the atmosphere was tense. Uncle George was arguing with someone,

or everyone, as he was known to do. Even at that young age, I knew that George was the source of the tension. Being a peaceful person, I felt that if I could calm him down everything would be O.K. I walked over to where he was sitting and timidly stood beside his chair. He reached over and scooped me up with his left arm and snuggled me into his lap. He was such a big man and I felt happy and secure as he held me and caressed me with his left hand. All the while his right hand was driving home his point as the argument raged on. Not even I could calm the bark of the bulldog, but I could make him wag his tail.

I remember the fishing trip Dad, Uncle George, and I took when he had a boat. It's funny how three different people can have the same fond memories. We ate clams and oysters until we thought we would burst. Dad and Uncle George stayed up all night drinking and talking. I remember I wanted to stand on the bow of the boat. Dad and Uncle George wouldn't let me, but little girls can be very persuasive…I remember the feel of the wind through my hair and the salty spray on my skin. The freedom I felt pressing my face into the wind, knowing that I was the luckiest girl in the world. I looked over my shoulder into the faces of two worried men who didn't have the heart to ruin my fun. Dad was holding on tightly to the end of the lifeline that was tied securely to my waist. Uncle George was looking nervous and proud as he steered the boat.

A few years later, I was at the farm and I wanted to watch him kill a chicken. The phrase "running around like a chicken with its head cut off" fascinated me. I argued and pleaded but he wouldn't give in. It was alright for me to stand on the bow of a boat, but there was no way I was going to watch something ugly, like a chicken getting its head cut off. Thanks to him I'll never know if they really do run around without their heads.

I can imagine what it was like for you and your brothers growing up in the Yukon. I can imagine the long cold winters, dark and forbidding. I can imagine the constant struggle to survive in a land that is unforgiving to those who do not respect it. I can imagine it was the winters that were the test of your mettle and if you survived, you were rewarded with the spring and the glory of the Yukon in summer. I don't know how accurate these imaginings are, and although I've never lived there I've felt a part of it my whole life.

To me, Uncle George was the Yukon. If you had what it took to tough out the winters of his disposition, you were rewarded, as I was, with the warmth and beauty of his summer. This is how I will remember him.

Love always,
Hillary

✦ ✦ ✦

John William 'Johnny' Hoggan, like his brothers, had little formal schooling. Over the years, when he needed to know something, he took correspondence courses and when he retired, he took night school courses. He had a collection of small pocket-sized books from which he learned many skills. Johnny spent all his working life in the Yukon doing a variety of jobs.

I am indebted to Marion May Dore, my friend since childhood, for the following, written by Johnny. He wrote it for the *Bear Creek*

Bucketline, a brief history of the people working in Bear Creek when the Yukon Consolidated Gold Corporation (YCGC) closed down in 1966.

This is a matter-of-fact list of the work Johnny did. It doesn't begin to do justice to his wit or personality. He did end the original document with a string of punctuation marks "to be used as needed." The value lies in the variety of ways in which he made his living—work which was typical of the times and the places. Like many Yukon men, he was willing to turn his hand to any work that needed to be done, and learned to do it very well.

Johnny—I went to work on the riverboats in 1917 and stayed with the BYN [British Yukon Navigation] as deck boy on the old steamer *Dawson* for two years, then on the *Casca* for another year. [He was only 14 in 1917 and would have gone to school when the boats weren't running, as the family lived in the Dawson City area at the time.] In 1920, I was pilot and purser on the *Hazel B.*, on the Stewart River run to Mayo. At that time, the Yukon Gold Company operated a silver mine on the top of Keno Hill. The next summer, I was with Emil Forest and Cam Smith on the lower Yukon River as pilot on the old *Sabila* mail launch and the *Hazel B.*, as she was not needed on the Stewart-Mayo run that summer. We ran from Dawson City downriver into Alaska, Anvik, and Nanana, where the mail was transferred to be carried to Fairbanks by rail and from there to places not covered by water routes. That ended my career as a sailor.

I went to Mayo that fall [1921] and cut logs in a logging camp at Fraser Falls that winter, then made a long trip into the Wind River country next spring and trapped rats [Muskrats] until break-up. We arrived back in Mayo the first week in June 1922 and I started my career as a dredge man on the old steam dredge on Hyatt Creek, which was owned by Harry Jones, Finlayson, L. Titus, and McVicker. Everyone at that time worked 12 hours a day. The oilers rate was 50 cents an hour, and we had no deckers, just a winchman, steam engineer, oiler, wood buck, and one shore man. We had no set payday and the outfit finally went broke in September, so we were all broke for the winter. With Frank Osborn, who had worked with me and was also broke, I started

Working dredge—the buckets on the right take gravel into dredge
and tailing piles are formed on the left; power pole and lines leading
to the dredge can be seen just right of centre

for Dawson with a poling boat and all our worldly belongings 6th of
October. We had very good weather all the way down the Stewart
River and, when we got to Ogilvie, on the Yukon, the caribou run
was on so we were able to stock up our winter's meat. We landed in
Dawson around the 15th, just ahead of the ice run. Frank and I both
wintered at home that winter.

On April 1st, 1923, I got a job with the North West Company on
Dredge #1 at Paris on Dominion Creek. Bill Moore was Dredge
Master. At that time they were still thawing with steam points, but had
experimented with cold water thawing the previous year. The steam
thawing was not very efficient and very expensive and was not used
after 1923. I decked on the dredge that summer until we closed for
the winter on November 1st. Then Walter Troberg, Eric Johnson, Paul
DeBressay, and I walked to Whitehorse [Johnny had a reputation of
never walking a trail, but trotted along it and could cover 50 miles a

day, a pace that one learned trotting after a dog team] and from there went out to Vancouver. For Walter and me, it was our first trip to the great Outside.

I met Gladys that winter in Vancouver and we decided to get married the following summer. [Johnny told me that he met Gladys at a "soda shop" where she was to meet someone else who had been North for the summer. But it was love at first sight for both of them. They had an exceptional rapport and very strong marriage.] We were married at my home at Stewart City, on the Yukon River on September 4th, 1924. We're numbered among the fortunate few who spent their honeymoon in Paris—Paris on Dominion Creek!

Joann—It is worth noting that there were many males and only eight females at the wedding. This probably reflects the proportion of Caucasian males to females in the whole of the Yukon. It was largely a male society. The *Dawson News* wrote this report of the event:

Dawson News   September 5, 1923

John Hoggan & Miss Gladys Gaundroue wed at Stewart City. Arrive on Steamer Casca. Greeted by many friends at the dock amid a shower of rice.

Among the passengers arriving on the Casca this afternoon were John Hoggan and bride. The young couple were married at Stewart City yesterday at 3 o'clock at the residence of the groom's parents, Captain and Mrs. J.E.F. Hoggan. The bride was Miss Gladys Gaundroue of Vancouver, and the groom is one of the best known and popular of Dawson's young men. At the wedding Walter Troberg was best man, and Miss Florence Hoggan, sister of the groom, was bridesmaid. The following guests were present: Captain E. Morrison, J. Scotland, J. Murray, A. King, W. Wilson, Captain J.E.F. Hoggan, Mrs. J.E.F. Hoggan, Dawson deWitt, A. Davidson, Mrs. D.C. Shand, J.C. Lawrence, S. Card, Marjorie Hoggan, George Hoggan,

Johnny and Gladys' wedding—Ned second from left,
Kate, Johnny, Gladys, and Florrie in centre

Gladys with gold pan on her
honeymoon in Paris

Gladys beside sluice box

Macgregor Hoggan, L. Bouvette, Constable Cruickshanks, Rev. W.H.L. West, Scott Heaver, Alex Lesperence, Mr. and Mrs. H. Woodburn, Yvonne Woodburn, L. Scott.

At the wedding supper a toast to the bride was proposed by Rev. West and responded to by the groom. The toast to the bridesmaid was responded to by Walter Troberg, best man. The occasion was a happy one and all drank to the health of the young couple.

On arrival of the newlyweds at the dock in Dawson this afternoon, they were greeted by dozens of their friends and landed amid the pealing of bells and the blare of trumpets and showers of rice, confetti and serpentine.

Johnny—After finishing the season on Dredge #1, we lived in Dawson that winter. Went broke again and moved to the creeks in March 1925. That year, the North West Company was about on the rocks and the only dredge to start the spring was old #5 at Granville. I sent Gladys out to Vancouver and worked on Dredge #5 until Dredge #1 started up on the 4th of August. Dredge #2 started up in June that year.

That fall, I left for Vancouver where our daughter Peggy was born in December 1925. Son Frank was born in Dawson in 1928. I stayed in Vancouver until the spring of 1927, then headed north again. I will always remember that Lindberg landed in Paris, France the same day I landed at Skagway. I arrived back in Dawson on May 29th, on the steamer *Casca*, after spending a few days stuck in the ice in the middle of Lake Laberge.

At that time, the North West Company had bought their first tractor, a five-ton Holt and I was their first driver. About this time, Mr. A.N.C. Treadgold came back to the Yukon after an absence of 13 or 14 years and started the North Fork Ditch and some shovel mining at Quartz Creek, but after a couple of years he finally lost out.

Joann—This was the time when several, often competing, interests were formed into the Yukon Consolidated Gold Corporation, YCGC, or the Company. In a letter to his mother Eleanor, dated August 18th, 1927, Ned wrote:

> John and his wife are settled in Bear Creek. He has come back to the North and landed a job as the Head Caterpillar Driver for the North West Corp. a big mining outfit up here. He gets $225 per month and $1 per hour for all overtime over 9 hours work a day so that is good.

Johnny—I worked on a lathe and welding in the shop in 1928 and part of '29. The Company was short of winchmen at that time and I went to Dredge #2 as winchman until 1936 when I took over as Dredge Master from Amede Dubois [Middy] who then became superintendent. [When I spoke to Alex Van Bibber in 2010, he told me he worked for Johnny on #2 dredge for a number of years. He described both Johnny and Gladys as very fine people.] I ran Dredge #2 until 1942, except in 1941 when

I turned it over to Bob McLaren for the summer and went on to the construction of Dredge #4 to install all machinery and piping, working under Gus Erickson and Grant Barrett. When Dredge #2 finished operating at Bear Creek in 1942, I worked in the shop that winter, then took over Dredge #4 on Bonanza Creek the following spring. The Company would not pay for my gas to get to #4, some distance away, so I quit there on June 1st, 1943 and went to Whitehorse.

Joann—Johnny worked at Aishikh airstrip as mechanic. Then he supervised the building of the Snag airstrip. The airstrips were part of the airfield system used in ferrying US aircraft to Alaska. Later, he and Gladys bought a house in Whitehorse which Johnny added to over the years. It became their home base for a number of years.

In the post-war years, Johnny was dredge master at Thistle Creek, Henderson Creek, and Clear Creek. Each of these closed when costs exceeded the value of what was being taken from the ground. Johnny and Pete Foth, who was also a dredge master, had known each other for many years. They bought the dredge, one claim, a dragline, and two Cats from Mr. Patty, shut down Clear Creek, and worked Henderson. The investment paid off when the price of gold rose.

In 1959, when Superintendent for YCGC and Johnny's friend, Middy Dubois died, Johnny was asked to take over. He and Gladys moved back to Bear Creek, not into their cabin, but to a bigger, more modern company house. Gladys was delighted to be back among old friends.

For many years, Johnny played Santa Claus for the Bear Creek children and both Bobbie and I remember the year one of us said, very loudly, "That's not Santa Claus, that's my Uncle Johnny!" I remember the beard was made from binder twine, yellowy and rather thin. Maybe a new beard was bought because the next year we knew it was the real Santa. He was being Santa for a new generation of children when a perforated ulcer nearly killed him.

Brownie Foth, wife of Johnny's former partner Pete Foth at Henderson Creek, remembers the event very clearly except for the exact year, which would be about 1963. Medical services in the Yukon were scattered and doctors worked only where there was enough population to support them. I don't remember that there was any provision for critically-ill people to be moved by air. There was no doctor or hospital in Dawson at that time. There was a nursing station at the old RCMP barracks and the head nurse, Rona Millar, decided that Johnny would have to be taken the 146 miles to Mayo, which had a doctor and a hospital. Johnny agreed to do that if Brownie, a nurse, would go with him. Brownie had come north in 1951 and, as soon as she saw Pete, she knew she would marry him, which she did the following year. Pete and Brownie lived and mined in the Dawson area for many years before retiring to White Rock, BC and spending the summers in the North.

Christmas morning, Johnny was put on a stretcher in the back of the RCMP station wagon with Gladys in the front seat, and Brownie in the back with Johnny. Brownie says it was the hardest thing she had ever done, kneeling beside Johnny and trying to keep the drip going and managing to clear it each time it stopped. Johnny was losing blood and Brownie was not sure they would make it to Mayo in time to save Johnny's life. She says he was a great patient, never spoke, but just opened his eyes long enough to see that Brownie was still with him. When they got to Mayo, Brownie had a short rest at the Tim O Lou Motel then she and the RCMP officer returned to Dawson. When she got back to Dawson, Tommy Nakashama, a neighbour, had a Chinese food Christmas dinner all ready for the Foths (Pete and Brownie had two young daughters). Brownie says this was the most wonderful thing he could have done as she was so exhausted.

Dr. Evans, who apparently had a offbeat sense of humour, said that although Johnny should have had a blood transfusion there was no one in Mayo "with enough blood in their alcohol." Johnny, thanks to his strong constitution, survived the ordeal and, after some time at home recuperating, went to Vancouver for surgery and made a complete recovery.

The scarcity of medical and dental services in the Yukon was a fact of life even into the 1950s. Communities were often too small to attract or support services. The population was scattered. Long, dangerous, and painful trips for medical attention were the norm. I experienced some myself when we lived on the Alaska Highway in the 1940s. Over the years, when Johnny and Gladys lived in Whitehorse, they housed those of us who needed dental or medical care which we could get only in Whitehorse. I stayed there several times, as did Bobbie and our cousin Dale, Jack Ward Jr.'s daughter. She had cut her hand very badly on an axe and had to go to Whitehorse to have it looked after. There was no medical service in Atlin at the time and Dale stayed with them while getting penicillin shots several times a day. Her mother Eileen stayed with them before Greg was born. Johnny and Gladys always had an open house for those in need.

Johnny was active in the Masonic Lodge, the Eastern Star (along with Gladys), and the Yukon Order of Pioneers (YOOP). He was a well-known raconteur and at a talk he gave at a YOOP meeting, probably in the 1950s or '60s, he told the following stories.

Johnny—One summer when Pierre Burton, (born and raised in Dawson City) who is now managing editor of *Maclean's* magazine, was a student at high school he worked for the Company. At that time, we had an engineer, Jack Simpson, who was fond of playing practical jokes. One morning on his way to the office, he saw standing on the warehouse platform a big brawny gullible boy. Simpson was immediately interested and asked who he was and whence he was going. It was Pierre on his way to work on the thawing plant on Dominion. Simpson told him he should be weighed, tagged, and have a bill of lading. He weighed him, got a tag from the warehouseman, and filled out the data: Pierre Burton, Labourer, Age 16, weight 175 lbs., Assigned to Dominion thawing. He pinned the tag to the lapel of Pierre's coat, made out a bill of lading, and told him to stand in a prominent place on the warehouse platform so when McCormick's truck came along to hand the bill of lading to the driver, he would be taken to his destination. Fortunately a good Samaritan came along, took pity on the poor boy tagged like a piece of merchandise, and told him it was merely one of Simpson's bad jokes, to discard the tag, and to sit in a comfortable chair in the office until transportation was available. Both Mr. Simpson and Pierre have travelled far since that episode, but the story is still told in Bear Creek when old-timers are reminiscing.

Joann—I remember reading an account Pierre Burton wrote about that job, which was a miserable one. The soil had to be removed then the permafrost thawed before the ground could be worked. The men had to stand in deep cold mud while using 'points', long hollow probes to thaw the ground with, as well as in the early days, steam, and later, cold water.

Johnny—For many years, Percy DeWolfe carried the mail from Dawson City to Forty Mile. During the summer, he used a launch and, in winter when the ice was safe, a dog team. During the break-up in the spring and freeze-up in the fall, he packed it on his back and travelled the shore ice. On one such trip, the going was heavy. He had broken through the ice and been in cold water up to his knees and worse several times. Somewhere about the halfway point he met Bishop Stringer walking from Forty Mile to Dawson. "Hello, Percy," said the bishop, "how is the trail?" Percy said it was the damndest he had ever known and for several minutes swore fluently about it. Then, he asked how it was ahead. "It's just the same, Percy. I endorse every word you said." [Percy DeWolfe carried mail by dog team from 1910 until 1948].

When Ed Holbrook was operating the dredge on the Sixty Mile, the crew lived in Dawson during the winter, usually spent the nights visiting different bars in town, and slept during the day. One winter, I was boarding at the Arcade Café and quite often they would be having supper while I was having breakfast. Once, one of the group who shared with Holbrook the winching of the boat [dredge], each working a twelve-hour shift, broke the silence with "Everyone thinks that me and Ed are the best two winch men in the country." And when there was no comment, he added, " . . . and me and Ed agree."

Joann—Johnny and Gladys were remarkable people. They retired and moved to Maple Ridge, BC in 1966 when the YCGC shut their gold-mining operations in the Yukon.

Gladys and Johnny, Whitehorse, 1945

9

WORLD WAR II:
DAWSON CITY AND WHITEHORSE

My cousin, Viola Margaret 'Peggy' Hoggan, daughter of Johnny and Gladys, was born in Vancouver in 1925. She was nevertheless a true Yukoner. She lived in Bear Creek and went to school in Dawson City, eight miles away, as my mother did when she lived with Johnny and Gladys, and as my sister and I did when we lived in Bear Creek. Gordon Tubman, whom she later married, came to Dawson City in 1940 and writes of his experience as a newcomer there and his later experience in Whitehorse when the Alaska Highway was being built. Their memoirs were given to me by their daughter, Maribeth Tubman Mainer.

The accounts written by Peggy and Tubby of the beginning of World War II illustrate the impact the building of the Alaska Highway had in Dawson City and especially in Whitehorse. It changed the Yukon forever. I was especially interested to read about the role Dawson City and the Yukon River had in delivering supplies for the construction of the highway into Alaska, something I was unaware of. Nor did I know there were American soldiers in Dawson. I do remember having to get immunized, but have no memory of the role the army played.

Gordon Tubman, always called Tubby, was only twenty years old when he went north. He was housed at first in an old hotel. Dawson

City is built on permafrost. As heated buildings warm the underlying soil, it starts to thaw and results in buildings settling unevenly, leaving them leaning at odd angles. Tubby had an abrupt and often frightening introduction to the life and the work he was expected to do in the Yukon. He obviously had what it took to become a true Yukoner.

Tubby—After three years working in a Victoria hardware store, I went to work on the Ogden Docks. I hadn't worked there long, perhaps a few months, when a stranger came up to me. He said he had heard I had a good knowledge of the hardware business. If that were true, would I like to go to Dawson City to work? I said, "Sure, but where is Dawson City?" He asked if I had heard of the Klondike. I said "Yes", but to me it was to Hell and gone North. I was on my way in a week, April of 1940.

On the *Princess Charlotte*, I met Pete Kereluk who, unlike me, was heading North with no work lined up. On arrival in Skagway, we boarded the White Pass Railroad, bound for Whitehorse. From the train, we went directly to the paddlewheeler *Whitehorse*. This was a beautiful way to travel—the scenery was beautiful during the two-and-a-half-day journey downstream to Dawson City.

As we came around the bend, we spotted Dawson. Had we had the money, Pete and I would have turned around and gone home. There had been a big fire on Front Street—what we first saw was the blackened ruins. All the buildings seemed to be leaning against each other and threatening to tumble down. The Northern Commercial company (NC) did not have my room ready above their store so they put me in a hotel close by. This was a hotel unlike any I had ever seen. The floors sagged here and rose there so you went down the hallways like a drunk. There were big gaps top and bottom of the doors. There were no locks on the doors. There was no plumbing in the rooms for washing, just a crockery basin and pitcher. The bed was not bad, but all night my door kept opening as people checked to see who the stranger was. They meant no harm, were just inquisitive, so I couldn't get hostile about it.

The Company I had come to work for was an old established firm with head offices in Seattle. They were similar in operation to the Hudson's Bay Company. The NC had large mercantile stores in Alaska and the

Yukon, located in the larger towns, with trading posts in the smaller settlements. You could buy almost anything you could ever need in the larger stores: huge sacks of food, clothing, china, hardware, building supplies, anything you could name. They also had the Caterpillar dealership, Ford, Chrysler, and the Aeronca line of aircraft! At one time, they also had a fleet of river steamers plying the Yukon River.

Above the store in Dawson, there was an apartment for the manager. The single men had good accommodation up there, too. Even in the coldest weather, we kept comfortable as the heating was by hot water, furnished by a large, wood-fired boiler. We had all the hot water we needed. We only had to go out to eat in the restaurants nearby.

Because Dawson was still dependent on the steamboats and some winter Cat trains and the NC was the chief supplier in the area, they had to carry huge inventories. The main store complex, including warehouses, freezer rooms for meat, space for building materials, and plumbing supplies, covered one city block. Other large warehouses were scattered through town.

I hadn't been with NC for long when I was asked if I would like to go on a delivery to Sixty Mile. There was a load of parts to be delivered and I might as well go along. The fellow who was to drive the tractor was out on the town the night before. Come morning, he was either too hungover or too drunk to drive, so he gave me a quick course in how to run the tractor. I had never been on one, let alone driven one. One of his instructions worried me more than the other: if I was going downhill and the load started to push the tractor, I was to throw the tractor into reverse.

Once we were off the ferry, the driver moved back to the trailer, curled up, and went to sleep. After a few miles of driving, I said, "To Hell with this," stopped, went back, woke him up, and told him he was on his own. "What are you going to do?" he asked. "Walk back," I replied, and proceeded to do so. By the time I got back to the ferry, it was shut down for the night. I bedded down for the night. When the ferry came over in the morning, I was informed I should have just fired my gun and he would have come across for me. I figured that was not necessary, under the circumstances, which got me on the good side of the operator right then and there.

Another time, a scraper came in on the boat for one of the mining concerns. Once the thing was unloaded, the Cat and the scraper had to be connected. There I was, with the book in one hand and a cable in the other, connecting them, with Ed Schwartz shaking his head. I must have done it right because it worked. They got someone from town to load it on the ferry and drive it to the camp. Later, the NC would send me to Caterpillar school, but it was just the book, the cables, and me that day.

In Dawson City, as in most northern towns, drinking was probably the number one pastime. If there were no excuse, you invented one. The arrival or departure of a riverboat was always a good one. At the sound of the boat's whistle, much of the town came to a standstill as folks left their stores to go to the docks for the boat's arrival. Most of the boats came from Whitehorse, not so many from Alaska.

The hotels in town each had bars, illegal but usually tolerated by the RCMP If there were to be a raid, the hotel was usually forewarned. Second Avenue had its red light district but V.D. apparently was not a problem.

There was other recreation, lots of it. I did lots of hiking on the hill, fishing, and hunting. As I used to do a lot of running in Victoria, I continued in Dawson. Often I would take off on a summer evening, on my own, and run over the hill to the Indian settlement of Mooshide. I never did clock the distance but would guess it would be four to five miles. Most of the fellows thought I was crazy.

In winter, we did a fair amount of snowshoeing, bobsledding, and skiing. I became a member of the Midnight Sun Ski Club. Although I was never any good at skiing, I got along. I had two memorable ski sessions. The first time, the fellows who had been at it awhile asked if I wanted to give skiing a try. They were to ski to the top of the hill behind the town (the Dome). As the sport appeared easy, I agreed to give it a go. Of course, I outfitted myself with proper ski-clothes but I refused to wear longjohns, as I had not yet felt the cold. I did manage to make my way to the top of the hill but, in so doing, froze (not badly, but damned painfully) my exterior plumbing system. I guess I was concentrating too much on keeping up and not enough on what was happening. I fell on every turn back to the ski club cabin. The next occasion was when my Norwegian friend, Arne Anderson, conned me into making a ski jump. He made it look simple, as he had been doing it since he was small. I completely wiped out, breaking a ski. The wrist that took the brunt of the fall still bothers me. I still had to get back to the cabin so Arne told me to place my feet directly behind his skis and to hang onto him and follow his moves. We went down the hill just fine but, when we hit the narrow ski trails in the bush, I was lost on the first turn. Winding up among the bushes, I elected to walk in the snow back to the cabin. Everyone but me got a kick out of it all and, as I recall, after a hot rum or two, I could see the humour of it too. After living over the NC for some time, four of us decided to rent a house and move. We were Pete Kereluk, Frank Cody, Harry Fatt, and I. The move worked out pretty well and we all got along fine.

Pete and I had become very close friends. Pete was the one directly responsible for my meeting Peggy Hoggan. Pete was going with one of her friends, Avis Hulland, and thought I should get into the act. I did. The trouble was, Peggy lived eight miles from Dawson (in Bear Creek). To the rescue came an old, crippled NC employee for whom I did many things. He let me use his old Model A Ford as my own.

This started at least weekly trips to Bear Creek. The mechanics of getting the car mobile in the extremely cold weather were sometimes a problem, but we managed. At least twice on the drive to Bear Creek, I was accompanied by coyotes running either side of the car, close enough to touch with a yardstick. They seemed to enjoy it as much as I. Luckily, I hit it off with her mum and dad and her brother Frank, and I'm sure I came close to eating the Hoggans out of house and home, but Peg's parents became like parents to me.

Peggy—On the 'day of infamy', December 7, 1941, Japan bombed Pearl Harbor. This triggered the building of the long-planned Alcan Highway. In late November, 1942, Tubby received a telegram from the NC head office in Seattle, instructing him to go to Whitehorse. He was to help set up a Caterpillar parts depot to service the highway construction equipment.

He asked me to wait until he could get back in one year. I was truly upset, but knew it was our chance to get ahead. It was the longest year of my life. I completed my grade eleven. We said nothing to anyone of our plans to marry. We wrote each other weekly. We were lonely but we survived.

Tubby—Arrival in Whitehorse was a real shocker! When I last saw Whitehorse, it had a population of four hundred and fifty. This had now risen to twenty thousand with a mix of US troops, US contractors, Canadian troops, and Canadian contractors. Probably ninety percent of the population was American. It seemed like all the flat ground was covered with army barracks and tents. In spite of the bitter winter cold, at this stage, there were still acres of tents for American army personnel. My first home was the Whitehorse Inn, occupied mainly by Americans. One thing to be said for it: it was warm. My roommate turned out to be Pat Bell, the guy who opened his big mouth and got me transferred. I had met him in Dawson when he was on a trip through the Yukon for the NC. He was the Company 'big gun' in Seattle, as far as Caterpillar parts were concerned. I was to assist him in their new venture, or at least try.

When I arrived in Whitehorse, a nucleus of a parts depot had already been set up. Its main business was with large US contractors, working on separate contracts on the highway system: airports, pipelines, an oil refinery, and on the road itself. The location of our parts setup itself was in the so-called Dowell Area, named for the major contractor there. In this area were warehouses (large reused, prefabricated structures, dismantled and moved from the States), huge machine and repair shops, mess halls, army barracks, etc. Our warehouse contained our parts depot at one end and a US army engineers supply base at the other.

I was asked to show my driver's license. I had never had one. They ordered me to get one and I did. I had been driving for several years by that time. I don't think anyone in Dawson had a license back then.

Peggy—In June 1943, my Dad [Johnny] left for Whitehorse and his job superintending the construction of the airports at Ashiak and Snag. Mum,

Frank and I moved to Dawson City. Our Bear Creek cabin was on YCGC ground so we could no longer live there. It was an interesting summer.

Nearly every able-bodied man either joined the armed forces or moved to Whitehorse for the highway construction. I received my engagement ring August 20, 1943. We set our wedding date for November 15. Suddenly I was very busy, as all my stuff had to go to Whitehorse on the last boat.

Dawson City was involved in the highway construction, even though the actual highway was many miles away. Much of the machinery and lots of US soldiers who provided most of the manpower, were moved by barge and steamboat from Whitehorse to the lower Yukon River in Alaska. These had to stop in Dawson as only two of the steamboats had a shallow enough draft to push the barges through the lower river. Many of the soldiers were from the deep south. We had trouble understanding them. One fellow asked where he could rent a "pie-anny." I couldn't figure out what he meant until he mimed playing a piano. They were organizing a dance for the town. Late that summer, typhoid broke out in Dawson. With only one resident doctor, this became a real problem. The US army medics volunteered their services. In half a day, they had rounded up everyone in town for inoculation.

With Dad and Tubby miles away and Mum busy with war work, I had to make all our wedding arrangements myself. My Anglican minister insisted that I have banns read. I told him I doubted my intended even knew where the church was located in Whitehorse. He replied that Tubby did as he was helping Arne Arneson build Arne's house near the church. Reverend Alsop had already been in touch with Reverend Chappell in Whitehorse! The banns [a notice of an impending marriage so that any objections may be lodged] were duly read.

Tubby and Dad were to fly to Dawson one week before the wedding. The weather was so bad, they spent the week pacing the floor in Whitehorse. The day before the wedding, I went to Sunday services and asked Rev. Alsop for a postponement. He got up to make the announcement and the sun came shining through the church window right on me. He did not make the announcement. As I left the church, there was a message for me to go to the post office for my ride to the airport. The plane was

Charlie Williams, Tubby, Peggy, and Marjorie

coming. As the plane landed, a snowstorm was right on its tail. We were married in St. Paul's Cathedral in Dawson.

The church overflowed with our friends who then proceeded to our house for the reception. For two days before the wedding, a steady stream of people had been helping make sandwiches and bringing cakes and liquor for punch.

Because of the snowstorm, we had to wait for a plane to Whitehorse. Finally, on December 1st, the plane arrived. It was dubbed the 'Honeymoon Express' because of the two sets of newlyweds aboard. We took a taxi down the hill to the Whitehorse Inn. My first impression was of men and women all dressed in GI issue, lined up around the block to get their two-bottle ration of Christmas liquor. There were bonfires every few feet to keep those in line from freezing.

When we arrived in Whitehorse, Tubby's good friend Arne Andersen held another reception for us. The guests were a mixture of old Dawson friends and Tubby's workmates from the US Engineering Department.

What started as a simple punch was constantly reinforced by whatever people uncorked and poured in. Occasionally, someone would add water. It was a great reception. Everyone chipped in to a collection for us. The $126 collected bought us a second-hand radio.

The first meal I cooked was for Dad, who was leaving for Snag the next day. I was slicing a loaf of bread when I heard a CRUNCH. I had cut through a very well-baked cockroach. That was the last time I bought bread in Whitehorse. The next morning, Dad stayed over and Arne came to help. The cookstove was installed and bread set. With the bread-making came visitors. Harry Fatt used to call in to walk to work with Tubby. He'd casually remark, "That bread baking sure smells good!" That night, friends would 'drop by', having been to the army mess to acquire jams one couldn't buy in town. Others would bring chocolates, hot chocolate envelopes, apples of a size and juiciness we would not otherwise see.

Whitehorse was WINDY! Occasionally, the wind would blow over the Quonset hut next door and straight down the cookstove chimney. Once, the cabin filled with smoke and I ran out into the street clad only in my housedress. Across the street was a warm storage building. The GIs came running out of it, threw a warm coat around me, then went to see what was wrong in our cabin. They put out the fire in the stove, which was great. They also wanted, right then and there, to raise the chimney and would get us some more stovepipe to make ours taller. Canucks were not allowed to have any GI supplies, but Tubby did the job later that night with material supplied by the Americans.

The US army switched to all oil burners. We burned wood. There was a knock at the door one morning. "Ma'am, would you look the other way for a bit? I was told to take this firewood to the dump. I think I've found a good place to dump it." We had enough wood to last until May when we left Whitehorse [briefly, when Tubby was called up]. Another time, the U.S. Engineering Department found out I was washing clothes on a scrubboard. Next day, a gas-powered washing machine arrived. We didn't dare keep it as the customs officer was getting tougher.

Joann—Customs duty had not been paid on any of the supplies the Americans brought into Canada. The result was that there were huge dumps where perfectly good washing machines, refrigerators, stovepipes, and even vehicles were buried.

Peggy—Our first Christmas, Arne Anderson supplied a huge turkey, which I cooked at his place for him, Jack (pronounced 'Yak'), Jim Wake, two GIs, and ourselves. My Christmas pudding was well-received except that the overproof rum I poured over it didn't all burn off before the flames died down. The man who ate the centre helping broke out in a sweat!

Although there were some 18,000 American GIs and construction workers, and about 3,000 Canucks in Whitehorse, there was very little trouble. Whitehorse had been a town of 500 people at the most. Pearl Harbor and the entrance of the States into the war caused the big surge in population. The Alaska Highway had to be built and built quickly to get supplies to and from the Northern armed forces bases. Some Whitehorse facilities were severely taxed. Restaurants were full and not clean. Line-ups for a show [movie] would be blocks long.

As we lived across the street from the show, we soon got to know when to get over into the line before the cut-off. Our friends would gather at our place. Harry Fatt, the lone bachelor, would run over and get in line. When he got close to the door, we would join him. We all knew 'Big Nick', the owner, from Dawson. Arne's wife, Anita, was his usher. Nick would ask Anita, "Are the kids coming tonight?" If we were, he'd put reserved signs on a prime viewing row for us.

When Tubby first went to Whitehorse to work in the U.S. Engineering Department depot, he was the only Canuck there. As time went on and GIs were posted elsewhere, Tubby was able to get several Dawson fellows to replace them.

Every town has its local colour. Whitehorse was no exception. Back of our place, the Inn waitresses were running a 'night business', all night. The GIs kept cutting across our yard, causing us to lose sleep. I mentioned it to the RCMP who hadn't been aware of it. The RCMP spoke to the US army MPs. Guess who were first in line the next night!

Living in Whitehorse was very different for me. I had a lovely rose parka with white fur that fit right in in Dawson City. In Whitehorse, everyone wore army colours. I got stopped so often, the MPs told Tubby "for goodness sake, go draw an army parka for her." Tubby never did because spring came and I didn't need it.

Shopping was a real problem. Two cans of vegetables per week. Fresh vegetables were very rare. Kippy Boerner, the Northern Commercial company manager, had his own ration system. We ate a lot of onions, boiled, creamed, etc. At the meat market, we would line up and the butcher would ask, "What will you have, lady? We've got round steak and ground round steak. What'll it be?" We fared pretty well as our friends went to the army mess and the cooks would give them stuff to bring over.

The RCMP had a midnight curfew. Jim Wake (an RCMP officer) and some others were over one night when I realized it was 11:55. I alerted Jim, who was out of the door like a shot and down the alley. Unfortunately, sanitation in Whitehorse at that time was lax. The outhouse behind us had become overfull so the people had lifted the trapdoor and let everything run out into the alley. [This was an outhouse with a bucket, not a hole in the ground]. The trapdoor was there so the honey wagon man could get the bucket to empty it. Jim fell face-down into this mess. When he reached barracks, the boys had to wash him down with the garden hose. His dignity was bruised; the boys had a good laugh. Many of the RCMP had been transferred to Whitehorse from Dawson and we knew them well. They took great pleasure in telling us about Jim's problem. Jim's mishap accomplished what all my complaining had not. The next morning, a clean-up crew of prisoners was shovelling it all up. The sanitation trucks ('honey wagons') came regularly after that.

Tubby and Arne did a lot of skiing before we were married. Arne was the instigator of creating a ski hill and clubhouse across the river. The work and the skiing were great pastimes for everyone involved.

In April 1944, Tubby got called up. We sold what little furniture we had and packed all our goods to go to Vancouver. Tubby was rejected. To this day, we believe the US army had him deferred as he was vital in the 'spare parts' depot. He went back to Whitehorse and I stayed in our wee flat. In late July, Tubby left the US army's employ to run the machinery department for the Northern Commercial company. This came with an apartment. It didn't take me long to pack and fly home. With Maribeth on the way, I had a margin of twelve days to fly or wait until after her arrival. I made it.

September 1, 1944, my brother Frank came into town to go to school and stayed with us until November when Mom and Dad came back to town from Snag, where Dad was superintendent. Mom and Dad then bought a small house and settled in. That little house started out on Lambert Street next to Arne's. Dad moved it to 505 Jarvis Street and spent the next 15 years enlarging and improving it, before selling it and returning to company housing in Bear Creek as the last superintendent of YCGC.

We stayed in Whitehorse another 12 years. Our son Franklin (named for my brother, but always called Skipper) was born severely brain-damaged, which took its toll. We had to place him in a BC institution in 1955. In 1956, with the economic future in the Yukon looking bleak, we made the decision to leave for BC ourselves.

✦ ✦ ✦

Joann—My cousin Frank, John Edward Franklin Hoggan, Peggy's brother, was enough older than me that I did not get to know him as well as I would have liked. But, like the rest of the Hoggan men, he was very family-oriented and I always enjoyed the time I had with him. Frank would complete high school in Whitehorse and Seattle, where he lived with our aunt Florrie, and go on to graduate in the first class of mining engineers from the University of Alaska. Mining being at a downturn at the time, he returned to complete a second degree in civil engineering. A university degree was unusual for a Yukoner at the time. It was expensive and there was no assistance from the government as there is now. He would have had some encouragement from his father Johnny and from the Chancellor of the University of Alaska who was, coincidentally, both Johnny and Frank's employer on 'the creeks' during the summers. Frank was a true northerner whose career as a soils engineer kept him in the North where he worked extensively in the Arctic as an expert in permafrost. He and his wife Jean Gilbert, whom he met at the University of Alaska, lived in Edmonton and had four children.

Peggy, Tubby, and Frank died within days of each other. Frank in December 2007, Tubby, then Peggy in January 2008.

* ✦ *

Maribeth Tubman Mainer, daughter of Peggy and Tubby, great-granddaughter of Ned and Kate, contributed greatly to this book by transcribing Ned and Kate's letters, scanning many of the pictures used in the book, and contributing her parents' memoirs. She also wrote of her childhood in Whitehorse.

Maribeth—It was 1998 and I had returned to the Yukon for the first time since 1956. We were heading for Dawson on the Klondike Highway when I looked up from changing my granddaughter's diaper and said, "The Clear Creek turn-off is just ahead." It was.

Such is the nature of my memories of my Yukon childhood—flashes with incredible clarity: standing in a crib with intense winter sunlight streaming from behind me; coming into that same room a year later, now darkened with blinds drawn, to meet my new baby brother. I remember staggering down the hallway, wearing a green housecoat, seeing the sparkle of candlelight on crystal and wondering why the adults looked so shocked. (I had been semi-conscious with red measles and had just awakened.) Mom got up immediately and cooked the double-yolk farm-fresh egg one of our neighbours had brought for me. That was the only egg that I willingly ate in the Yukon.

My mother used to tell of the time when I was three and got separated from her, surrounded by a pack of dogs fighting, and how she knew enough not to intervene unless they noticed me. They moved on; I was unscathed and unafraid. Dog fights were common and the sound of them stays with all of us. We were taught to keep away and never try to stop a fight. I had a rather eclectic exposure to school in the Yukon.

Kindergarten was only available at Christ the King, the Catholic school, so I went there. Lambert Street School was next. I had to start school on my own because I was boarding at the convent for three weeks during a family emergency. Lambert Street School, for me, was leftover army huts with the bathroom in the main building. The main building was the same school my grandfather Johnny and his siblings attended in 1909 when the family left the Kluane country. I finished off that school year in Brooks Brook in a one-room school, staying with my aunt Marjorie and uncle Curly during another family emergency.

In August 1952, when Prince Philip opened Whitehorse Elementary/ High School, I was there, standing for hours in the hot sun in my starched dress and white gloves. Finally, the washrooms were accessible! In the same building as my schoolroom!

Raised in an apartment downtown, above the Northern Commercial company business office, I had to be quiet at home. If I played with other kids, it was at their houses or at my grandparents' house. Living as close to the river as we did, even after the NC days, the prohibition against going onto Front Street was absolute. After all, a child had disappeared with only his tricycle ever found on the dock. Looking back, I have to chuckle at how this prohibition guided my childhood habits.

At six, I was being paddled in a makeshift boat on the ponds at the refinery end of town. No life jackets. No adult supervision. I remember walking over those same ponds after they froze but before the snow, and being able to see every plant through the clear ice. At nine, I was going down to the shipyards to lie on the riverbank near the laundry, fascinated by the river currents. Many times, I walked the railway tracks to the Whitehorse Rapids and lay on the bank, fascinated by the white water. In winter, I would walk a circuit from town, across the Whiskey Flats ice bridge along the road to the other ice bridge and back home.

In spring, there was the crocus-watch. I think I was four when I first climbed Burns Hill with the Burns and St. Jean kids to pick my first crocus (mountain anemone or pasque flower). I never missed a spring crocus hunt until a slide put the patch out of bounds about 1955. That same hill was our sledding and tobogganing hill—trees, rocks, and all.

Even as small children, we knew that playing there held danger and did not go there alone.

One of the dangers was the blue clay 'stream' at the bottom, behind the graveyard. Adults learned about it when the graves sank; kids knew that you could get stuck in it or, worse, lose a shoe or boot in it and have parents discover where you had been.

Children look at risk differently than adults, take their own messages from what they hear. We may not have understood what tuberculosis or TB meant, but we did understand that if someone "went out to the san" (sanatorium), they were unlikely to return. Polio epidemics of 1952 and 1953 closed the swimming pool and Takhini Hot Springs and kept us from gathering for the Coronation Day parade. One of the mommies we knew "went out to the san" and did not come back. I suspect the milder polio cases were kept quiet. I certainly do not remember the yellow quarantine signs for polio that went up for chicken pox.

No one was supposed to leave town during the 1953 polio epidemic, but this was not enforced. We went to our grandparents' on Henderson Creek, flying from Whitehorse to Dawson City then taking the steamboat to Stewart. En route, we visited the Dubois' in Bear Creek.

Now Whitehorse, at that time, had no soil except what was trucked in from McIntyre Creek. We had no lawns; gardens were rare. I had never eaten a carrot that had not been weeks in storage. 'Uncle Middy' Dubois took me out to his garden, at Bear Creek, pulled a bunch of carrots out of the ground, knocked most of the dirt off against his overalls, sluiced them off under his garden tap, and handed me one to eat. Mom was just beaming! Many times, she had tried to describe this but her words could not capture the taste and the crunchiness. It was everything she had said and more!

Our six weeks summer at the mining camp at Henderson Creek where Johnny and Pete Foth were mining, where my brother and I were the only children, remains one of the highlights of my life. Barrel chairs were true barrel chairs—made by nesting a nail keg inside a larger barrel cut to chair-shape and daintily slipcovered. The heater was a converted oil drum. The cabin was relatively new; frame and floor of the preceding tent cabin still stood a few feet away. [This would have been a white-walled canvas tent probably not much different from the one from which Kate chased a bear when Johnny, Maribeth's grandfather, was a small boy. These tents, which could have a woodstove in them, were often used by the Natives as they moved around to their traplines or

Maribeth, Henderson Creek, 1955—
tailing piles and dredge pond in background

fish camp. Coming across some poles a certain length in a clearing was a sign that such a tent had been used there.] There was no electricity so Nanna [Gladys] was happy to have Mom there to take her turn at hand-wheeling the Singer sewing machine. Ice cream was hand-churned, using ice chipped from the permafrost when stripping and thawing the ground on the flats. The 'cream' was evaporated milk but that is what we were used to.

My most memorable wake-up call: "Hold your brother!" There was a bear coming through the bedroom window and Nanna had the rifle aimed between his eyes. One shot through the brain but he made it a dozen yards up the hill before dropping. Six bears were shot that summer, one of them by Mom as he raided the vegetable garden.

The lessons learned that summer stayed with me. The camp deep-freeze was an old mineshaft into the permafrost. I glimpsed my first wolverine. I saw the damage a wolverine did to the mess hall storeroom and was glad my wolverine had passed the cabin by. Each time a bear carcass was dragged to the dump, the last one was already gone. If we were picking blueberries, we retired to the truck if a bear was picking that patch. However, one grizzly would leave his berry patch on the Henderson-Stewart road to race the pickup, apparently just for fun. I had my first collective action experience: the squirrels did not like the cherry pie we had put out for them (we couldn't cut into it). They came to the cabin and protested, noisily, as a group.

I wish my first and Mom's last trip on a steamboat had been a positive experience. For some reason, we were given a cabin with steam pipes running through it. It was very hot and even dangerous for small children. We couldn't get another cabin even though there were some empty ones, so the trip from Dawson to Stewart was very uncomfortable. With many years of family history on the boats, Mom was devastated. However, being flown out of Henderson by Pat Callison was a fantastic experience, including my little brother taking us into a nosedive over the Indian River. This happened when Pat put Skipper on his lap to show him the controls. Skipper, who was very strong, grabbed the stick and Pat had a hard time getting him to release it.

It was good for Mom to have enjoyable flights. Twice, she had flown my brother to Vancouver for emergency medical treatment. The only concession to an emergency was priority on the regularly scheduled flight, which could take 12 hours to Vancouver. On one flight, Skip was taken by ambulance to the plane and met by ambulance but denied oxygen on the flight. "It's for the pilot."

In 1954, Dad left the NC, having bought a Snap-On tool business. We moved into the old Harbottle house. No more running water or flush toilet. Pump the water for washing; buy it for drinking. Have the honey wagon stop by regularly. Skip and I loved having our own rooms, being able to run and yell at home and to dig in the dirt. However, when the heating bill overtook the rent and the kitchen pump froze, broke off, and fell out the kitchen window, it was time to give it up.

We spent the last year-and-a-half in the apartment behind my uncle's drugstore. Not much warmer but it had running water in the bathroom and the rent was affordable. We even had a yard—the woodlot across the alley was great for building playhouses. If the 'business lady' the other side of the woodpile had no customers, she might serve us cookies. If she had customers, though, we had to stay on our side of the woodpile.

In 1955, Mom took Skip outside for the last time. We could no longer care for him at home. After three years, he had finally been accepted into Woodlands. Our relatives in Vancouver had booked Mom an obstetrician's appointment as she was pregnant again. Skipper's difficult birth had left him brain-damaged so the obstetrician was very firm about the plan he laid out. Mom remained at her aunt's and I stayed with my grandparents for three months. I spent another summer at Clear Creek where my grandfather was mining. Heather was born by Caesarean section in Vancouver, safe and healthy.

The winter of 1955 was COLD! Business was bad enough without everything grinding to a halt for weeks at a time. On a trip to Vancouver to scope out new business opportunities, Dad decided that the boom was over in the Yukon. He suggested moving Outside. Mom started packing. They sold the Snap-On business, swapped the tool van for an old pick-up, loaded all they wanted to take with them, and headed off down the highway in May 1956. I stayed behind to finish grade six, then flew out to join them. The night I left Whitehorse, a double rainbow filled the sky over what is now Riverdale.

10

BEAR CREEK

The first 10 years of my life were spent in Bear Creek, Yukon Territory, a place which has almost disappeared from history even though it was the centre of gold mining and processing in the Yukon from the early 1900s to 1966. My uncle Johnny lived there from 1927 until 1943, then returned in 1959 as Superintendent of Dredging and lived there until the Company closed in 1966. My mother went to school from there to Dawson City from 1928 until she graduated. In 1934, when she married my father, she returned. My uncle Greg Hoggan lived near there working for the Company, from the late 1930s to about 1942.

The history of Bear Creek and the people who lived there deserves to be recorded. My interest lies primarily in the people but it is necessary to introduce the settlement and the Company, the Yukon Consolidated Gold Corporation (YCGC), as well. To that end, I have started by giving a brief history of Bear Creek and the YCGC, followed by short histories of some of the people who lived there when I was a child, followed by some of my childhood memories.

The map I have drawn is the Bear Creek I remember, circa 1940–45. Most people moved at least once and some many more times, so my memories may not be compatible with others who lived there at another time. The Mays, Craigs, and my sister Bobbie vetted the map and are in general agreement with it. What I term 'the camp' is the collection of Yukon Consolidated Gold Company buildings, not all of which I have included as many had no significance to me as a child.

Bear Creek, a tributary of the Klondike, was staked in 1896. By 1906, a small settlement was established. A merger of various companies over time became Yukon Consolidated Gold Company in the mid-1920s. The majority of the gold was obtained with the use of gold-mining dredges. Bear Creek was the centre of operations and remained that until 1966 when dredging ceased. It was eight miles from Dawson City on the old road, six miles by the new road (about 1943) over Jackson Tailings, tailings being the gravel left by the dredges which had worked the ground in earlier years. Dawson, as capital of the territory depended on the federal government and the YCGC for its livelihood. Dawson City, Bear Creek, and the Yukon Consolidated Gold Company were interdependent.

Dawson City was the capital of the Yukon Territory until 1953. It had both a Catholic and a public school, churches, a hospital, stores, a post office, docks, hotels, and tourist services. Tourism was an important resource, even before the Klondike Highway was completed, with the riverboats providing transportation for tourists. As the capital of the territory, it had the administration building (now the Dawson Museum) and all the business of government and administration of the territory took place there. According to Betty Fournier St. Jean [2009 interview], there was a lot of patronage and a change of government meant a change of employees. Upper management of the YCGC lived in Dawson, not Bear Creek. There was a complex social hierarchy because of the relationships between government, YCGC, merchants, and church interests. Dawson was a white-collar, government, YCGC, and business centre. Bear Creek was its blue-collar neighbour. Betty St. Jean and others say Dawson residents saw themselves as superior to Bear Creek residents despite the interdependence.

The Great Depression, starting in 1928, left the gold-producing area of the Yukon pretty well untouched. The price of gold rose during that period from about $25 an ounce to $35 an ounce. There was full employment in the gold-mining industry. Those of us who grew up in the North didn't hear any stories about the Depression from our parents or grandparents and knew almost nothing about it until we learned about it in school or from people Outside who had lived through it.

The little that was written about Bear Creek was in magazines such as the *Western Miner,* which published the following in January 1953:

> "The Bear Creek shops, offices, and community bear testimony to the importance of Yukon Consolidated [the Company] in maintaining the Dawson district . . . the Company supplies utilities in the form of light and water to the City of Dawson."

Electricity in Dawson was costly but Bear Creek residents had free electricity. Woodstoves were necessary for heat. There were no electric stoves.

One of the families that came to Dawson as part of the Company management were the Arnold Nordales. They were from Alaska, but had roots in the Yukon, as Arnold Nordale's father had been exploring in the Stewart River area in 1896. Young Arnold, after his birth in Seattle, came to the Yukon in 1899. His father later opened a restaurant in Dawson. When it burned down in 1901, the family moved to Dominion Creek where they lived until returning to Alaska in 1904 during the Fairbanks rush. After completing his engineering degree at Stanford University, Arnold went back home to Alaska. In 1935, he returned to Dawson as a civil and mining engineer for the Company, bringing with him his wife and daughters Joann and Marilyn. The senior Nordales lived in Dawson until 1959 when they retired to Seattle.

The Nordales lived in Dawson City in a company house at 7th and Princess which is now a Parks Canada building. My parents and the Nordales were not socially connected—my father operated heavy equipment and drove trucks for the Company and there were definite class distinctions, not just between management and employees but often between those who lived in Dawson and those who lived in Bear Creek, as noted above. It was a small world and I was named Joann as my mother liked the name. Joann and Marilyn, her sister, often rode their bikes from Dawson to visit Dodie Creamer, their Bear Creek school friend, to play tennis. Afterwards Dodie's mother, Pat, served them root beer and cookies. It would have been quite a ride, eight miles of gravel over the old road around the bluff.

Some management and administration staff for the YCGC, who were involved in the day-to-day operations, lived in Bear Creek. Andrew Baird, the Company's chief accountant, was one of them. I remember him as always dressed in a suit, a very erect and proper man. The Nordales used to visit him on Sundays. Marilyn remembers that he was originally from Australia and an early stampeder in 1898. He regaled the family with tales of the early days and often spoke of the strong men of the North. He was one of them, having seriously injured himself after falling down a gold-mining shaft. One leg was amputated and during his hospital stay, he studied accounting. Mr. Baird also took up knitting and it was said he knit a pair of socks a week for the war effort during WWII. The Nordale visits often included knitting instructions for Mrs. Nordale. Mr. Baird opened his house one afternoon a week to the women of Bear Creek to use in the war effort. Evy Craig took her sewing machine and I remember my mother going off to roll bandages. The Baird house was a large one so I suppose that is why it was used.

Bear Creek was in most ways a company town as everyone worked for the Company, save the Fourniers who owned the roadhouse. But Bear Creek residents had to go to Dawson City for all services and while the Company 'owned' some of the land, most was Crown land. The Company provided some housing for the small contingent of local administration and skilled staff and there was provision for single men with a bunkhouse and mess hall. Most families had to provide their own housing. Later in the 1940s, the Company built more houses for staff and built a community hall where movies were shown about once a month.

Before that, however, the Company provided few extras for employees. The mess hall was used for community events like plays, dances and Christmas parties for the children. I even heard stories that the men had to move the bunkhouses from one creek to another on their own time when the mining sites changed, as they did when one piece of ground was played out. The men supplied their own bedding. In the late thirties, my uncle Greg, working twelve hours a day as a bow decker on a dredge, made 50 cents an hour, seven days a week. Board allowance was $45 a month. My father made $5 a day as a truck driver. As a heavy-duty machine operator (Caterpillars, drag lines, shovels etc.) he probably made more. Costs were very high—butter was 45 cents a pound as was coffee. Eggs were 75 cents a dozen, and $1 if they were flown in. There was a period when the Company couldn't pay anyone for three months. It was the beginning of WWII, taxes had gone up, the Company was in poor shape, and the equipment was wearing out and hard to replace. The Company had to dig up the gold before the men could be paid. The Dawson merchants allowed credit to the workers.

According to my uncle Greg, there was an informal work stoppage in the late 1930s to protest the poor working conditions and pay. The strike lasted for about ten days, after which pay went up to 60 cents an hour. I have been told that Arthur Hand, who supervised the machine shops and mechanical works, supported the workers and was then fired by the Company. He moved from Company housing to the roadhouse as a paying guest. Later, he worked for my uncle Johnny at Clear Creek and Henderson Creek.

The camp was situated on an arm (we called it the slough) of the Klondike River which was to the North. Water courses were constantly changing as dredges worked the ground. There was an island and a bridge to the island over the slough. From the hill to the North of Bear Creek, the Klondike Siphon, a large flume, brought, or had in the past brought, water from the North Klondike to the workings in Bear Creek or Bonanza Creek. Dredging required huge amounts of water as the dredges floated and operated on water and water was used in sorting the gold from the gravel.

The only road from Dawson and beyond went through the yard, which was a large space flanked on one side by the machine shops, administration building, and others. Across the yard was the bunkhouse and mess hall. There was some Company housing there too. Mr. Gloslie, the assistant resident manager, lived on that side of the yard. His wife Hazel always had a wonderful display of flowers. Mr. Baird's house was just around the corner near the bridge to the island and other staff lived nearby. Jean Fournier's roadhouse was next to the yard, on the road that went through the camp and on to the airstrip, his brother Archie's farm, the Arlington roadhouse, then on to the creeks and mining areas. The roadhouse was the only non-YCGC business in Bear Creek.

The yard was a common meeting ground, like a main street, since mail came to the administration building and the freezers for the community were located in one of the buildings. Houses not owned by the Company were scattered around, placed wherever the owner wanted to put it.

✦ ✦ ✦

According to my mother, about 45 families lived in Bear Creek at the time we did, 1934 to 1945. I don't remember that many, probably because they were not family friends or did not have children in my age group. Some people I remember very clearly. I begin with my parents, followed by the Craig, Chapman, and May families, the parents and grandparents (in the case of the Craig grandparents who, like mine, came to the Yukon in the early years of the gold rush), then the first playmates my sister Bobbie and I had. As small children, we all lived near each other on the bench, a flat area above the Camp. We are still friends.

My mother Marjorie worked at the Arcade Café in Dawson City after she graduated from high school, the only work she could get. Had her father Ned been able to afford it, she might have gone Outside for further education as her sisters Dorothy and Florrie had done.

My father John Cochrane 'Curly' Stevenson, went north in 1932. His brother Jimmy was already working on the dredges. They were from Langley, BC, where they had lived on the farm their father bought through a land purchase programme for WWI veterans. He died in a traffic accident in New Westminster in the early '20s leaving them, their two brothers Bob and Stanley, and their mother. Jimmy later went to Colombia in South America, as did other dredge men from the Yukon. My father was always called Curly because of his

Frank Hoggan, Bobbie and Joann Stevenson, and Marion May on the
Klondike slough, with the siphon in the background

Mr. Baird's house, 1989

The yard: administration building is on the left, gold room is behind the tree—the old road to Dawson, around the bluff, ran between the gold room and administration building, the road over Jackson's Tailings was on the right of the gold room.

Machine shop, 1989.

thick very curly hair. He drove truck and became a skilled Caterpillar and heavy equipment operator. One winter, he worked on the Cat trains with my uncle Johnny.

My parents met and married in Dawson City, 1934, and I was born in 1935. We lived in a log cabin that my father had disassembled and rebuilt on the Bench in Bear Creek. When my mother was pregnant with my sister Roberta (usually called Bobbie), my father decided she should be born Outside. So, several months pregnant and with me about 8 months old, she went Outside for the first time on the last boat up the Yukon river that fall. My mother had never been beyond Whitehorse before, and it was just a small village at the time. The whole thing must have been quite an unnerving experience for her. Fortunately my father's family were very welcoming, especially my grandmother Mary who, as my mother has said, "became a dear friend." My father joined us later and we all returned to Bear Creek in the spring of 1936.

◆ ◆ ◆

The Craigs, like my grandparents, were early Yukon residents too. They met in Dawson City and were married there.

Benjamin Craig arrived in Dawson City in 1898, when he was 21, as part of the 'Ogilvie Party'. Ogilvie was a surveyor and had spent years in the North. Benjamin was a distant relative of his. It seems Ben did not have a specific role when he arrived but became a postal clerk in Dawson. Ben is credited with doing everything in his power to make sure all the incoming mail got to the addressee. He never became Postmaster but he was a list-maker and kept extensive records, including lists of names and locations of the men on the creeks and camps.

Rosanna Marek was born in 1878 and emigrated from Czechoslovakia with her sister Anna in 1896. The sisters went first to the US, where they had relatives. Both were adventurous and decided to go to the Klondike to look for work in 1900. Rosanna worked for Skookum Jim Mason, one of the discoverers of gold in the region. Tom Dickson, a former NWMP member, was married to Jim's niece Louise. Tom was, according to Rosanna, helping Skookum Jim with his businesses.

Rosanna's English was poor, but she was hired to care for Skookum Jim's daughter Daisy. It was there, with Daisy's help, that she perfected her English. Later, she worked in a boarding house in Dawson with her sister. When the owner wanted to leave the North, the sisters bought the boarding house.

Benjamin and Rosanna married and had two sons—Benjamin, who died at age 15, and Clarence (Clary), born in 1905. Ben worked in the post office until 1924 when the family moved to Vancouver where they bought a lot at 39th and Dunbar.

The following year, 1925, Clary, who was then 20 years old, and his friend Ralph Zaccarelli decided to return to the Yukon. They didn't have much money when they got to Whitehorse and they needed to get to Dawson City. It was winter and Cat trains were carrying freight from Whitehorse to Dawson and Mayo. They hired on to care for 150 cases of eggs and keep them from freezing as far as Stewart Crossing, four days from Whitehorse. Each night, the eggs had to be unloaded and taken into the warm roadhouse. (There were 11 roadhouses on the winter road between Whitehorse and Dawson.). At Stewart Crossing, the Cat train turned to go to Mayo. Clary and Ralph then had to walk to Dawson, about 100 miles away. It took them three days.

Clary went Outside again and apprenticed at Heatley Machine Works in an industrial area of Vancouver. By the latter part of 1929 and the start of the Depression, there was little work in Vancouver. Clary decided to return to the North in 1931 and gives this account of his first job in Bear Creek. All the Craig papers are in the Yukon Archives, but I was given the two pieces in this book, written by Clary by his daughter, Lorraine Craig Mackie. This first piece is a good description of the work in Bear Creek which changed little over time.

Clary Craig—Now without a job and not a chance to get one in Vancouver, I decided to head back to the Yukon again. The gold-mining business had not declined during the Depression, in fact it was the reverse. The price of gold remained stable . . . I was certain I could get a job with the big dredging company in the Klondike.

After a fine trip up the coast to Skagway, Alaska, and on the narrow gauge White Pass Railroad from Skagway to Whitehorse—110 miles and down the Yukon River 400 miles on the steamer *Casca*—I arrived in Dawson on June 25th, 1931. It was good to see the old town again.

As our boat was being tied to the dock, I spotted one of my old school chums, Franklin Osborn. He was surprised and glad to see me. Franklin was an automotive mechanic for the mining company located at the Company's headquarters at Bear Creek eight miles east of Dawson on the Klondike river. This was my lucky day.

When I told Franklin that I was looking for a job, he said that a tractor driver was needed for hauling freight to the mining operations on the creeks. I told him I had never operated a tractor. He said if I came along with him to Bear Creek on one of the tractors, which were being loaded at the dock, he would show me how to operate the tractor.

So, after the three tractor (Cat) trains had been loaded [the trains would have been at the docks to be loaded with freight from the barge pushed by the *Casca*], I put my suitcase aboard and off we went to Bear Creek. I watched Franklin take over. He explained the operation to me, and by the time we reached Bear Creek, Franklin said he would recommend me for the job. I knew Mr. Baird, the mining manager, since I was a small boy. For a time, the Baird family lived across the lane from the Craigs on Church Street in Dawson. When talking with Mr. Baird, I mentioned that I had several years experience in machine-shop practice and he said that an opening in the machine shop might come up. In the meantime, if Franklin thought I could operate the tractor, the job was mine. I was now a 'Cat skinner'.

This was the start of my many years experience in the operation, supervision, and maintenance of heavy-duty equipment, involving tractors, Cat trains, bulldozers, shovels, dragline, trucks, etc. Prior to the mid-1920s in the Klondike mining area, hauling freight was done by horses. The big gold-dredging company had to house, feed, and maintain a large number of large heavy draft horses to haul everything to all their operations in a radius of approximately fifty miles. When track-type tractors became available, the horses were gradually phased out.

For the first few years, when tractors came into use, the trailers used were the heavy wheeled wagons drawn by the horses—altered so the wagons could be coupled to form a train—usually two or three

Clarence Craig with Lorraine, *photo courtesy of L. Mackie*

wagons, depending on the road conditions. The roads in the Klondike mining area at this time were poorly-maintained gravel roads with many potholes and swampy areas on which trucks could not possibly be used. Small pickup trucks and cars could be used but often ran into difficulties, especially when roads were wet. In winter, of course, sleighs were used for heavy hauling.

The main placer mining company in the Klondike at this time, under the name of Yukon Consolidated Gold Corporation, operated and maintained at the most twelve large bucketline floating dredges, a number of hydraulic operations, and an 18,000 HP hydroelectric power plant to supply electric power to all operations as well as power to Dawson City.

The dredges were located on a number of the tributaries of the Klondike and Indian Rivers which flowed into the Yukon River. At each location, there was a camp with bunkhouses, mess, etc. The headquarters for all operations were located at Bear Creek camp, about eight miles from Dawson City, up the Klondike River. All the outlying operations were serviced by Bear Creek. The huge dredges which operate 24 hours during the mining season required constant maintenance and repairs, so a very large and fully-equipped machine and forging shop, warehouses, spare parts, etc. were located at Bear Creek Camp.

I started my job as a 'Cat skinner' the next day under the direction of the transportation foreman, Dan McDonald, a former teamster who really knew the freighting business—a really nice guy. He didn't know much about mechanics but he surely knew how to secure a load and secure the freight wagons. Franklin Osborn, the automotive mechanic, at times would drive one of the Cats.

In the 1931 season, the Company was operating five dredges and two hydraulic operations. There were three freighting tractors and one smaller service tractor. The normal working hours were ten hours per day, seven days a week. Pay—labour—was $4.50 a day and board; others $5.50 a day and board. Cat skinners received $200 per month and board, but no overtime, and had to service their own 'Cats'. Transportation had its own maintenance and repair shop with a well-stocked supply of repair parts. Major overhauls were done mostly in the late fall and early winter, before sleighs could be used for heavy winter hauling.

+ ✦ +

Joann—Ernest Chapman was born in Northhampton, England in 1884. When he was 20 years old, he emigrated to the US, but then moved to Ontario. He worked on the railroad to get across Canada, then went north to Dawson City. Once there, he set up a supply business which became a store. Over time he also established some trading posts.

Christine Wiklund was born in Goddede, Sweden in 1884. In 1902, her brother sent her the fare to join him in Seattle, Washington. She spoke no English and worked as a waitress, a maid, and in a logging camp. Later, she got a contract to work in the Yukon and went to Dawson City to work as a waitress.

Ernest and Christine married in 1913. Evelyn ('Evy') was born in 1916, and Virginia ('Ginny') in 1918. Ginny is one of the friends who went to Stewart with Marjorie one summer after Kate died and, as Ned wrote in a letter to Lill, "It is good to hear laughter in the old home again."

Clary Craig and Evelyn Chapman married in 1934. Lorraine was born in 1935, six months younger than me, and Anita in 1936, six months younger than Bobbie.

Gramma and Grampa Chappie, as we called Lorraine and Anita's grandparents Ernest and Christine, were well-known to all us children. We remember the 'jump' seats in their car and how Lorraine and Anita fared at Easter, where they benefitted from the store the Chapmans owned. I remember a large dog filled with candy which made me quite envious. The strongest memory of Grampa Chappie is the plane crash just after take-off on January 31, 1941. He and the pilot, Lionel Vines, were killed. Grampa Chappie had been on his way to his Bonnet Plume Trading Post. This was a great shock to all of us and Bobbie, Marion, and I remember going to Archie Fournier's farm where the plane had crashed behind the barn to see the plane. Lorraine and Anita were not allowed to see it. It was our first experience of the death of someone we knew.

+ ✦ +

The Mays, like Curly Stevenson, came north in the late '20s and early '30s when the Yukon Territory and Alaska were still large areas with small populations, relatively isolated from the rest of Canada and the USA All were part of the 'old' Yukon.

Sidney Walter May, the eldest of six, was born in Birmingham, England in 1905. The family emigrated to Toronto in 1906. In the 1920s, he rode the freight trains and took whatever jobs he could get. When he got to Vancouver, he planned to work his way to China on a ship. He and his friend were so broke they bought a loaf of bread to share, then went to a movie matinée to sleep. After walking the streets all night, they saw a recruitment poster for the RCMP and decided to join rather than go to China. Sid was accepted, his friend was not. Sid went to Regina, still the home of the RCMP, to be trained, and was posted to Dawson City about 1929. From there he was sent to Old Crow. Old Crow is a very old Native village located well above the Arctic Circle and close to the Alaska border. One of the many duties of the RCMP was to care for and assist anyone who needed help and investigate the cause of any death. An old trapper had died of unknown causes and Sid had to take his body to Fort Yukon in Alaska, the nearest hospital, for an autopsy.

Clara Hayes Dickenson, whose family had emigrated from England to the US, graduated from her nursing studies at the Good Samaritan Hospital in Portland, Oregon in 1927. She nursed in Anchorage, Juneau, and Ketchican, Alaska. When she saw an ad for a competition for a nurse in Ft. Yukon, Alaska, she applied and was chosen over 200 applicants.

The body Sid was responsible for had to be transported sitting up as it was frozen solid. The body was put in the basement in the hospital to thaw, which it did, slowly and with some movement as it did so. This caused the Native women working in the hospital to refuse to go downstairs for supplies or stoke the furnace. Clara thought that the Mountie who had accompanied the corpse was a strange fellow. He wrote that he was impressed by the new nurse. Clara, when she got to know him, changed her mind.

The RCMP had very strict rules about any of the men marrying and permission had to be asked for and approved by their commanding

Sid and Clara May, *photo courtesy of M. Dore*

officer before a marriage could take place. Sid had the required amount of money in the bank and was old enough to marry so he applied, fully expecting to be granted permission. The distances involved meant that it would be some time before official approval would arrive.

Not expecting to be denied, Clara and Sid married in Fort Yukon, Alaska in 1932. She went with Sid, by dog team, to Old Crow. That caused some problems for her years later when she applied for her Canadian Old Age Pension. One of the questions was "How did you enter Canada: Ship, Rail, Road." Her answer, of course, was "dog team". Since that was not on the list, the bureaucrats didn't know how to deal with it.

Much to Sid and Clara's dismay, permission to marry was not granted. It was said that his commanding officer is reported to have said, "I have other plans for that young man." That may have been because Sid was one of the RCMP members who were part of the five-week search for 'The Mad Trapper of Rat River', Albert Johnson.

Albert Johnson was a mysterious figure. He arrived in the Yukon in 1931 and built a cabin on Rat River. He was accused of trapping and destroying traps on a Native's trapline. When questioned by the RCMP, he shot and wounded one officer, eventually fleeing and killing another officer. This prompted a massive search, starting on December 31st, 1931, and ending on February 17th, 1932. It covered a large territory, some 150 miles and was widely covered by radio and press all over North America. It was the first time an airplane, piloted by 'Wop' May (no relation to Sid), was used to track a killer. When Johnson was finally found and shot to death, Sid was delegated to approach the body, rifle at the ready, and turn the body over.

When word came that Sid and Clara were already married, Sid was arrested and taken to Dawson. The arresting Mountie had little river experience and Sid had to show him the ropes. Sid was fired. He returned to Old Crow and worked as a trapper. Later, he was told he could be reinstated if he apologized. He refused as he believed he had done nothing wrong.

People who live in relative isolation have to be inventive and think fast. On one such occasion, Sid was duck hunting and a gun on the bottom of the boat discharged, blowing a hole in the canoe. Sid grabbed a duck and stuffed it in the hole where it proved to serve as a perfect quick fix.

With the birth of her first child imminent, Clara made all the arrangements she could including saving kerosene for the lamp to make sure they would have sufficient light for the birth, went ptarmigan hunting, came home, and on March 2nd, 1934, gave birth to Marion, the first white baby girl born in Old Crow. The kerosene lamp would not work so the birth took place by candlelight. Clara later said that Marion's birth was the easiest she had. The two Native women in attendance were, according to Marion's birth registration, Mrs. Persis Kendi and Eliza Ben. They had Clara squat, got behind her, held her around the waist, and supported her. Everyone came to see the new baby, "looks like May" was the refrain. They brought gifts: a rabbit bunting (a hooded blanket that closed so that only the baby's face was exposed), an egg (probably kept from the previous September), a moose heart (considered a delicacy), and a tin of pineapple. Later, the women from Old Crow used to visit Clara when they came to Dawson and Bear Creek. She always used her good china when she served them tea.

When Marion was a month old, an American bush pilot said that if they wanted to leave Old Crow where the opportunities were limited, they had a few hours to pack [he would have to fly during daylight hours] and he would take them to Dawson City. They decided to take the offer and left Old Crow. On arrival in Dawson, they were not allowed to stay because the pilot, flying from Alaska, had not cleared customs there. If they did not go back to Alaska, the plane and all their belongings could be seized. Marion, still a small baby, could have stayed in the hospital in Dawson City, but Clara and Sid said no. They were a family and all would go to Circle City, Alaska and clear customs. Which they did. They lived in Dawson for a brief time, then moved to Bear Creek to a cabin on the Bench just down the trail from the Craig and Stevenson families.

✦ ✦ ✦

While the Craigs, Chapmans, and Mays were very significant to me, there were other people I remember too. Some have already been mentioned, others follow in no particular order.

Mr. Hand, who has already been introduced, was always dressed in a suit and tie and sat in the lobby of the roadhouse. One of my earliest memories of him, I was probably only two or three years old, was at Christmas. He and some other men were visiting us and had brought a box of chocolates. The box had a very shiny gold seal and I licked it—I suppose I thought it would taste as good as it looked. It didn't. Recently I learned, from my cousin Maribeth, that a ring I often wear was made by Arthur Hand. The band is made from a Canadian quarter and the top is a dime showing the *Bluenose*, much faded now. My father brought the rings to Langley after working at Clear Creek the summer of 1945. Maribeth has the same ring, made for her by Arthur Hand at Henderson Creek in the 1950s. He was then working for Maribeth's grandfather, my uncle Johnny. Maribeth said Mr. Hand was a man who treated children with respect and as if they were adults. Perhaps that is why I remember him from when I was a very small child.

Bill and Nora Hare moved to Bear Creek from Mayo with their children Alec and Betty. They became close family friends. Bill was originally from South America. Nora, née Ross, was born in Elsa, Yukon. Alec and Betty were older than Bobbie and me, Betty was our baby sitter. I remember that Alec, who would have been in his middle teens, belonged to the Pacific Militia Rangers, started at the beginning of WWII, where he learned to use a sten gun. My father didn't belong to the Rangers, although I remember both of my parents took Red Cross training. I remember Alec taking Bobbie and me out in a canoe on a dredge pond and the huge fish we saw. Bill listened to the Metropolitan Opera on shortwave radio every Saturday. Nora was very well-read and a deep thinker although she, like many Yukoners of her age, had little formal schooling. In a way, the Hares typified what was common to many of the people I knew as a child. Aware of their isolation, they, like my parents and others, made a great effort to keep up with world events. I can remember my mother saying, "Hush, Churchill is speaking," while listening to shortwave radio. Bill became a well-known Yukon photographer. Much of his work is in the Yukon Archives.

Jean Fournier and his wife Gertrude owned the roadhouse. I found her to be a formidable woman. She presided over the small

Bill and Nora Hare, *photo by W.S. Hare*

bar—I suppose this was the registration counter—in the lounge of the roadhouse, which was the only place to buy gum, candy or ice cream so I had to face her on the rare times I had money to spend. Once I bought a package of gum only to discover it had already been opened. My mother had me take it back. I was terrified but Mrs. Fournier replaced it without question, much to my relief. The lobby always had some men in the bar section and it and smelled of cigar smoke.

Bud and Esther Rogers lived below our cabin on the Bench. Esther's family, the Grants, were early pioneers. The Rogers came to the Yukon about 1920. Their daughter Rosemary married Alan White, the son of McLeod White who was the Resident Manager of the YCGC from 1943 to 1948. Rosemary is older than I am, but her brothers Jimmy and Bobby were close to my age and we sometimes played together. Marion May Dore and I recently visited Rosemary and Alan in Whistler, BC. We had a great time talking about the people we had known. Esther was on the softball team with my mother. Bud and Esther were the last people to live in Bear Creek Camp, where Bud had a garage. They left in 1978.

There were other families too. The Lewises' daughter Marnie, whom I spoke to recently, was our age. The Lewises moved into my uncle Johnny's cabin when they first came to Bear Creek. Johnny had left to work on the flight strip at Snag when the Alaska Highway was being built. Later, Bill Lewis built a house on the island on land he leased from the Company. According to Marnie, when the Company wanted to end his employment with them, they rescinded the lease and the family had to leave the house. The Lewises moved to Dawson City where Bill began a career with Canada Customs.

Children roughly in my age group included Jack and Danny Drott, Darlene and Gordon Pritchard, and Shirley Hill who lived next to the Hares on the Bench. There were other adults whose names appear in this chapter, and other children, big or little, who were known to us but played a small part in our lives in Bear Creek. The Craigs and the Mays were our primary friends.

The three families lived on the Bench above the camp. From our cabin, there was a trail to the Craigs and then to the Mays. The cabins were quite small. Marion remembers the cellar in theirs which was used as a cooler and accessed through a trapdoor. While the Stevenson and Craig cabins were not even in sight of each other the Mays' was, as I remember, one in a row of cabins. There was a stairway down to the camp near the Mays'. Bobbie remembers the big poppies which grew beside the stairs. We all remember the sweet peas Pete Huley grew beside the mess hall. Pete had worked as a stand-in for Charlie Chaplin. We aren't sure if that had anything to do with the way Pete's feet splayed out. Pete was a friend to all the kids. He saved the scraps from the mess hall for our dog Tony.

While we don't remember being put out to 'air' when we were very small, our mothers have told us about having to potty each of us when we were older. This involved removing all our winter layers including the longjohns made out of our fathers' old yellow Stanfield's underwear. And dressing us again in all those layers. We probably spent as much time getting dressed, then undressed for the potty, and re-dressed than we actually spent out of doors. Lorraine remembers how Anita, who was rather chubby, being dressed in her snowsuit, scarf, and mitts and placed out to air, just stood there as she couldn't move.

When we lived in the cabin, Dad and Clary Craig carried water up from the Klondike slough, with buckets hung from a yoke over their shoulders. In winter, they had to keep the hole open by chopping the ice out of it before they could fill the buckets. Sid, Marion's father, carried water up from the camp as they lived just above it and he had access to running water.

When we were all about six or seven, we moved to houses off the Bench. The Mays moved to the island into a house that Sid built which was moved to Dawson after YCGC closed. The house featured gable windows which Sid was determined to have. When Peggy and Frank Hoggan, my cousins, were younger they and the Dubois were the only children on the island. Later, other houses were built, most of them Company houses built for the administration personnel, and the number of children on the island increased.

Stevenson cabin on the Bench

Joann and Bobbie Stevenson

Marion May, Joann Stevenson, Lorraine Craig, and Bobbie
Stevenson standing, Doris May in tub, *courtesy of M. Dore*

Joann, Bobbie, Marion May, Anita and
Lorraine Craig, *courtesy of M. Dore*

The Craigs and Stevensons moved down near the slough and the road which ran from Dawson and through the camp. Clary built the Craigs' house and, in letters to his parents, goes into some detail about it. He was especially pleased to have running water and a bathroom. The Craig house was also moved to Dawson later. Our house had been a bunkhouse in Guggieville, the headquarters of the Guggenheim mining company, which had been closed for years. It was just over the Ogilvie Bridge from Dawson, on the road to Bear Creek. Dad moved it to Bear Creek. It was built of laminated 2x4s. We had a sandpoint well so water did not have to be carried in buckets as it was when we lived in the cabin. On a trip to Dawson, in the late 1980s, we talked to the current owner who reported that the well was still working. There was a bathroom in the house but we never had 'real' running water with a hot water tank and taps, nor was there a sewer system.

Over the years, our house was, by turns, a near ruin in 1978, well-maintained and added onto in 1989 and 1997, and a near-ruin again in 2010. The corrugated steel garage my Dad built was still standing in 2010 but rusting, leaning, and appeared to be sinking into the ground. The garage was where the fall moose was hung before being cut up. Bobbie and I used to enjoy poking the fat bubbles which gave a satisfying pop, much like bubble wrap does now.

Looking back, I wonder when our fathers had time to build houses. I think they worked six or seven days a week in summer. In winter, there was less work but the weather would have made building difficult. Each family had a woodlot from which trees were cut and hauled home then sawed into stove lengths. There was a community saw which was moved from house to house to saw the logs. I remember the day my uncle Johnny lost two fingers using the saw. The saw could cut four-and-a-half cords of wood an hour. Then of course, they had to split and pile the wood. Since all heating and cooking was done with woodstoves it required a lot of wood. Just to live in basic comfort in the North required a lot of work.

Our mothers worked hard too. In the early years, we did not have a washing machine. Water had to be heated on the stove and clothes were washed in tubs with the aid of a scrubboard. Even in winter, the washing was hung out to freeze and partially dry, then brought in to finish drying. Just the diapers alone would have been a lot of work. My mother and Evy Craig would both have had two children in diapers. Clara May may have had it a bit easier with Marion four-and-a-half when Doris was born and Nancy two-and-a-half years younger than Doris, but it was still a lot of work. Our mothers canned too, making jam, jelly, and pickles and doing other preserving. Lorraine remembers canning season as a time when hungry children would plead for something to eat and mothers, being so busy canning, would ignore them. Lorraine was very skinny and, since Evy was always concerned about Lorraine's weight, I doubt if she would have let Lorraine go hungry.

When we lived on the Bench, it was not possible to have a garden as there was permafrost too close to the surface, but my mother brought soil up to the cabin so she could plant sweet peas. There was enough water on lower ground down around the camp and the island to thaw the ground. There were streams, sloughs, and dredge ponds, water courses which changed as ground was dug up for mining, which melted the permafrost and made it possible to have basements and gardens.

All the families had big gardens. The root vegetables were canned or kept in sand in the cellar. The cabbages were hung in the cellar. Lorraine, Anita, Bobbie, and I would go to the island to raid the gardens there. Only recently, I learned that Marion and the island kids raided our gardens. Lorraine says probably the parents knew what we were doing but didn't care because we were eating vegetables. I'm sure the Stamelens knew we raided their strawberries which, as I remember, were right in front of their house—and there was nothing to hide behind. The strawberries were prized because they were so big and the wild ones so small.

Berry-picking was done to harvest the wild high and low bush cranberries, blueberries, raspberries, red and black currants, and gooseberries. I don't remember wild strawberries being picked much. Maybe there were too few to make it worthwhile. Mushrooms were picked on Archie Fournier's farm, brought home, and fried in butter. The farm was also the source of the real cream used to make ice cream with the ice cream maker my mother had brought from Stewart Island. It was like no other ice cream I have had since, probably because it was real cream right from the cow. Our usual milk was Klim, a powder mixed with water which none of us liked, and canned evaporated milk.

Moose was a staple. I think all the families depended on a moose each year. There was a cold room in camp where the meat was kept, each family having a locker. We never had caribou—my mother thought of it as dog food. Bobbie and I had to eat everything on our plates before we could leave the table. I remember gagging as I tried to eat some things, especially liver. As an adult, I realized the liver was moose which is very strong. A happy food memory is canned peaches which were the only thing I could eat after I had licked the doorknob one winter and lost the skin off my tongue. I remember the doorknob was just the right height. The peaches were a treat, but not one that prompted me to lick the doorknob again. Marion's tongue episode was not as salubrious. She did not want to tell what she had done and when canned pineapple was served that night, she experienced considerable pain.

There were limited resources for meal planning with most vegetables coming from cans, except in the summer. Potatoes and other root vegetables could be bought, but they would have been shipped a long way and were expensive. The staples for baking were always available so cakes, cookies, and pies were always to be had (but not in our house as Mum did not have good luck with pastry). Of course, breadmaking was a regular event in all households. Women would test the temperature of the oven in the wood ranges not only by looking at the gauge on the front of the oven door, but also by putting an arm in to double-check the temperature. Some, like my aunt Gladys, had elaborate dinner parties served on good china with sterling silver tableware. I don't know how she could have managed it from the tiny kitchen, a woodstove, and no indoor plumbing. I asked my mother why so many people had expensive china and silverware. She said because it cost as much to ship as cheaper products. There was also a competive element I expect.

Most of the mothers sewed. My mother made most of our clothes, especially our summer dresses, on the old pedal sewing machine from Stewart. It was important to be well-dressed. We did not go to town (Dawson City) without having our good clothes on, which meant dresses, and when we were small, the capes she made which we wore

Greg and Frank Hoggan with Moose, *photo from the Frank Hoggan Collection*

with the ermine furs trapped by our father. I remember Dr. Snyder, a dentist, taking movies of Bobbie and me playing in a small park in Dawson dressed in our finery. In my childhood memory, it was about lot size and had flowers and small statues. I have never seen the movie but it is probably still in existence as Dr. Snyder shot many movies and used to show them at Yukoner meetings.

When the Dawson City flood of 1944 happened, I'm sure I remember it because we went to town to see it and were allowed to wear pants. Into town!! Then we went to visit the Lelievres. Alice Lelievre was such a good cook. I could even enjoy the vegetables, cabbage, and carrots she did. Later, I realized she never spared the butter or salt and pepper. Alice's daughters Vivien and Arlene were very surprised to hear how I remembered their mother's cooking. My mother, when she had to leave her home at Stewart, had always been made welcome by Alice's family, the Burkhards, who had a bakery in Dawson.

Most of us have warm memories of a small community where our families were all known to each other, in some cases even into the second generation. I don't remember ever being told to get out of the way and play somewhere else, even when we played in and near the yard and camp. We didn't go into the machine shops and garages in the yard but were free to roam about the warehouses, and we have fond memories of Benny Gladwin allowing us to come into the gold room where the gold bricks were made. When Mr. Gladwin became ill with mercury poisoning and could no longer work in the gold room he was fired. This despite the fact that he had processed hundreds of thousands of dollars worth of gold over the years. The Company would not even keep him on as a watchman. The YCGC was not a benevolent employer.

Another man we remember is Hariyama (phonetic spelling). He was the cook at the mess hall. When Pearl Harbor was attacked, there was trouble in camp. Some of the men decided he was an enemy and were harassing him. At the time, it was thought he was fired because he was Japanese but Marilyn Nordale Stacy told me he was fired for drinking and gambling in the mess hall, which was forbidden, and after he had been warned many times. Hariyama then opened a restaurant in Dawson City. Once, Bobbie and I were in a pickup outside the restaurant waiting for our dad, who was a drinker, to leave the beer parlour and take us home. We were there for a long time and Hariyama invited us in and gave us pie. He was a kind man. Later, according to Marilyn, he became a Christian and was hired back by the Company. His nieces Winnie and Marlene were hairdressers in Dawson for many years.

Under the oil storage warehouse, which was open and raised above the ground, was a great place to break rocks open to find the fool's gold—which have cubic crystals which means they are all squares and rectangles—hidden within iron pyrites, quite fascinating to us. There was old machinery which we climbed around on, the bone yard (a dump in which treasures could be found), a small shack which we found and where we somehow managed to light something which allowed us to melt tar which some of us chewed. We were banished from there when found. Years later, Nancy May and her age group found and used the shack for a similar purpose. I remember a pipe warehouse where Bobbie and I spent some happy times climbing around with Danny and Jackie Drott.

Our aunt Gladys was a well-known seamstress, having been a shirt tailor. Doris May Chorney still remembers the dress Gladys made for her when she was a little girl. Doris liked the print in a dress Gladys made for herself, so Gladys, who had some fabric left, made one for her. Nancy

Gold room, *photo courtesy of D. Chorney*

Gold bars on table, *photo courtesy of D. Chorney*

May remembers the cloth hen sitting on a fabric nest that my mother sewed for her when Nancy was about two years old. We had Bantam chickens at the time so my mother put a little Bantam egg in the nest. We were all fortunate as children to have significant adults in our lives.

Nora Hare taught me to sew when I was about eight. I made an apron, with embroidery, for my mother. My first part-time job was in her brother's jewellery store in Whitehorse. I always called Nora and Bill by their first names, as my parents did not require us to call unrelated adults, friends of the family, 'aunt' or 'uncle'. The Hares lived on the Bench above the Stamelens. The Stamelen cabin was built by Archie Fournier. Betty, his daughter, told me the formula for caulking between the logs was newspaper pulp, flour, water glass, and formaldehyde (as an insecticide). This was applied both inside and outside. That cabin, now added to, is still there and in excellent condition. The Hills lived beside the Hares on the Bench. Alec Hill was a lineman. His wife Meg was on the softball team and Shirley was a playmate of ours. I don't remember either family living on the Bench when we did.

We went to school in Dawson City. Our bus was a small van-type vehicle, not at all like the big yellow bus known to those living Outside. Ed Hickey was the driver at the time. He smoked large foul-smelling cigars and my memory of the ride to Dawson is permeated with the smell. The bus stopped outside our house and Bobbie, who gagged when trying to swallow her morning egg, became an expert at storing her egg in her cheek and spitting it out on her way to the bus. She remembers that the bus was crowded and she and Anita had to take turns sitting on Rosemary Roger's knee in the front seat as they were prone to car sickness. Rosemary (whose nickname was 'Rosebud') was one of the 'big kids'. Of course, for many months we left home in the dark and came home in the dark. Once a year 'Jerusalem Joe' Knotis, (phonetic spelling) who was a miner from one of the creeks, got a ride on the bus into Dawson in the morning, which cost a dollar, returning with us after school. He was, as I recall, always dressed in a suit for his trip to town. On the way back to Bear Creek, he would pass out bags of candy to all of us. During WWII, he gave us savings stamps for our War Saving Books. Children were always well-treated by the old men from the creeks. When Doris May was working in a bank in Dawson, Jerusalem Joe gave her a large gold nugget.

The Mays remembered an incident that occurred after we left Bear Creek. 'Uncle' Gene Fournier was driving the bus. A wolf was hit by the bus on the road between Dawson and Bear Creek and, thinking it was dead, and there being a bounty on wolves at the time, he stopped and picked up the wolf, placing it behind the drivers seat. The wolf, as it happened, was not quite dead and began to stir. Gene reached behind his seat while he was driving, and whacked it with a big wrench. Another time, when Danny Drott misbehaved, Gene had him get off the bus and walk in front of it. The Bear Creek bus was definitely not the usual yellow bus. Gene had also driven the bus for a time back when my mother went to school in Dawson. She said he used to get excited and turn around to talk to someone, not watching the road at all which must have been frightening as it was the old road that curved around a bluff, the 'skinny road' in Bobbie's memory. Later, the road was moved and went over Jackson's Tailings which was two miles shorter and straight.

The Dawson school was comprised of all the grades from one to twelve. Mr. Hulland was the principal, and later became Superintendent of Schools for the Yukon. Mr. McGinnis was the janitor and Marion remembers that he was especially good to the Bear Creek kids. I remember him clearly; he had a warm presence. The teacher I remember most is Miss Jean. She and her sister, Miss Betty, were new to the Yukon. Bobbie had Miss Betty as her teacher and remembers her reading *Winnie The Pooh* to them. Miss Betty later married Charlie Williams who, coming from an 'old' Yukon family had been in school with our mother. It was in grade one that my sister decided Bobbie was a baby name and she wanted to be called Roberta from then on. I think she also felt it was a boy's name because of Bobby Rogers. Marion, Lorraine, and I still call her Roberta, but most people call her Bobbie, maybe because the rest of the family continued to call her that. My strongest memory, shared by Bobbie, is of our cousin Peggy telling us "pull up your socks" every time she saw us in the hall.

I remember a Valentine's Day when we were having our party and eating ice cream. When we looked out the window and saw that a dog, well-known and liked as it hung out at the school, was struck by a truck and killed. For years, I could not eat ice cream without that memory. A very different and happier memory is the day someone brought balloons to school. This was during WWII so we hadn't seen any for some time. These were different. They were sort of a clear colour and long, not round and coloured. When we described them to our parents that night, we got the distinct impression they were not really balloons and somehow wrong. Just what made them wrong wasn't clear to us. We never saw any of those balloons again.

My cousin Peggy remembered that there were three grades to a room when she was in school.

Peggy—The Indian kids were brought from far and wide to Dawson for schooling and lived in a hostel run by the Anglican church, where Indian kids could stay if their parents wanted them to go to school. [Actually, the hostel apparently housed children of mixed race only, who were sent there by their parents who wanted them to get an education. It does not appear to have been a residential school where children were sent even without parental consent as was the school in Carcross. I have not been able to find further information.] In winter, the warm classroom air got a little heavy with the smell of wet moccasins. We got along well. Many of these children later died of tuberculosis. I thought I was the only survivor of my grade one class until Maribeth (Peggy's daughter) met up with Ray Blackmore, a classmate of mine in Enderby, BC in 1973.

When I was talking to Marion recently, I mentioned the crush I had on Clifford Geddes when I was about fourteen and living at Mile 830, Brooks Brook, on the Alaska Highway. She brought out her grade one picture: Clifford was her classmate in grade one in Dawson and was living at the hostel. Also in Marion's picture is Aksel Porsild who was a classmate of mine at Brooks Brook years later. Marion's picture, taken ten years after Peggy's, when Marion was in grade one, shows that seven of the nineteen children in her schoolroom were Native. I barely remember the hostel children, probably because they were just others in my class, like all the Dawson kids. I didn't know many of the Dawson kids very well except for John and Mary MacDonald, the Frys, and the Lelievres because we spent little time there. My friends, who were at the school longer than I was, remember feeling sorry for the hostel kids who came to school with their heads shaved and looked as if they were not cared for. Alex Van Bibber told me that he was beaten every week for bed wetting. He left school after grade five. He received monetary compensation through the Residential Schools Settlement Act for the abuse he received.

The school Christmas concert was held at the Eagle Hall. In Bear Creek, there was a party for all the children in the mess hall, with gifts from Santa Claus (a.k.a. my uncle Johnny). It was held in the mess hall as there was no community hall then. At home, we got an orange in the toe of our Christmas stocking every year but my strongest memory of them is that they were starting to go bad in the middle, and how they smelled.

We had the piano that my mother brought from Stewart Island, which the family acquired when they lived in Dawson. It had quite a large burn on one corner and the story was that it was caused when a dancehall girl knocked over a lantern in the early days. It had a water stain too, from the flood on Stewart Island that Lill wrote of in Chapter 3. We had piano lessons from Sister Clementia at the Catholic school. Bobbie and I remember getting our knuckles rapped with the sharp edge of a ruler. Marion said she never got rapped. She thinks that was because she was such a bad student that Sister Clementia knew she was a hopeless case. After three years of lessons, Sister called Marion's mother to tell her that she was wasting her money and Sister's time: Marion would never be able to play the piano. Marilyn Nordale Stacy dreaded her lessons on Mondays and Thursdays but was saved when Sister Clementia called her mother to tell Mrs. Nordale that Marilyn, like Marion, was a hopeless case. Bobbie and I did not last even that long. Evy cancelled Lorraine's lessons after she was given the same piece to practice for eight weeks, but Anita persevered and still plays. They got the ruler treatment too. Lorraine remembers that Sister came into the lesson one day very upset, and told her that President Roosevelt had died.

Our winter play was not much different from others raised in a cold climate except that it sometimes took place in the dark, or in the near-dark, in the middle of winter. When it was very cold, we played indoors. The smell of Crayola crayons is an indoor memory. On Halloween, we went trick-or-treating—in the dark, of course—I remember we were allowed to carry a 'bug'. A bug is made by making a jagged hole in the side of a big can, held lengthwise. The candle goes in the hole, and a handle goes from one end of the can to the other. The candle flame is sheltered and the light comes out of the open end of the can.

My mother, always up first in the morning, was a clattery person and the rattle of the cookstove lids and the crackle of kindling woke us, but we stayed in bed as long as possible so the kitchen would be nice and warm when we got up. My mother was an excellent firestarter whether in a stove, or in the woods.

In summer, we woke to the sound of birdsong and played outdoors all day, revelling in the endless sun and the freedom of little clothing. And there was more to do. When we got too hot we could go to the place Bobbie remembers as the "jumpy hole" that Clary Craig, Lorraine and Anita's father, scooped out of the side of the slough with a Cat, creating a nice pond near their house for us to play in. There was a dredge pond, which we did not go to alone as it was dangerous. I remember, when I was very small, floating in the dredge pond perched on Phil Creamer's large belly. There was a forty-five-gallon drum with a fire going as the dredge ponds were very cold, warm for about 18 inches down and icy after that. Marion says there was ice in the bottom. They are the excuse I use for still being a non-swimmer. The brief summers did not allow much swimming time.

In a 1983 interview with Michael Gates of Parks Canada, my uncle Greg told of learning to swim in a dredge pond, probably a different one closer to Dawson City. It would have been while the family lived in Dawson before they moved to Stewart Island.

Greg— . . . at the upper end of the pond, there was a narrow spot, oh 25–30 feet wide, I guess. That's where the little kids, of which I was one, took the test. The bigger kids would watch us from the other end. When you thought you could swim the narrow part you went up there and swam it. If you didn't, well they were there to help you, and if you swam it then you passed the test and nobody worried about you anymore—you could swim.

Joann—The sandbars and islands in the rivers and sloughs are a strong memory. They seemed quite magical maybe because they were not covered with dense bush but were quite open. They were the site of soft sand, some wild flowers, and the snipe and sandpipers which tried to lead us away from their nests and young, doing the 'wounded bird', a wing dragging, as a way to lead us away. These magical places were destroyed by the dredging that started in the area about 1943 and no longer exist.

My mother played softball on the Bear Creek Team. Joan Minet, Donnie Grant, Esther Rogers, and Meg Hill are the names I remember from the team. While they played, we climbed around on the old machinery near the ballpark. The team played against the Dawson team and at places like Granville where there still had enough people to make up a team. Bobbie and I also remember the beer barrel parties that were held on an island near our house. Our parents and others created a lot of noise as there was a lot of singing and talking and drinking. In my mind they were related to the ball team, so it was probably the same group of people. My mother was not a drinker though there was a hard-drinking component in Bear Creek. Betty St. Jean told me the men always went to work the next day.

Dredge Pond swimming hole—Joann on left, Curly on right

Lorraine, Evy, Anita Craig, and Joann
Photos courtesy of L.Mackie

Bobbie Stevenson, Lorraine Craig, Joann Stevenson,
and Anita Craig, *photo courtesy of L. Mackie*

There were many wild flowers in the woods: columbine, daisy, pine drops, larkspur, 'orchids', baby's breath, and more which I can't name, but especially bluebells. The scent is unforgettable and while lupines are found everywhere (I've seen them in the Andes), bluebells seem to be a special northern blossom. They are not the same as those in the British Isles 'bluebell' woods.

Grandma Chappie figures in my strongest memory of the Northern Lights. A group of us were with her on the road below the Drotts' house. It was dark but not very cold, probably early September. The lights were dancing in all their colours, very beautiful, the best I have ever seen and I was sure they could be heard too. A kind of crackle or, to Marion, like the crack of a whip. We knew what a whip crack sounded like because there were still some horses in Bear Creek, although I don't remember them working. Mr. Coutts, who looked after them, would exercise them by taking them out of the barn located at the end of the machine shop on a long lead and cracking a whip to get them running in a big circle around him. The horses, apparently retired, were treated better than some employees.

The Company had a lot of power. When Doris and Nancy May, Marion's sisters, were followed home one night, their father Sid reported it to Mr. Nordale and the man concerned was on the next plane out. Swift justice was meted out to dogs too. When the Roger's dog Jack bit Bobbie right through her winter jacket, leaving scars she still has, Bud Rogers took him and immediately shot him. Jack must have had some wild blood as the Mays had one of his pups which, as a grown dog, turned on Clara for no reason, actually taking her to the ground and going for her throat. Fortunately he had a choke chain and Clara was able to hold him away. He met the same fate as his father and just as quickly.

The 17th of August Discovery Day celebration in Dawson City was and still is an annual event. It was started by 1901 at least, although Ned, my grandfather, called it the Pioneer Parade in a letter he wrote to his mother in 1927 when he was about to return home to Stewart River after a lengthy stay in St. Mary's Hospital in Dawson City:

St. Mary's Hospital   August 16th, 1927

Dearest Mother,
    I have just completed my 67th day in hospital but everything having gone well with me, I am now convalescent and am going home to Stewart River tomorrow. I would like to stay in Dawson for the big Pioneer Parade and celebration but the steamboat has to meet the mail boat on the coast so she must get out at 10 a.m. I have not been in Dawson for the celebration since 1901—when one of my friends won the ring out of the basket on the top of the greased pole. We were down to $5 apiece at the time, but we sold the ring to put half the price down on the roulette wheel. Three spins and by the time we were through the three rolls had won $600 if I remember rightly. So we sent $500 to his wife and kids in Victoria and paid our bills with ½ of the original stake and took $50 apiece and had a great time . . .

Joann—The Seventeenth was a big event for the whole area and Bear Creek always had a float in the Discovery Day parade. About forty years after Ned's letter, Marion and Doris May, Bobbie and I, and I think Shirley Hill were the first 'Bear Creek Nuggets', dressed in yellow on a large float with a gold pan tilted up behind us. We were the colours—the gold in the pan. My cousin Peggy was on the 1942 float and said Bear Creek usually won first prize. Lorraine remembers being a nugget on a later float and being so afraid that she would not be able to find her mother in what to her was a huge crowd. Her mother took her off while the parade was still going. None of us was used to seeing large groups of people except on the 17th of August, but Lorraine does admit she was a bit of a coward. There were displays of fruit, vegetables, jams, and jellies. The year I was seven or eight, I won a prize for my currant jelly and for the birdhouse I made myself, except that my dad used his brace and bit for the hole. I was not strong enough to do that. Carpentry held my attention. Domestic things like jelly-making did not last. There were races, softball games, and more, but I don't remember a greased pole such as my grandfather described—I expect they had gone out of fashion.

We did not go to the August 17th celebration in 1944 as we were living at North Fork for the summer where Dad was cleaning the ditch with a dragline. The ditch was a trench that brought more water from the south fork of the Klondike River to the north fork where there was a power plant which supplied power to the dredges, to Bear Creek, and to Dawson City. It was there that Bobbie and I were told we must not go into the woods as there was "nothing out there." I remember Pierre Burton writing of a similar warning from his father. We did venture into the woods a short way, keeping the camp in sight. Remarkably, the woods looked the same in 1989 when I camped there with my mother as they did in 1944, small poplar or aspen trees. I suppose they grow only to that size there. I'm sure children growing up on the edge of wilderness have a concept of 'nothingness' different from others. By 'nothing,' we understood that there was nothing but endless wilderness. No people. No landmarks. No way to find our way home.

In April 1945, my parents decided to leave Bear Creek where we had lived since I was born. We flew to Whitehorse where we stayed for a few days visiting our family, Johnny and Gladys and Peggy and Tubby. I remember Whitehorse as being a very busy place with the smell of sawdust and the sound of hammers pounding. One of the Cyrs or Seeleys rushed up to tell my mother that Roosevelt had died and they talked about what that could mean for the war. We went by train to Skagway and down the coast by boat to Vancouver. We were bound for Langley (30 miles from Vancouver) where our grandmother Mary Stevenson lived. Bobbie and I remembered the winter of 1939–40 we had spent there, so we were looking forward to going back to the mild winter, the smell of cedar trees and pennies which were not used in the Yukon.

My Dad remained in Bear Creek, where a new dredge was being built. This was seasonal work so he joined us in the fall in Langley, thinking he might want to stay on the Coast and we would make our home there. After two years of spending the summers in the Yukon and wintering Outside, he realized the wet winters were not for him and decided we would all move back to the Yukon where the climate was much more to his liking.

I did not go back to Bear Creek until 1978. There was no sign of any of the cabins which had been on the Bench. Our house was derelict, the Craigs' house was gone, the Mays' was gone. No one was living in Bear Creek. Parks Canada had the camp all fenced as, while it is not a National Historic Site, it is a 'Protected' one. A sad sight at the time.

The Craigs moved to Vancouver in 1950. Sid and Clara May lived in Bear Creek until the YCGC shut down in 1966, then moved to Kamloops, BC. Marion, their daughter, went Outside to Vancouver for grade twelve in 1951 and then took her nursing training at St. Paul's Hospital. In 1957, she returned to Dawson City with her husband, who was 'in the bank'. Men in the bank and RCMP often married local women, although Marion met Ray Dore Outside. Marion nursed there and was able to help some of the people she had known as a child. Her daughter Christine was born in Dawson in 1958. Doris and Nancy May completed school in Dawson and went Outside for further training. Doris married Stanley Chorney who was 'in the bank' in Dawson and later worked in the gold room in Bear Creek. They married in Vancouver where he was working in a bank again. Nancy married an RCMP officer, Brian Pope. She worked for the YCGC after her secretarial training. Nancy and Brian are retired and live in Tagish, Yukon. Their children, Monica, Debra Coyne, Christopher, and Jenny live in Whitehorse. The rest of us Stevensons, Craigs, and Mays all live Outside.

Bobbie, Marjorie, Curly and Joann Stevenson, 1945, *photo by W.S. Hare*

11

THE END OF AN ERA

When we left Bear Creek, the Yukon was undergoing many changes. It was as if it were entering the modern age. I know that I have felt at times like an anachronism. My early childhood was so different from that of my contemporaries living below the 60th parallel.

Isolation from the Outside world was still a factor and even though air travel came in the 1920s, the rivers were the main connection to Outside. The last boat out and the first boat in were very important events. My mother Marjorie's account of the yearly cycle serves as a record of what the harsh climate meant to everyday life.

Marjorie—In the Yukon, everyone used wood for heating and cooking. In the winter, one had only to look out a window, after thawing a peek hole in the frost, to get an idea of the temperature. In extreme cold, the smoke would be going up in a straight line as there was seldom, if ever, any wind during a cold snap. There would be a stillness in the air, as though we were waiting for something to happen. What everyone was really waiting for was a break in the weather and hoping the woodpile would not diminish too quickly!

The memory remains with me of one November when I was a young mother living in Bear Creek. It was 45˚ below the whole month and what a long one it was—in a small log cabin with two little children it was confinement to the point of what was known as 'cabin fever'. I believe that expression probably originated when two trappers were house-bound due to the cold. All I can say is—just try it with a young family—Robert Service didn't write about that! November at the best of times was a dreary dark month. December at least had the excitement of Christmas to relieve the monotony but there were only about two hours of daylight and about three hours of twilight. January was often very cold, though I remember one year when there was a chinook wind which brought a brief thaw, then turned cold again, just to show us it was still winter and we had a long way to go 'til spring. But *ah!* In late January one might see, and rejoice in, a brief ray of sunshine gleaming through the kitchen window! What a lift that gave our snowbound spirits. February could be changeable, windy and cold, lightened by Valentine's Day and the annual dance held in the Oddfellows Hall in Dawson where there was a good dance floor and lively music provided by the local orchestra. March was usually brighter, though a blizzard was likely to arise any time, to show us again that spring was still another month away. In April, the sun shone more brightly and the snow began to settle. In the morning, it would be crusted and gleaming, a bad time for dog teams as the dog's feet could be cruelly cut unless they wore the canvas moccasins which we made and tied on. The animals were reluctant to carry these strange additions and would tear them off at every opportunity. Still, spring was in the air and spirits were lifted by the returning sunshine and the looking forward to the exciting day when break-up would occur.

In early May, the snow would be going, the creeks running, and the North coming to life again. I think one needs to live where the winters are long and snow all around to feel the joyous surge of spring. The little crocuses would be pushing up the tips of their furry coats in bare patches on the hillsides, even through spots of snow in some places. The scent of that downy covering and the sight of the purple petals arising was a celebration of spring triumphant.

Then, in Dawson, there would be bouquets of leaf lettuce available from Schmidt's greenhouse. For 25 cents, one carried home on the school bus the first green signs of summer wrapped in pages of the *Dawson News.* The greenhouse would have been started in April, the woodstove carefully tended, and the seedlings watched over with dedication. Later, in July, the luscious tomatoes would be ready. Surely there is no more delicious flavour than that of a Yukon tomato! The long daylight hours of summer make for quick growth and all vegetables grown in the North have an extra succulence.

Of course the big day in May, or very rarely, in late April was when the siren sounded, the fire whistle blew in Dawson, and the schools erupted with shouting children, followed by no less excited teachers. The ice was moving! Break-up had started! The whole town turned out and the riverbank and White Pass dock were crowded. It meant that the long exile of winter was over and, after May 24th, the first steamboat of the season would be coming 'round the bend, bringing fresh fruit and those perishables we had been longing for. Friends and family who had been Outside for the winter would be coming home. Our months of isolation would be at an end.

At Stewart, we first saw the puffs of white smoke coming around the bluff above Stewart Island. We'd had no fresh food since the last boat in October. By the time the first boat arrived with fresh vegetables and fruit, the sacks of potatoes had begun to sprout, the carrots were finished, the cabbage from the garden hung in the cellar then put out to freeze was gone. The cabbage, while it lasted, was sliced and put in a heavy cast-iron pot on the back of the kitchen range with a generous chunk of butter then laced with vinegar and became a near-substitute for sauerkraut. The six cases of eggs would have developed a flavour all their own even though they would have been turned regularly. The moose meat and other meat would have been thawed and canned for summer use.

Now we would have apples and oranges again, and perhaps even bananas, a special treat. The cases of dried fruit, apples, apricots, prunes, and peaches would have been used up over the long winter. There would be no lettuce until the garden produced it in July. There was a large greenhouse attached to the living room but it was never used as mother was not a gardener. There would be no tomatoes or cucumbers until the greenhouses in Dawson had them for sale. Vegetables grew so quickly in the twenty-four hour days, they had a flavour quite distinct to the North. So did the eggs for quite a different reason!

Before the ice moved, it would have lifted a bit along the shore. We fished for greyling using the lead from a twenty-two shell polished until it shone as a lure. What a great treat it was to have fresh fish! One winter, my brothers chopped a hole in the ice along the shore. They may have caught greyling, but what I remember was a strange large fish my mother called "inconnu", meaning, she said, "the unknown." Later, a net would be strung across Andy's slough and we could have pike and whitefish.

The storm windows and doors would be taken off and put away until the next winter. Bedding would be hung out to air—not only in spring, but through the winter when there was a wind, the beds would be stripped and all coverings hung out to freshen up, clothespins cold on one's fingers. Doors would be flung open to air the house. My mother was very fussy about this and my parent's bedroom window did not have a storm window because it has to be aired every day. With a wind blowing through the house, my father would say, "Kate! What are you trying to do, warm the great outdoors?" No use, mother would do it anyway.

June was the month of flowers and high water and 24 hours of daylight. July—mosquitoes and swimming. August—the 17th celebration, dark nights, northern lights. September—taking in the garden on Labour Day, leaves falling about the middle of the month. October—the freeze-up, the last boat out and winter isolation beginning. November, the month heralding the onslaught of winter.

Joann—Winter was a time of going to school in the dark and coming home in the dark. Winter also meant layers and layers of clothes. Undershirt, long underwear, combinations (an undergarment with garters attached), long stockings, blouse, sweater, skirt, snowsuit, felt boots under our moosehide moccasins. And that was just to go to school, eight miles away. We went to school every day unless it was colder than minus 50 degrees Farenheit. We played out in winter too and I can remember being so cold on my way home that I wet myself just to feel warm for a minute or two. As I was about seven at the time I got spanked with a piece of kindling when I got home. When it was especially cold, colder than 20 degrees below Farenheit, we could stay indoors to play.

One year, the snow must have been pushed off the roof because there was a pile beside the house. My mother poured water over it and because it was very cold, the water froze making a hard crust. We then dug the snow out and had a snow cave in which we had a candle.

We had a dog named Tony and a sleigh and harness so we would sometimes hitch him up, but he was not a willing sled dog and would pull us only if he heard the whistle at the end of the workday and he knew my Dad was on his way home. Then we got a brief ride as Tony ran to greet him.

Spring brought the smell of melting snow and the sound of water trickling. Our mother showed us how to tap the birch trees for the sap that had started running. We tapped a small tube into the bark and hung a small can from it to catch the sap. I don't remember that we got a lot but the experience stays with me. Spring, when the sap was running was the time to make whistles from the willows. We would cut a length of knot-free willow, slip the bark off and cut a small slice off one side then cut a notch to provide a way for the sound to come out. The bark would be carefully put back on and the bit of bark over the notch cut out.

The ice going out in the Yukon River and the arrival of the first boat generated the same release from school and rush to the waterfront that Marjorie describes.

Summer was a time of shedding the many layers of clothes. It was wonderful to run out to greet the day wearing only underpants, shorts, and a top. Such lightness and freedom. The early morning was filled with birdsong. Sudden 'sunshowers', rain falling while the sun was shining, were a summer feature.

The best thing about the end of summer was the arrival of the Eaton's catalogue order with our new winter clothes. The snowsuits, wool, had an oily not unpleasant smell. New beaded moccasins, bought from Native women, were welcomed too. They had the smell of tanned moosehide, not an unpleasant smell either.

I was not a happy winter person. My mother said I got cranky in September and stayed that way until spring. Years later, I took part in a University of British Columbia research study on Seasonal Affective Disorder, which confirmed that I suffered from the syndrome. The long dark winters with only a few hours of light at that latitude (about 64 degrees) is very difficult for some to bear.

◆ ◆ ◆

The current concept of recycling is relatively new. My 1984 *Webster's New World Dictionary* defines recycling as: "1. To pass through a cycle or part of a cycle again, as for checking, treating, etc. 2. to use again and again as a single supply of water in cooling, washing, diluting, etc." A 1961 *Funk and Wagnalls* does not even list the word. Still, the Yukon of my childhood was what could be called a 'waste-not society'.

In the Yukon, everything possible got used, reused, and used again. Nabob coffee cans used for baking the Christmas cakes that were in the hampers made for the old bachelors on the creeks were only one of the many containers re-used by Yukoners. It can be fairly said that nothing went to waste. Shipping costs were very high, and what came north stayed there. Stores and trading posts were few, nothing could be easily replaced. This was true for cars as well as other goods and Dawson City and area was a bonanza of another sort, not gold, but cars brought into the Yukon from the early days and never taken out. Car collectors, when the all-weather road to the outside world was built in the 1950s, soon discovered the old models and took them to be restored. Dawson City was the end of the line for movies too, and a great cache of them was found in later years.

Apple boxes became cupboards. Butter boxes were prized for their sturdy construction and dove-tailed corners. The big round cheese boxes were especially important to children like my uncle Greg who would cut the box in half and make a toboggan with a board tacked on. Kraft cheese came in little wooden boxes, with a sliding top as I recall.

Forty-five-gallon drums were water barrels, furnaces, or were sometimes used as floats. The barrel furnaces were laid on the side, legs were welded on, a door was fashioned at one end, and a chimney hole cut in the top. These furnaces held logs of a size and number that kept a fire alive for many hours. That was our furnace in our house in Bear Creek and in many other houses.

Five-gallon gas (and kerosene) cans, which were square, not round, were shipped two to a sturdy wooden box. The cans became water pails, slop buckets, and with the sides peeled back, dog food was cooked in them. Water was heated in them. Used upright, according to Uncle Greg, smudges (smoky fires using green wood and leaves) were made in them and, when the bugs got bad, the horses would make a noise by knocking the cans around with their noses until someone came out and made a smudge to keep the flies away. Flattened, the cans were used as roofing. Christie's crackers used to come in oblong tins with a tight-fitting lid and along with coffee cans were used as baking pans.

Nothing got thrown out if any possible use could be found for it. The only things which were discarded had no further use. There was a 'bone yard', not a garbage dump, in Bear Creek. I think the term was used elsewhere but 'bone yard' was evocative of what was there—bones, broken dishes, tin cans that had no further use.

People leaving the Yukon usually left any large pieces of furniture and household goods behind as the freight costs made it uneconomical to ship goods Outside. In fact, one man who must have been either a newcomer or just stupid took the motor out of a washing machine, filled the space with stolen gold and tried to ship the machine Outside. Shipping something of that size Outside just was not done and raised the Mounties' suspicions. His cache of gold was soon found.

I still have trouble throwing out something that looks useful. Before I go to a store, I think about how I could make what I want with whatever I have. Sometimes I am surprised to find something in a store that I have been trying to fashion myself. This is not all because of my Yukon history, as I am an inventive person, but my past is still with me and a part of me.

Not only were things used and reused: sometimes they had to be taken apart, moved piece by piece, and put together again as happened with log cabins—and in the following case, a car. The Klondike Highway follows the old stagecoach route quite closely. More than 20 years before there was a winter road suitable for motor vehicles between Whitehorse and Dawson City, Clary Craig and his friends took a car over the route. This trip was probably the first one by a motor vehicle between Dawson City and Whitehorse. It seems fitting to end this part of the book with the following account by Clary Craig, a preview of what was to come.

Clary Craig—The steamboats on the Yukon had closed down for the winter, but the overland stages could not be used due to some of the river crossings not being frozen over because of the mild weather. The Company had an old Model T Ford touring car that was not being used, so I asked Mr. Baird, the manager, if it was for sale. He said if it was of any use to me I could have it for $50. I had been talking to three dredge men who were waiting for transportation to Whitehorse, Bob McLaren, Bill Grafton, and John Hill, and suggested we buy the old car and drive to Whitehorse. They all agreed.

It took us several days to get the car in condition. We tuned up the engine and cut off the rear seat and replaced it with a wooden box to form a kind of pickup truck that would accommodate a double mattress. We took my tool box, a roll of haywire, some old blankets, a piece of canvas tarpaulin, a spare wooden spoke wheel, tire and inner tube, tire chains, 2 shovels, axe, tire pump etc., some canned food, our hand baggage, and two cases holding two four-gallon imperial gasoline cans. We also took an empty four-gallon can to melt snow in.

The weather had turned a bit colder so we figured that the larger river crossings would be frozen and safe to use. We set off on our four-hundred-mile journey to Whitehorse in early November 1931. After noon, approximately eight inches of snow covered the ground, which gave us no problem. All went well until we reached Flat Creek, where a long and quite steep stretch of road went up the hillside, out of the Klondike valley, and on to a much higher level. After hours of shovelling and pushing, we finally reached the top, built a fire, and melted snow to refill the radiator, which had boiled almost dry. After dark, we reached Crooked Creek roadhouse, where we spent the night.

Next morning, we headed out in a more southerly direction for the McQuesten, a small river, and the Stewart, a much larger one, where we had our first major problem. After crossing the McQueston and heading for the Stewart, a small sharp upturned stick pierced the radiator core, causing a leak. We had to stop and melt snow for water. Thankful for our four-gallon gasoline can, by adding snow we were able to make water by keeping the gas can on the engine transmission. We finally came to Findlay Beaton's wood camp. Findlay contracted for cutting cordwood for the steamboats that operated on the Stewart River. Here we were able to work on the radiator by pinching the pierced tube together and adding about one-half a can of mustard—it stopped the leak. Findlay wanted us to stay overnight but, after a short stay and a snack, we wanted to push on. A short distance from Findlay's place, the trail had washed away and we had to make our way through the woods, around the washout, over some very rough ground. I was driving the car and the other guys were walking ahead to find the best ground to travel on. All at once the right rear wheel went over a short stump and down into a hole with a loud crack. Several of the wooden spokes were broken and the wheel collapsed. We were surely lucky we had the spare wheel and tire pump.

We found a good smooth crossing of the Stewart at the Stewart roadhouse and, being early in the afternoon, we decided to push on to the Pelly Crossing, the Pelly being a tributary of the mighty Yukon.

Here, I must describe this old car we were driving. It was an early 1920s Model T Ford with a 'fold-down' top, a hand-crank for starting the engine, a two-speed transmission (low and high gear), with a built-in generator in the transmission to power the engine and the headlights. To start the car, two small dry-cell batteries gave power to spark plugs and after starting, switched over to the generator. It had no fuel pump—it was gravity-fed from the fuel tank located under the front seat. There were two main springs, front and rear, which were linked crosswise over the axles and attached to the frame of the car with two large bolted clamps. The rear-wheel drive to the rear axle was attached to the transmission with a slip-on universal joint. The front axle had a metal support shaped like a wishbone, attached back to the transmission

Model T Ford, 1929, *photo from Library of Congress Prints and Photographs Division*

housing. The engine and transmission were bolted together in a unit, and were held in place in the car frame with only four bolts. Thus, the front and rear axle and spring assemblies, as well as the engine and transmission unit, could be removed simply with few tools. I would say the weight of the car was less than 800 lbs.

During the past summer, the long stretch between the Stewart and Pelly had been ravaged by a forest fire. We spent hours avoiding and clearing windfalls (fallen trees) to make our way. In the late afternoon, we arrived at the Pelly roadhouse, situated on a high bank of the Pelly River.

The owner and operator of the roadhouse was a large pipe-smoking woman known as 'Ma' Shaffer, a well-known character who ran a strict house and took "no lip from no one." Shaffer's roadhouse had been a trading post and a store, which supplied the people in the area. It was known as Pelly Crossing. Ma and the people here were surprised to see us arriving in a car. Nobody used a car to drive over this winter trail. They didn't think that we would be able to cross the Pelly because the river had only stopped running ice the night before and being only about -5 degrees Farenheit. it was not cold enough to make a safe crossing. We decided to stay the night and see how things were in the morning.

Ma was low on gasoline, but she sold us one ten-gallon case. She fixed us a really fine dinner and we had a good night's sleep. She prepared a huge breakfast. After breakfast, we took a long iron bar and went down to the river to test the ice. The river at this place was about 150 yards wide. At this time of year, the water in the river is at its lowest, which leaves a wide gravel bar on each side of the river. The ice cakes floating down had stopped very peacefully and frozen together, making a fairly flat surface. The ice freezing the cakes together tested three to four inches. We were dubious about this. However, we decided to unload and carry everything from the car across the river.

The roadway from the roadhouse going down to the river had a steep grade and I figured that if I could get up a good speed down the grade in the empty car and keep it going, it would make it across, and just did—water following the rear wheels near the far side. Without the steep grade and speed, it wouldn't have made it. Ma thought we were crazy! And maybe we were!

Our troubles were not over.

Between the Pelly and Yukon Crossing, we encountered many problems by having to clear our way through many windfalls and make many detours through the bush around washouts, etc. We arrived after dark on a clear moonlight night at Yukon Crossing to find the Yukon river open and running ice. What a disappointment!

We saw no one around the roadhouse across the river, but a light was seen and smoke was coming from the chimney. On our side was a small log hut with stove, oil lamp, etc. and a large 18-foot freight canoe with paddles, poles, etc. The temperature was still around -5 to -10 °F, so we made a fire in the stove and heated up the last of our canned beans and sized up our situation.

Looking at the river upstream in the bright moonlight, a few hundred yards away there was a bend in the river. When the ice cakes came around the bend, at times an opening through the ice cakes would form, which would make almost a clear passage across the river. We watched this happen a few times and figured we could make a crossing with the canoe. The shore ice on both sides of the river extended into the river to where the ice was running. We dragged the canoe down on to the shore ice and upstream some distance to compensate for drifting downstream while crossing, and loaded our baggage. We waited for an opening to appear, then shoved off. With Bob McLaren in the bow with a pole to shove ice away, John Hill in the middle with paddles, and me in the stern with paddle, we crossed the approximately 100 yards without trouble. Securing the canoe for a landing was a problem and we drifted downstream a short distance to a driftwood pile, where we were then able to drag the canoe up on the shore ice. We carried our baggage up the shore ice to the roadhouse and surprised Harold King, the caretaker of the roadhouse, who had not seen or heard us. The river still being open, the stage line was not in operation, so he was astounded to see us. When we told him where we had come from, he said he had been told by the owner of the stage line, T.C. Richards, that four men left Dawson by car for Whitehorse, but he didn't think they would get very far. If we did come along, he was not to give us any help whatsoever. T.C. had the only means of winter transportation between Whitehorse and Dawson City with his horse-drawn stagecoaches. He did not want any competition.

What to do now?

The river was still running ice—the weather was too mild to freeze the river—the stage line would not operate until the river closed and was safe enough to cross. Maybe we would be stuck here for—how long?

Harold showed us to two rooms for the night. It was getting on toward midnight. Harold went upstairs to bed. We sat and talked. None of us wanted to stay here for however long. Maybe we could take the car apart and bring it across in the canoe. Let's give it a try!

Without notifying Harold, we went down to the canoe and dragged it on the shore ice upstream and crossed without trouble. We pushed the car down to the shore ice and upstream to where we would dismantle it to be loaded into the canoe. We figured we could take it across in two trips.

We made a good-sized bonfire to give us more light to work by while dismantling the car—which we did as described earlier. Our first load consisted of front and rear axles and wheel assemblies, radiator, gasoline, and miscellaneous items. It went across without too much trouble, landing at the driftwood pile. I don't think we would have made it without that driftwood pile being exactly where it was. It made our tie-up place, poles for skidding the loads onto the shore ice, and firewood to give us light. The second load consisted of the engine and transmission assembly, body and frame. This was the tricky one, being the heaviest one. The body and frame, being wide had to be loaded onto the gunwales protruding over the sides of the canoe. In order to stabilize the canoe, the heavy engine and transmission had to be placed on the bottom. It was a scary crossing because of being top-heavy. We had to be very careful and alert to keep things in balance. We were very lucky!

By about eight o'clock in the morning, we had the old Lizzy back in running condition and then who comes down the shore ice from the roadhouse but Harold King with a long face, "How did you get that across the river?" he asked. I told him that, after he had gone to bed, we decided to steal his canoe and try and ferry the car across. "I know," he said. "When I heard you guys leave the place after I went upstairs, I figured you were up to something so I stayed up and watched the whole procedure from the upstairs window. Well, now that you are here, we had better go up to the house and have breakfast." When we got there he had everything ready, bacon and eggs, pancakes—everything.

We paid for a night's lodging and our meals and wrote a letter to T.C. Richards, which we all signed, stating that we had, during the night, taken his canoe without his permission, dismantled our car, and transported it across the river in his canoe. That letter would clear our friend Harold of any responsibility.

Harold stated that the road from here to Carmacks was good and from there to Whitehorse even better, so off we went and arrived in Whitehorse the next evening.

Whitehorse at this time was only a small town at the head of navigation on the Yukon River and the terminus of the White Pass Railroad between Whitehorse and Skagway, Alaska. When navigation on the Yukon closed for the winter, traffic on the railroad was also affected, which resulted in bi-weekly or weekly trips between Whitehorse and Skagway. We arrived in Whitehorse the same afternoon of the day the train had left, so we were stuck in Whitehorse for three days.

The next morning we drove around town and what a dead place! Back at the Regina Hotel, we sat and talked to some of the locals—nothing to do! Bob McLaren had relatives who operated a general store in Carcross, on the lower end of Lake Bennett. The railroad to Skagway, 110 miles, ran right through Carcross and Bob was hoping to see his people when we would stop there on the train. We found out there was a wagon road between Carcross and Whitehorse but it was used very little because of the railroad. I don't remember the exact distance, but I would estimate it to be less than fifty miles, and we decided to try it. After a quick lunch, we set off. This road was no problem compared to what we had been going through, except when we were a short distance from Carcross. We lost the trail, and soon it would be dark. We headed for the railroad which was on our right and, finding it, we figured Carcross must not be far off. We drove right up to the railroad, lifted the car to straddle the narrow gauge rails, and headed off down the track bumping over the railroad ties for several miles until we arrived at the station in Carcross.

Carcross is a small town located at the northern, or lower, end of Lake Bennett on the Nares River, a small river that joins Lake Bennett with Marsh Lake. Lake Bennett is a large, beautiful clearwater lake thirty miles long. The White Pass Railroad runs along the east side of the lake for the full thirty miles. Across the Nares River at Carcross is the Indian village. The original name was 'Cariboo Crossing', which was later shortened to Carcross.

The only hotel in Carcross was close to the station, and everyone was surprised to see a car pull up at the railway station!

We had now reached the end of the road. No one had ever driven a car between Dawson and Carcross before. Another full day was ahead of us before the train would arrive to take us to Skagway. Late the next morning, we visited the general store operated by Matthew Watson who was married to Bob McLaren's sister. They were very surprised and made us most welcome. Later, we wandered to the Nares River and looked across to the Indian village. The river, approximately 100 yards across, was frozen over and the Indian kids were out playing on the ice which was like a sheet of glass. We went down to the ice and found it safe. The Indians were crossing with their horses. "Let's bring the car down on the ice and give the kids a ride," somebody suggested. This is what we did. The kids were thrilled! They would pile on the car and we would get up a bit of speed, then take a sharp turn, and the car would spin around in circles while the kids would be laughing and screaming. This brought the whole village out and soon everyone was taking part. We were also having a lot of fun.

One of the Indians, apparently one of the leaders of the band, became very interested in the car and wanted to know what we were going to do with it. He would like to have it. Having paid only $50 for it, we told him he could have it for $50. He said he didn't have $50, but would give us five mink skins, which he said were worth a lot more than $50. We made the trade for the five skins. This Indian was Johnny Johns who later became quite a successful big-game hunter and guide on the survey for the Alaska Highway. I think he was quite sharp as well. We got $10 for the five skins.

The next day we boarded the train, proceeded along the east coast of Lake Bennett, through the Coast Mountains, over the White Pass to Skagway. We stayed at the Golden North Hotel overnight and, next day, boarded the *Princess Mary* for Vancouver and home.

It was a rough trip, but I would not have missed it for anything.

12

THE CHANGING YUKON

We lived in Langley for two years, with my father returning to the North every summer to work and spending the winters with us. Then he got a job on the Alaska Highway working for the Canadian army which was responsible for the maintenance of the highway. We returned to the Yukon in July 1947.

In 1947, the highway was five years old and was open for general traffic, trucks hauling freight, buses, and tourists. It also drew what my father called "pilgrims moving to the Promised Land," Alaska. Many of them were unprepared for the realities of the distance, expense, and lack of services on what was then little more than a gravel track through the wilderness. The highway was very hard on vehicles and passengers alike. My father helped more than one family by patching worn tires and doing other minor repairs. He probably gave a little cash when there were hungry children. I had read some Steinbeck by then and always thought of them as comparable to the 'Oakies', with the cars piled with household goods, spare tires, and gas cans.

It was 918 miles from Dawson Creek in British Columbia, Mile Zero, to Whitehorse which was the supply point for the central and northern sections of the Alaska Highway. There were mile posts, painted white with the miles in black paint, every mile so referring to anyplace by its name as well as its mile number was common, *e.g.* Swift River, Mile 733. The mile posts were also necessary so that a problem on the road could be quickly located. Ft. Nelson, Mile 300, Ft. Liard (an old trading post), and Watson Lake, where there was a flight strip, about Mile 600, had existed for some time. Stopping-places where gas and other services could be had between those locations were infrequent. They were usually located where there had been a construction site, which meant there was a clearing and usually some old army buildings. These were very primitive facilities. Maintenance camps and Canadian National Telegraph (CNT) repeater stations were located along the route at the same locations, about one hundred miles apart. They too were located at the sites of former construction camps. CNT was responsible for the maintenance of the telegraph lines and forwarding of telegraph messages.

The housing in the maintenance camps was built from the remains of army barracks and was very crudely made. 'Apartment' seems a misleading term for these shoddy buildings which often had a tarpaper outer covering. Camps had a foreman, a mechanic, and grader operators. There were perhaps six to eight families. Families with school-age children were posted to those camps that had a small school.

My mother found living on the highway difficult. She had been working in Langley at Berry's store and was used to having my grandmother, her sister-in-law Irene, and other friends for company. She found little to do on the highway. There were no jobs for women. Bobbie and I were old enough to require little care. When my father was camp foreman, there were certain constraints on her as his wife. My mother wrote the following account of living at Swift River, Mile 733.

Marjorie—After two years of Curly working in the Yukon in the summer and spending the winter at the Coast, I was not surprised to get a letter from Curly in the spring of 1947 saying he would be moving to Swift River, mile 733 on the Alaska Highway, and that the girls and I would join him at the end of the school year.

Curly's description of Swift River was not too encouraging but as I had always been able to make a home in whatever circumstances I found myself, I had no qualms about moving back north. He described the apartment we would have and sent measurements of the five big windows so that I could bring suitable curtains. To this end, I bought about twenty yards of unbleached cotton and made the curtains up on a treadle machine in the kitchen of the farmhouse. I got some variegated wool and finished them off with two lines of cross-stitch—I finished the last one on the boat to Skagway where we boarded the train to Whitehorse, where Curly met us.

It was an interesting drive but, just around the bend from Swift River, Curly stopped the pickup, turned to me, and said, "Marge, this is an awful place to bring you and the girls to live!" I must say my heart sank a bit, but remembering how my mother had moved around the North with my father and her many children I realized that whatever Swift River was like, it was bound to be better than some of her homes had been. So I answered, "Any place with oil heat, indoor plumbing, and a shower can't be too bad, let's go!" [The farm, like our Bear Creek houses, did not have indoor plumbing.]

Joann, Bobbie, and Curly on Alaska Highway, 1947

So on we went and I must say, I did not expect to see an unfinished board floor with wide cracks oozing dust, nor a bedroom with walls of odd pieces of celotex, a heavy paper-like wall-covering in black and tan! However, I tried not to show my dismay and said, "We are all together again and that's the main thing."

My mother had always said that the first thing she did in a new location was to hang curtains, for that is the start of making a home. Heeding her advice, that is what I did. We had our first meal at the foreman's house, the only separate living quarters in the camp, as the maintenance crew had apartments in long buildings which were divided into three apartments each. Frank and Agatha Speer were to become lifelong friends. They were fine people with a daughter, Millie, a little older than ours, and an older son, Bill.

Our unit was on the end of the building, and on the other end was the Couch family who had two children, Carol and Leslie. Our girls soon became acquainted with the other children in camp and, though I look back on our sojourn there with few happy memories, I was surprised to hear they had many good times in that place, climbing mountains and hiking around and really enjoying themselves. Though Joann, who was to become my fishing partner many years later, said she doesn't know why she didn't fish in Swift River which was right behind our apartment.

We had been there only three weeks when Joann developed a high fever and we took her to Whitehorse Hospital where, to our dismay, she was diagnosed as having the dread polio. I remembered that coming up the coast, there was a little boy who seemed to be feverish, whined, and cried and I wondered if it was from him she caught polio. I stayed with my niece, Peggy Tubman, and Curly returned to camp.

Dr. Roth told us not to tell anyone as it could start a panic among parents. Nevertheless, somehow word did reach Swift River and Bobbie heard from other children that her sister had polio. Later, she told me, "Mum, when they told me what was wrong with Joann, I went inside and cried and cried, remembering that boy we knew who had been crippled with polio." Her father was unaware that she knew, so there they were, neither letting on to the other. How much easier it would have been if they had openly talked about it. How clearly I remember that terrible night of crisis when the doctor told me that was the turning point, and next day we would know how much damage had been done. Fortunately, she suffered no ill effects, though it was some time before she became strong again.

The next crisis came in the fall when Joann was once again rushed to Whitehorse. This time, she had appendicitis. She came home with her appendix, only to be rushed back a few months later when her appendix was removed.

I did what I could to improve our apartment so, when a truck turned over in a ditch, leaving many rolls of coloured paper only nine inches wide scattered about, Curly brought these home and I papered one wall with them. As I recall, it was quite a job but it did brighten the room a bit!

The CNT repeater station was across the road from the camp and the two young men there were most congenial. We heard that Al washed his money before passing it on! That seemed to be one way of passing time. The young men there were friendly and a good addition to the community, if such it could be called. [My father often brought men home for coffee, including Billy Smith, a Native trapper who lived near the airstrip.] The teacher was Mr. McNiven, who put on the traditional Christmas concert which was appreciated as he had so few students to work with.

In January, the middle apartment was taken by a young couple from the southern area of the highway. When we heard them moving in, Curly said, "Marge, this isn't the most friendly place we have ever lived, I'm going to help them and ask them for coffee," We had both been raised in very hospitable homes and our coffeepot was seldom cold. So that is how we met Ches and Helga Campion, who became close friends, with whom we were to share weddings, births, deaths, and all the many things that constitute living. I can still picture Helga stretching out her legs in brown ski pants and commenting in a fascinating accent, which I later found out was Icelandic, that she would go each month to Whitehorse for a check-up as she was pregnant. The use of a pick-up was provided for necessary trips. Ches was a quiet man from Winnipeg with a good sense of humour.

We were told by a young couple from the Prairies of the dreadful cold winter of the year before—little did they realize we were seasoned

Yukoners and had been through many such winters, and without the benefits of oil heat and indoor plumbing! We found it delightful here in the morning to step out of bed onto warm floors, never mind the dust, it was warm! The oil heater in the living room kept us quite comfortable. Though the kitchen stove was wood-burning, it was no problem. We had ample dry wood and I was accustomed to such a stove. The soup pot could simmer on the back and the oven turned out many a pan of well-browned bread. The communal laundry room was adjacent to our building and there was always plenty of hot water. One thing I greatly missed was my sewing machine, for we had left it in Bear Creek. It was an old treadle machine of my mother's and had probably been transported over the Trail of Ninety-Eight. I used to make all the clothing for the girls and myself. Aside from missing my sewing machine, housekeeping was not difficult.

I was quite shocked, as any old Yukoner would be, to hear that one's groceries came out from Whitehorse, cash on delivery, from Taylor and Drurie's store. We had always had a charge account at Fred Caley's store in Dawson, which was the custom there. We had not thought of making a similar arrangement in Whitehorse, but perhaps it would not have been possible anyway. To us, this was a real demonstration of how the Alaska Highway had changed the North. People came and went as they had not done previously and perhaps the merchants had been left with unpaid bills, hence the change. [I have heard that those with debts in Dawson were sometimes prevented from leaving on the last boat by the RCMP unless their debts were paid.] It was not a nice feeling to be treated as strangers. I must say that our stay at Swift River was the one and only time I ever felt somewhat poor. Certainly it was the worst living accommodation we had ever had. Still, we were together as a family so it was worth accepting the situation and, as it happened, we were there for only one winter. First, we moved to Brooks Brook, Mile 830, then to Marsh Lake, Mile 883. In 1956, we moved to Whitehorse.

+ ◆ +

Joann—We were back north but Swift River, on the Yukon–BC border, was very different from Bear Creek and Dawson City which were some 400 miles north as the crow flies. Bobbie and I did not feel like we were back 'home'. Everyone else in Swift River was from places like Saskatchewan and Alberta. They were not from our Yukon.

Swift River had been a large camp during the construction of the highway and there were many buildings, one of which held a ping-pong table. Another building was used to show movies. It is still a maintenance camp, one of the few left since the highway was paved and the maintenance requirements changed. The houses are very different from our old places. When I last went through in 2003, the garage where my father worked was, much to my surprise, still standing. We had very few possessions when we went back north as all we took to my grandmother's house in Langley were two large trunks that had belonged to Ned and Kate, packed with the good silver, my mother's Mixmaster, and other small household goods. I think our Bear Creek house was rented and then sold furnished. Even if we still owned the house, to get our possessions would have meant a trip back to pack them, get them on a riverboat to Whitehorse, and then have them trucked down the highway. Fortunately there were enough army goods left around to furnish, if minimally, our 'apartment'.

Swift River stands out in my mind as a place where it rained every afternoon in the summer and the mosquitoes and black flies were fierce. In winter, we took sleds and toboggans and used the hill on the highway leading down to the camp as our play space. I made a sign for the top of the hill saying 'Children Playing', or something like that. We were quite safe as there was very little traffic, mostly trucks, and we could hear them coming. Once, we were out on the river, quite a small one, and one of us either fell through the shell ice or there was a hole. We explored a wonderful ice cave where the river had frozen, then the water level dropped, and a further layer of ice formed.

A novelty for Bobbie and me was going home for lunch, as we had always had to take a bus to school. Now our one-room school was just a minute away. One of our classmates was Mathew Thom, a Native whose parents were trappers. They camped and trapped at Swift River for the

Swift River School. *Back Row:* Unknown, Mr. McNiven, and Matthew Thom
Front Row: Glen and Dale Simpson, Bobbie and Joann Stevenson,
Carol Couch, Gay Simpson, and Leslie Couch

winter, living in their white-walled tent, so Mathew could go to school. Bobbie remembers visiting their camp that winter, but I must have been in hospital otherwise I'm sure I would remember it too.

I remember the hospital trips my mother mentioned only too well, especially the polio trip in an old American army ambulance, 185 miles over the rough road. There was a flight strip nearby but there was no plane available, or medical evacuations simply weren't thought of. I later heard another polio patient say she had a headache 'as big as a house'. An apt description. The appendix trips, or at least one of them, were in the back of Al Halladay's new car, a more comfortable ride even though I threw up all the way. Al, who worked at the CNT station, was very generous to provide this very ill and messy child a ride in his nice car. I think there was snow on the highway so the rides were not as rough, at least for the second trip.

Our new neighbours, the Campions, were to become such close friends that when we had a small family reunion in 1989, Ches and Helga, who happened to be in Vancouver at the time, came as part of our extended family. By then, they knew many of my aunts, uncles, and cousins.

When there was an opening for a grader operator in Brooks Brook where my father was foreman, the Campions moved there from Swift River. Fortunately, they lived in the unit connected to ours by a common porch and the frequent back-and-forth visits were not obvious to others in camp. Social relationships in very small communities have to be delicately handled, especially between a foreman and other workers.

Ches had a major role in building the Atlin Road in 1950 while they were at Brooks Brook. Later, they were at maintenance camps in Watson Lake and Beaver Creek, Mile 1202. In 1957, Ches became Superintendent of Highways for the Yukon. That was the beginning of a time of extensive road building in the Yukon and when Ches retired in 1980, all the current Yukon highways were in use. In 1970, the Alaska Highway ceased to be the responsibility of the Canadian army and was turned over to territorial and provincial governments. The BC section became an extension of BC Highway 97 and the Yukon section became part of the Yukon highway system. The Campion children, Brian, Ann, Greg, and Jillian, were all born in Whitehorse. Brian later became a well-known lawyer and pilot. His untimely death in 2002 was a shock to all of us.

The mountain climb my mother mentioned took place the summer after we moved to Brooks Brook. Bobbie and I were visiting the Campions at Swift River. The BC–Yukon border had recently been surveyed, leaving a wide clearcut which led above the treeline on Mt. Swift Horn. We were roaming around with the Couches and Yvonne and Paul Russell, whose father was cook at the CNT camp. Someone got the idea to climb the mountain which did not look very difficult as it looked like a smooth green expanse above the treeline. So off we went, not thinking to tell anyone where we were going. It was an easy climb and I remember a very pretty small round pond with a large boulder in it below the treeline. Farther up, above the treeline, there was a small patch of snow which never melted. We got to the peak, had a look around at all the wilderness and started back down. Unfortunately, Carol Couch fell and cut her knee quite badly on a sharp piece of the shale which covered the mountain at that level. This slowed us down but since we were in no hurry, we continued to enjoy ourselves. We also felt quite pleased with ourselves. Helga Campion, carrying Brian, was waiting in camp, very worried about what had happened to us, as were others. Carol's mother, Helen, was quite angry (and worried) as I recall, especially as Carol had cut her knee quite badly.

• ✦ •

Brooks Brook, where we lived from April 1948 to the fall of 1951, was on the shore of Teslin Lake, a very pretty spot. Brooks Brook no longer exists as a camp and the dip in the highway where it lay has been filled in, making it hard to find unless you know where it was. The housing was still old army buildings no bigger than the ones in Swift River and certainly just basic accommodation, but better finished on the inside. Hospital trips were shorter—only 85 miles rather than 185 miles. The first one was when I was running, fell, and dislocated my shoulder. The second time, I was putting on my coat and dislocated it. My father, not surprisingly, was getting tired of taking me to hospital and tried to fix it himself but didn't succeed. The third time, I was wrestling with Charlie Rear over a ball. I said, "I can't go home, my dad will kill me." So I wiggled my arm around until it went back in the socket.

Brooks Brook, with people we knew from other parts of the Yukon, seemed more like 'our' Yukon. Unlike Swift River where all the people were from Outside places, we had as schoolmates the Porsilds: Aksel, Ellen, and Johanna. Aksel and I had been at school together in Dawson City. Dick and Buddy Morris were known to us from those years too. They all lived at Johnson's Crossing, which was commonly called 'JC', six miles up the highway.

Elly and Bob Porsild had a lodge, or roadhouse, at JC which had been assembled from the Quonset huts left on the site. At that time, most of the lodges, inns, or roadhouses on the highway were started in the same way. Later, the family built a large roadhouse, mostly from salvaged lumber on the site. Ellen Porsild Davignon's book *The Cinnamon Mine*, written about that period, is a child's eye view of that time. The Porsilds were very hospitable and had at least one party and dance a year for their neighbours—who lived miles away. Bob served pickled greyling from the river and Elly played the piano.

The Hares, friends from Bear Creek, came to Brooks Brook when Dad needed a mechanic. They lived in the apartment the Campions had vacated when Ches went to Watson Lake as foreman. Because we were closer to Whitehorse, we sometimes had visitors from Dawson City and Bear Creek, who had traveled to Whitehorse by riverboat and came to stay. The Lelievres, Alice, Vivien, Arlene, and Judy came, as well as others. Rose Kelly, from Minto, whom Mum had known at Stewart Island, lived in the area. She made us a coffee table which is still in the family. The Morris kids would sleep at our house when there was a party at the recreation hall. The houses were very small and I wonder now how we all fit in, but Yukoners are hospitable and there was always the floor space.

One of the families at Brooks Brook were the Rears. Glen and Ella had a large family. Alex and Charlie were about our age. My mother met Mrs. Geddes, who her parents knew at Hootalinqua when Mrs. Geddes served as midwife to Ella Rear. Both Bobbie and I remember Ella as someone who radiated calm and warmth. Ella was a Profiet from Mayo. This was another connection to our past, as Mayo had been home to my aunt Dorothy who taught there, my uncles for a time, and was where my grandfather was buried.

There was a CNT repeater station at Brooks too and in the summer there might be some young men stationed there. This was of great interest to us girls when we got older. Also a source of great concern to our parents. Bobbie remembers that an American army convoy, on its way to Alaska for maneuvers, camped in the yard for the night and how our father refused to let us out of the house. He had to go to the garage and we were allowed to go with him so we got to see some of the soldiers, but that was it—no contact was allowed. Sometimes, convoys of American soldiers would go by on their way to Alaska and throw us candy bars if we were on the highway.

Teslin, Mile 804, was the site of an old Tlingit Native settlement. My father, who was interested in many things and meeting new people, often gave rides to the few hitchhikers on the highway. Most were Natives and he was especially interested in talking to them. One old man told Dad that when he was a small boy, men from the village took their furs over the mountains to the coast, and traded them for such things as copper pots. At that time, Alaska was still a Russian territory. Dad was also told that there used to be great potlatches at the end of Marsh Lake where the army camp is now situated. July 1st, Dominion Day (now called Canada Day), was a time of celebration in the village, probably because it was close to the summer equinox. There were games and a dance that night which we took part in. There had been a special dance early in the morning, a sundance I think, but it was closed to us Caucasians. My father had wanted to be there, but he respected Native traditions too much to push the issue.

There was a small Royal Canadian Air Force base at Teslin which, as I recall, was where the ballpark was. I kept score at the games which allowed me to watch Clifford Geddes, whom I found very attractive, without it being obvious. Bobbie remembers that there were strategically-placed oil drums with smudges (green wood and leaves) burning to give some relief from the mosquitoes and black flies. These were fierce, as they had been in Swift River. The only thing that made outdoor life at all possible at Brooks Brook was the annual spraying of a mixture of fuel oil and DDT which really made a difference. The spraying was done by a low-flying aircraft, probably from the RCAF base in Whitehorse. We were notified about the plane coming as everyone had to stay indoors until it was finished. One spring before the spraying, we had a contest inside the school: who could kill the most mosquitoes? The desks were old and had inkwells in which we put the bodies, which made body count easy. I recall my score was eighteen in maybe a one-week period.

We had such freedom all through our childhood, very different from what most children are allowed now. I'm sure the tourists must have wondered where we came from sometimes, when a group of us would suddenly emerge onto the highway after one of our rambles. Bobbie and I belonged to a group of other kids our age: the Rears, Georges, Karen Gebert, and Joyce Solodan. We spent hours roaming in the woods and on the lakeshore.

In spring, when the ice on the lake was breaking up, the 'ball diamond', really just a small clearing near the lake, sometimes flooded. We made rafts and had great fun on them. The water was quite deep and we did not tell any parents what we were doing.

A favourite summer spot was Jackson's Point where the Jacksons, a Native family, had a house, although they were seldom there. There was a beautiful little cove and a sandy beach. In winter, we would take some cans of beans, some bread, and maybe a few potatoes to roast and go off into the woods, build a fire, and have lunch.

The Brooks Brook one-room school was at the end of a long building that also housed the laundry area, recreation hall, and at the far end, the communal freezer. The first teacher we had was Alberta Cox who was a bit of a martinet and liked to enforce her edicts such as toothbrushing and clean fingernails, which she inspected daily. She also believed we should not have a snack before bed. Dale George would put his food in a toy truck and push it into his bedroom if Alberta was visiting. My parents simply ignored her rule and if she was visiting, we ate when and what we wanted before bed. I do remember some indignation on their part at the thought that we would be sent to school with dirty hands and our teeth not brushed. Alberta went on to teach in Dawson City. Our next teacher was Mary Gartside, who was very different and a very good artist. I have one of her paintings, *Yukon Roses*. She too went to Dawson to teach after leaving Brooks Brook and later taught in Whitehorse.

We had a movie in the recreation hall every week, the films moving up or down the highway from camp to camp. The films were prone to breakage and we rarely got through the whole movie without a pause to have the breaks spliced. There were dances in the hall, sometimes monthly although I remember they were cancelled for a time for reasons of 'bad behaviour' which we children were not privy to. I do remember some men with black eyes the next day. Still, we were allowed to go to the dances when they were on. This was a great boon to us girls as we got older and there were young men in camp.

My parents continued their hospitality with Dad often asking travellers in for coffee or a meal. This included a few salesmen of various products. One day he brought the Singer Sewing Machine salesman home for lunch—and bought Mum a Featherweight machine. She was so happy she got tearful.

Miss Hasell and Miss Sayle, the 'Brownies', were a pair of buxom ladies from England who drove their tiny grey van up and down the highway every summer conducting church services. I have since learned, through the internet, that the vans were designed under Miss Hasell's direction to fit a Ford chassis and that there were at one time some twenty operating in Western Canada where the ladies were called 'vanners'. Miss Hasell was responsible for the religious services and Miss Sayle was the driver and mechanic. We called them Brownies, a term I prefer, because they wore brown 'uniforms' much like a Girl Guide uniform. The van sign identified it as 'The Sunday School Mission Anglican church Yukon Mission'. It was a marvel to everyone how two such large ladies managed to live in that tiny van. Of course, they came for coffee too. One Sunday morning, Dad was still feeling in a party mood after the Saturday night dance. He was happily singing "Tennessee Waltz," his favourite tune, in the bedroom as the Brownies had coffee with us. All pretending nothing was amiss. The last time I saw the van, it was in the Whitehorse Transportation Museum awaiting restoration.

The highway was maintained by the Canadian army and surveying was still being done. Our house was where the surveyors came for showers, coffee, and maybe a meal when they came out of the bush. I was horse crazy and, as the surveyors used horses when necessary, I had a leg up, so to speak. The horses belonged to a big-game outfitter in the area and were used in the fall hunting season. They were left to forage for themselves in the winter and were hired by the surveyors in the summer. One summer, I was invited to go up the Canol (an abbreviation for 'Canadian Oil') Road with the survey crew. We went in trucks, with the horses being moved by the wrangler, Don Sheridan. Don drowned shortly after that while crossing the Ross River and Don Bassett, whose sister Willa was the cook, replaced him. Don and Willa were from the BC Peace River country. Another year, Bobbie and I saddled up and helped move the horses up the highway about eight miles. I think Lyle Westergard was the wrangler that time. We had lunch in the cook tent. The mosquitoes were so thick they kept getting in the food.

Dad could build or fix almost anything. At Brooks Brook, he built a small twelve or fourteen-foot boat. It cost 86 cents for the brass screws he needed. The plywood and paint, army grey, was scrounged from the camp. I don't remember if he built the boat with the plan to go from Brooks to Dawson City, but that is what happened. My parents took the boat from Brooks Brook to the end of Teslin Lake, down the Hootalinqua River (now the Teslin), and down the Yukon to Dawson, about five hundred miles. Marge's lessons in reading the water, learned from her father, would have been helpful on the rivers. The Five Fingers and Rink Rapids in the Yukon were well-known hazards to both small boats and the steamboats which were still running.

Bobbie and I were left at home. Some people at camp were sure Bobbie and I would soon be orphans. We were, however, well able to care for ourselves, having been brought up to be responsible and independent. This included being allowed to read whatever books came into the house. Our parents believed that if we didn't understand some parts that was fine, and if we did understand it was too late to worry about it. There were a lot of books available as the army had supplied the soldiers with paperbacks and, since we were all readers, we had a good collection. When

Curly waiting for Marjorie to take the picture and get in
the boat to go to Dawson City, 500 miles away

I was thirteen and in the hospital in Whitehorse to have my appendix out, I was happy to find a Zane Grey, an author I was already familiar with, in the small library—actually just a bookcase. The staff was shocked at my choice and, deeming it unsuitable, removed it and gave me a Cinderella castle to put together. That was my first experience of censorship. The second experience was *Kitty*, a risqué book for the period which my sister and I were not allowed to read. Of course, I went looking for it as soon as my parents left. I couldn't find it because Bobbie had beaten me to it and already had it under her mattress. I got to read it when she finished it. We may have been responsible and able to care for ourselves but we still took what advantage we could of our freedom from supervision.

Our parents had a good trip, although Mum got very sunburned and, as Dad was not the least concerned about comfort and there were no foam camping mats then, she did not sleep well on the robe that served as their bed. They left the boat in Dawson and, after visiting friends there and in Bear Creek, flew back to Whitehorse with the outboard motor they had borrowed for the trip. They brought some wonderful tomatoes from Evy Craig's greenhouse in Bear Creek.

My dad would not ask the men to do any job that he would not do himself. One of his responsibilities was the maintenance of the emergency flight strip at about Mile 843. He was afraid of heights and I remember the first (and only) time he climbed the tall tower when the emergency light needed to be changed. I think he was still pale when he got home. Another time, after going to the flight strip, he reported that a young American couple were opening a lodge across from the strip. They were Bert and Ellen Law who had three small children and called their place the Silver Dollar. Dad was concerned about how they would make a living as the lodge was slightly off the highway and I know he told others about the young couple and urged people to stop there to have a coffee, a meal, or to get gas. The summer before we went away to school, some of the young men in camp wanted to take us to the Silver Dollar for a party. Dad would not let us drive there with the men, but said he would drive us there and pick us up later. Bert and Ellen had a good collection of records so we had our party and dance in complete safety with Bert and Ellen chaperoning. Bobbie later worked for them one summer.

Marjorie, Bobbie, and Joann
in Brooks Brook, 1951, *photo by W.S. Hare*

Mum, having had to go away to school at age 12, did not want to have to send us away from home. Our one-room school, however, went only to grade eight. I took grade nine through correspondence lessons, and the next year Bobbie and I, aged 14 and 15, were sent to high school in Dawson Creek, BC (830 miles away), along with Dale and Alden George and Joyce Solodan. There was dormitory housing, mainly for farm kids of high-school age from that area. Bobbie and I were not unhappy to leave home and found our year in Dawson Creek quite a lot of fun as we were 'new girls in town' and had lots of attention from the boys. It was also the first time in our lives that we had lived in an actual town. The next year, we had to go to Whitehorse as the BC Peace River School District decided to stop accepting children from the Yukon.

✦ ✦ ✦

Our family moved to Marsh Lake, Mile 883, fall of 1951, but Marsh Lake had little impact on my life. Bobbie and I boarded in Whitehorse with the Russells, whom we knew from Swift River. Bobbie finished high school in 1954 as one of four graduates from the new elementary/high-school on Fourth Avenue. She went Outside to work after graduation.

The Yukon Territory was undergoing many changes in the 1950s and the population was steadily increasing, especially in Whitehorse. In the space of a few short years, Whitehorse went from being a small town that was primarily a transportation hub—the railway, the riverboats, the small airport—to a community with many new functions and factions. The Canadian army had a strong presence there until 1970, when the Canadian section of the Alaska Highway was turned over to the territorial government. The air force was still a factor in the 1950s. The capital of the territory moved from Dawson City to Whitehorse in 1953, with an influx of federal government employees, most from Dawson. Other people came from Outside to start businesses in the newly-opened territory. Whitehorse was still a small town, though the army base was at Camp Takhini at the top of Two Mile Hill. The Department of Transportation housing was across the highway from the top of the hill. The air force base was across from the airport. Except for some army barracks, the fire hall, mechanical work shops, and a few other installations, the town itself looked much the same as it had prior to the building of the highway.

The social fabric of the town did change however. The addition of the army and the air force, especially the officer class, and the federal government resulted in a complex hierarchy similar to that which existed in Dawson City, just with different players, except for the federal employees. As someone who felt she belonged simply by right of birth, and my youth, the social structure was not a factor in my life. It was for other people.

Whitehorse was not an attractive town. It had gravel streets, wooden sidewalks (where there were any), and it was drab. There was little that was green as there was no natural soil, only what was brought in, so there were few lawns or gardens. Looking back, it seems to me that people just gave up on the old town, which has limited space because of its geography, a rough horseshoe, bounded as it is on one side by the river and on the other side by the clay cliffs. Suburbs now surround the city, across the river and up the hill. Much of the old town can be seen from Fourth Avenue to the base of the hill. There, it has changed very little.

I dropped out of school and started working at seventeen. I was bored with the school, did not feel I was getting anywhere, and skipped school whenever I could get away with it. I also missed a lot of school for legitimate reasons. A bout of pneumonia put me in hospital for two weeks because penicillin had to be administered, by injection, every four hours. My roommate in the hospital was Martha Cameron. She was a Ballentine from Dawson, had married an RCMP member, and lived at Fort Selkirk for many years. It was her husband, Cam, who once asked my mother why she had never caught 'scarlet fever'—which meant falling for a Mountie. Martha's father was living at Marsh Lake with his son Jim at the time. We still have a library-type table made by the elder Ballentine. Cam and Martha's daughter Ione Christensen was the first woman appointee as Commissioner of the Yukon. Commissioner is analogous to Governor-General in the provinces.

A month later, my four upper front teeth abscessed, probably because they had been improperly filled by a former Whitehorse dentist. I had to spend two weeks in the hospital to bring the infection under control. The teeth were extracted by the army dentist, not a gentle man, but there was no other dentist in the Yukon. At 17 and without my front teeth, I was not going to go back to school. Fortunately, we knew a former dental mechanic, Carl Gebert, who still lived in Brooks Brook. He was able to make me a partial plate. I was still reluctant to go back to school, so my dad gave me a choice: go back to school or go to work. I chose work.

My first full-time job, in 1952, was at Taylor and Drury Motors (T&D), the General Motors dealership, as a stock clerk. T&D had a large department store in Whitehorse and, in the early days, other stores and trading posts. I had the privilege of knowing old Mr. Drury, a lovely man. I next worked for Dr. Nori Nishio, new in town, as a dental assistant. This was a tough job with long hours. Nori, a very good dentist, was the only dentist in the Yukon and we were booked up months ahead. I was the only employee and was responsible for chairside assistance, developing the x-rays, billing, booking appointments, and everything else. Later, the practice expanded and moved to a medical dental building on Main Street.

When I first started working, I shared a two-room log cabin with friends: Millie Speer, whom I knew from Swift River, and her sister-in-law, Eunice. Then I moved to a house where I had a room but had to eat all my meals in cafés. This was very expensive and even after I started getting breakfast and dinner where I roomed, I got a part-time job, working at Mac's Books.

For many of us in Whitehorse in the middle 1950s, life was not so different from the way my grandparents and parents had lived in earlier times. In the winter of 1953/54, my mother, Bobbie, and I lived in the same small log cabin I had been in when I first started working. In April, I was to marry Don 'Rob' Robertson, whom I met the year I was in high school in Dawson Creek. My mother wanted to spend time with Bobbie and me, as Bobbie was in her last year of high school and we hadn't lived at home, except in the summer, for some years. Mum worked at Mac's Books. Later, after my parents moved to Whitehorse, she worked at Hougen's Department Store. The cabin had an oil heater but I don't remember how we cooked. Of course, there was a biffy in the porch and the water man and the honey wagon provided regular service. Our oil was delivered by Lloyd Ryder who was part of the 'old' Yukon. The floors in the cabin were so cold that I wore my mukluks indoors.

Rob and I were married at the Old Log Church on April 10, 1954, the same church where my uncle Johnny claimed to have been the first baby baptized in 1903. Our reception was at the Harbottle house which was currently being rented by my cousin, Peggy Tubman. Ardrie Harbottle had been my mother's bridesmaid.

Rental housing was hard to find in Whitehorse and it helped to know someone who was moving, and we did. We moved into a former American army hut with walls two inches thick and minimal insulation. It had an oil heater in the living room, but it was so cold that our heating bill was the same as the rent. The dog's water dish froze in the kitchen. We had a wood-burning kitchen stove, so had to buy wood for it. We had a biffy in the porch. We were lucky to have a well in the cellar for water. The previous renters had been Wynn and Alan Kulan. Al was the discoverer of Anvil Mines at Ross River. I had known them for some time as they used to stay at the Silver Dollar Lodge, Mile 843, with Bert and Ellen Law, between Al's exploring forays into the bush. Bert helped grubstake Al. The Kulans could move out because they had recently made enough money to buy their first house, just down the street. They gave us $50 for a wedding present, a huge sum to us.

Later, we lived in a log house in Whitehorse that friends, the Bremmers, were vacating. Another couple we knew, the Morgans, moved into our old place which was marginally better than their place on Whiskey Flats. The log house had a cellar with a forty-five-gallon drum wood furnace and was warm and comfortable except in the kitchen, which was a very cold add-on. We had a propane kitchen stove, no running water, and of course still had a biffy. As I recall, it was in the cellar and had to be brought up on the days it was due to be emptied.

In the 1950s, there were four hockey teams: the Army, the Air Force, the Legion, and the Town. Games were played in an unheated hanger at the air force base or at the town rink, also unheated. The Legion and Town had to 'import' men to get enough players. The young men were hired to drive cab and did other work to earn a living. Several times a year, there were formal dances held in the ballroom at the Whitehorse Inn. One New Year's night after the dance, a group of us decided to go to the hot springs at Takhini. It was 40 degrees below zero. The pool at the time was shallow and made of logs, with about three steps down to it from the changeroom. The pool was nice and warm. We soon had frost on our eyebrows, eyelashes, and hair which was a funny sight. Getting out and up the stairs was done very quickly.

Local radio came to Whitehorse when CFWH (Canadian Forces Whitehorse) opened. I'm not sure of the year. It did not have a wide range. Prior to that, we depended on shortwave radio or, if conditions were optimal, which usually meant the Northern Lights were not active, we could get a few regular Outside stations. KING Seattle was one of them. Bobbie returned to Whitehorse to work in 1956 and became a volunteer at CFWH. She credits Doug Johns, who was in the air force and trained many of the volunteers, for keeping the totally volunteer station on air. CFWH was to become a CBC station and some of the volunteers went on to become long-time CBC announcers. Terry Delaney, who became very well-known, got interested in broadcasting when he was a staff car driver for the army. He took the volunteers to the station which was located across the highway from the airport, in the air force area. Les McLaughlin, who was still in his teens, had the shift after Bobbie. He too became a long-time CBC employee. Cal Waddington and Rod Faulkner were others. Rod was part of the transition team when the CBC took over the station.

13

LEAVING THE YUKON

Bobbie returned to Vancouver, 1958. I left the Yukon in 1956 when we moved to Dawson Creek, where my children were born. Later, when my older children were small, I completed high school by correspondence courses and then at the local high school, where I had been in grade ten fifteen years earlier. In 1968, we moved to Vancouver where I attended Simon Fraser University as a mature student, graduating with a BA in 1973.

My father was a confirmed northerner and, since my mother was born there, it was unlikely that he and my mother would have left until retirement, if then, but my father died suddenly of a heart attack. He was only fifty years old.

Whitehorse Star   November 1959

Funeral Rites For Curly Stevenson Here

Yukon residents were shocked by the sudden passing on November 11 of John Cochrane (Curly) Stevenson. A long time resident in the North, he was well-liked and respected in many parts of the Territory.

Born March 17, 1909 in Toronto, the late Mr. Stevenson came to the territory in 1932. For many years he worked at mining in the Bear Creek area. While in Dawson City, he married the former Marjorie Hoggan in 1934.

The family moved to Whitehorse in 1947. [My parents didn't move to Whitehorse until 1956]. From that year, Curly worked as an equipment operator for the Northwest Highway System at points along the Alaska Highway. He joined the Department of Transportation in September of last year and was working for them at the time of his death.

Funeral services for the late Mr. Stevenson were held in the Presbyterian church with the Rev. J.B. Milne officiating. Interment followed in the Masonic plot of Whitehorse cemetery, where a Masonic service was held at the graveside. Walden Funeral Home was in charge of final arrangements.

Besides his widow Marjorie Mr. Stevenson is survived by daughters Jo-Anne [sic] (Mrs. Donald Robertson of Dawson Creek), Roberta (Mrs. Roy Cairns of Vancouver), brothers Robert in Vancouver, Stanley in Langley, and James in Colombia, South America, and two grandchildren.

My father's death caused my mother to think about her future as a single person. She had married at 18, now, at 43, she was on her own for the first time.

Marjorie—The fall of 1959 was to bring great changes into my life, for it was on November 11th that Curly succumbed to a sudden heart attack. We had celebrated our 25th anniversary that summer and of course looked forward to many more. But fate decreed otherwise and it was not to be.

We were at that time living in a duplex on the hill overlooking Whitehorse. Curly had always wanted to work around an airport and I was thankful he had the opportunity, though only for a year. Now there was a future for me to face alone and decisions to be made regarding my life without him.

I stayed with friends for several months 'til the legal affairs were concluded (we had been living in government housing). I decided to leave the North which had been my home for all but two years of my life. Joann and Bobbie came home for their father's funeral, both pregnant with Joann bringing Donald who was almost three, and Susan who was one year old. Those children were a great comfort in my time of grief. Both of my daughters urged me to "get out and live your own life"—I was, after all, only 43. This seemed to be sound advice, so I gave notice at the store where I worked and made plans to move Outside to Vancouver BC. It was the end of February before my affairs were in order.

I was not offered what I thought was a fair offer for my 1956 Pontiac, so decided to drive it Outside. That I would make the trip by myself in winter was a surprise to my friends, but I was determined, so packed my clothes and small sewing machine, an axe, a tarp, and dry kindling that a friend's husband supplied. So there I was, all set to go on March 1, 1960. The weather was promising, no storms were forecast, at least not where I was. It was to be quite different farther down the road!

The Alaska Highway was not new to me of course, and I relived memories as I drove past Marsh Lake, Brooks Brook, and Swift River. Life in those camps was quite different from any other way of life. I had also been up and down the length of the highway over the years.

On I went—the highway was always in good condition with snow ploughed off and should be no problem if I drove with care, which I did. In summer, the road often had rough spots and was always extremely dusty, if not muddy. I reached Watson Lake (Mile 604) in late afternoon, pulled into the hotel, booked a room, and prepared to spend the night. At that time, there were few, if any, women travelling alone on that highway and I encountered a few curious stares and met no one familiar. It was too early to remain secluded in my room so, after dinner, I thought I would go into the lounge and have a hot drink, hoping that would help me to sleep. There were two men at a table we had known from highway days who spoke to me and invited me to join them. But I wasn't used to being single yet, so I declined.

Next morning at breakfast, there were several people discussing the road, weather, and related topics. One man spoke up and said, "Oh, I cruise along at 80." I said nothing as I kept a somewhat slower pace, mindful of Curly saying most accidents were caused by excess speed and not paying attention to signs. So I was not unduly surprised at sighting, about ten miles from Watson Lake, a station wagon deep in the ditch, only the rear end in sight. Nor was I startled to see it was the fellow who 'cruised' at 80! Of course I stopped and asked if there was anything I could do, thinking I might be able to send help from farther along, but someone else was doing that, so on I went.

Only once, near Muncho Lake, I encountered ice and went into a skid, but I pulled out of it. I stopped at one of the lodges at Muncho Lake for lunch and to fill my thermos. I always found it reassuring to have hot coffee on hand. The afternoon wore on and it began to get dark, but I had planned to get to Fort Nelson, Mile 300, and really had no choice but to go on as there was no place to stop for the night. It began to snow quite heavily and it was difficult to see the road, which meant I had to drive slowly. By eight o'clock it was a real blizzard, so it was a great relief to see the lights of Fort Nelson ahead. I found the hotel, parked, and went in, sure I would find a bed for the night. This turned out to be wishful thinking, for the proprietor looked me over and said, "Lady, there's not a bed to be had in town—the place is full of oil men! It's a wild town."

It had not occurred to me to phone ahead since that had never been necessary on the highway. Needless to say, my heart sank so I asked him if there wasn't somewhere I could spend the night. He gave me directions to a place where there might be some accommodations, so off I went. First I had to scrape the windshield, as the snow had frozen on it and I could not see out the windows. I followed his directions and came to an assortment of tarpaper shacks—not a very likely place. I had quite a lot of cash with me and, though I also had a rifle, I did not want to go around knocking on doors! I didn't know what to do, but then I thought I had better get used to it—this is what it is going to be like from now on, so I better smarten up and do SOMETHING!

So I drove around 'til I found the police station, went in, and asked if I could park in their yard. The young man on duty didn't seem too surprised to have a woman wandering in alone at that hour on such a stormy night. "Yes, you can park there—just don't leave your heater running." Perhaps he didn't want to have a frozen female in his yard in the morning, but he really didn't seem to care at all.

I stayed there bundled up in the car for awhile, getting colder by the minute, then decided to see if I could find someone a bit more caring. I drove to the hospital, parked there for awhile, which was no warmer of course. Then I went in and asked to use the phone. By this time I thought Fort Nelson was the most cold and unfriendly place—not what one expects to find in the North, especially in winter. Then I called the manager of the Department of Transportation, told him who I was and why I was asking for help. I remembered a couple who we knew on the highway had moved to the Department of Transportation area here and I knew I would be welcome. He came down immediately with a map of the housing, pointing out where my friends were.

So off I went into the storm, finally found the place only to be told by a neighbour that they had moved to Musqua Garrison about four miles south. More scraping of the windshield and windows. Found the place right beside the road, knocked on the first door, and asked the lady who opened it, "Please, do you know where Swede and Millie Stranlund live?" "Yes, the second house in the next row." Well that wasn't far, so praying they would be home, on I went.

I knocked on the door, it opened, and I was never so glad to see anyone in my life as I was to see that big Swede and his tiny wife. "Have you got a bed for me?" "Of course! Come on in!" That was real northern hospitality, and I was made most welcome. They even wanted me to stay for a few days but, having got this far, I was anxious to get to Dawson Creek where Joann lived. After my bad experience in Fort Nelson, and before I found the Stranlunds, I had even thought I might drive on down the highway because there were other people I knew farther along, as well as a lodge. It's a good thing I didn't because the next day I saw that the lodge was closed.

When I passed through Fort St. John, I knew I was almost at the end of that leg of my journey. Joann was home and I was glad that part of my trip was over, but also pleased to realize that I could really cope with whatever fate had in store for me.

EPILOGUE

Marjorie made many trips back to the Yukon after she moved Outside. She took Bobbie's daughters to Whitehorse once. My daughter Susan went to Whitehorse and stayed with the Campions in the 1970s. In the 1980s, she and her husband Donato, with baby Christina, drove to Whitehorse and spent a week on Atlin Lake with Brian and Carol Campion. Some of the pictures we took over the years, from 1978 to 2010, follow.

My most memorable trip back was in 1978. Ches Campion and a friend had a riverboat they built for their annual moose-hunting trips down the Yukon River. It was a large boat and comfortably held the eight of us, Ches and Helga, Marjorie, my daughter Hillary, Bobbie, me, my partner at the time Jim Mackenzie, and his son Parker, and all our gear and food. We put the boat in the water in Whitehorse and were off to Dawson City. It was a leisurely nine-day trip, with many stops and time to fish and explore as we went. Four slept aboard and four in tents.

The first day, a storm came up on Lake Laberge and Ches, knowing the lake very well, pulled to shore at a safe place where the beach was covered with water-smoothed and worn small rocks. The wind was so fierce that the boat was driven right ashore. It had to be partly unloaded and pulled off the beach and reloaded when the storm blew over.

My mother, knowing the river and family history on it, gave us commentaries about the family connections and the old days on the river. At Lower Laberge, she said, "This is where Lill and Jack Ward got married."

Our first camp was at Hootalinqua where Ned and Kate had lived for a time and Lill had lived for about eight years. There wasn't much left there. The S.S. *Evelyn* was slowly rotting in the bush where there had probably been a slough. We fished and had greyling for dinner.

The Yukon is a broad and often shallow river below Hootalinqua—not at all like it is at Whitehorse. The action of the paddlewheels used to help keep the channels open, but even then running aground on a sandbar was a fairly regular occurrence. We did hit one bar—Jim had to get out, and with a rope tied to the prow and around his waist, pull us off.

Where the Little Salmon joins the Yukon, there is an Indian gravesite with the graves having little houses surrounded by picket fences. These are 'spirit houses' built over a gravesite. Those that have not been vandalized hold small dishes. The origin of the houses probably dates back to a time, before shovels were brought to the Yukon, when bodies were left above ground and covered so as to prevent animals from disturbing them. My uncle Greg once told me that when he was trapping in the White River country, probably in the late 1920s, that he saw from a distance what looked like an Indian village. On closer inspection, it appeared to be a burial site with piles of wood covering the graves. It appeared to be an old site. There were no picket fences and little wooden houses.

Both the Rink and Five Fingers rapids used to be quite dangerous with many a small boat and some steamboats coming to grief while navigating them. Since the hydro dam was built above Whitehorse, the currents have changed and they are quite tame now—just keep to the right through Five Fingers!

We stayed at Stewart Island, of course. Yvonne Woodburn, who lived at Stewart when Marjorie was living there, was still there, married to Rudy Burian. Yvonne had what she called her 'museum' with various things she had found, including a vase that Mum remembered was Kate's. We went to Andy's slough but it was no longer the wonderful place we had heard about. Having seen other sloughs, I can somewhat imagine what it had looked like when my mother was a child. We saw Kate's grave and the headboard which had been kept painted by the Yukon Order of Pioneers.

The White River is so named because it is white with glacial silt and after it joins the Yukon, when the motor was not running, we could hear a *sssss* sound as the silt-filled water went by. We stopped at a silt island where the silt was so fine and soft, it felt as if we were running on clouds.

I had not been to Dawson since we left in 1945. It was so changed that it felt only vaguely familiar. No longer was there any sense of the importance of the river as there were no docks, no warehouses. Small boats were simply pulled ashore. A symbol of how the Yukon had changed. Rivers were now of little importance. Roads had replaced them.

The hospital was gone, burned down. The school was gone, burned down. The stores that remained were left to lean over because of the unstable permafrost and propped up or had been straightened and painted in 'historic' colours: Victorian dark blue, wine, purple. In reality, stores had been white or cream with blue, brown, green, or yellow trim. The town was full of tour buses and new hotels had been built to serve them, although some old hotels remained. The government administration building where I remembered visiting my uncle George's telegraph office was still there, but now it was the Dawson Museum. The churches, the Bank of Commerce, and some houses remained. The old slide where a piece of the hill had come down countless years ago was still as prominent as ever.

We were not able to get into the camp at Bear Creek as it had been fenced by Parks Canada. We tried to get there on the old 'skinny road' around the bluff, but it had disappeared. We were able to get to our house, which looked as if it had not been lived in for some time. We could find no sign of our log cabin on the hill. Possibly it had been moved again, or had rotted away, although that was unlikely as cabins can stand for many years before completely disappearing. The Craig and May cabins were not there either.

In 1981, my cousin Babs, Lill's daughter, who was born at Hootalinqua, and her friend Doreen Waller, whom she had known at Hootalinqua, flew to Whitehorse and travelled down the Yukon River to Dawson with four others in a tour boat operating at the time. They stopped at the Thirty Mile (where the grizzlies hung out) and Babs caught a greyling. They camped across the Yukon from Hootalinqua and, in the morning, went to the cabin where Babs was born. The cabin was being restored and despite the threat of a fine and time in jail, Babs carved her name and the fact she had been born there on the cabin. She also took an insulator from the telegraph line and a piece of the wallpaper she remembered Lill hanging. She explored the creek, and visited the three-hole outhouse where she had her brothers take her as she didn't like going there alone. A doll had just been found by the restoration team and Babs remembered that it was hers, probably given to her by Captain Dan MacKay, her Godfather.

They stopped at Selkirk where she retraced her childhood steps, walking through the schoolhouse with the desks her father had built. Their log house was being restored there too. A Native couple were the caretakers and she asked if they used a dog team to get their food from Pelly River and felt foolish when they said no, they had a snowmobile. She remembered the time the RCMP was scouring the river looking for a missing person. They came across an old prospector in a cabin sitting on a chair over a trapdoor. The police removed him and found the body of the missing man in the cellar. They brought the suspect to Selkirk where they both, the Mountie and the prisoner, stayed with the family until they could take him Outside.

At Stewart Island, where Babs had also lived, they visited the Burians and Yvonne's 'museum' where there was an ice chest of Ned's and some of Kate's china. In 1990, Babs and the other three women who had made the river trip in 1981 met in Whitehorse, rented a car, and drove to Skagway. Then they drove back to Whitehorse and up to Dawson City, stopping at every little spot along the way to talk to people, most of whom had lived there only a few years.

In 1989, Helga Campion and Marjorie drove Mum's van from Vancouver to Whitehorse. I flew up to Whitehorse to go to Dawson with my mother, and drive the van back to her home in White Rock, BC. We went to Mayo and the Pioneer Cemetery where Ned was buried. The cemetery was overgrown and unkempt, but we did find the grave. As at Stewart, the headboards had been kept painted, and Mum and my uncle Greg had found the grave on an earlier trip. My mother decided that she would have a permanent marker made which would read 'Yukon Pioneers' and give both of her parents' names because her mother's grave at Stewart Island had been washed into the river since we saw it in 1978. In 1989, Mayo was little more than a ghost town. The only person we saw was a woman about Mum's age. After the "what family are you" questions were asked and answered, we found she was May Van Bibber, Alex Van Bibber's older sister who, it turned out, had been taught by Dorothy, Mum's sister, in Mayo in the 1920s.

We were camped at Moose Creek when a pick-up pulled in and a very good-looking man got out. He, it turned out, was Jimmy Rear who was one of the 'little kids' in Brooks Brook when we lived there. The previous day, we had visited his mother, Ella, in Whitehorse. Jimmy said he had wondered sometimes what happened to the kids at Brooks, so we got caught up, talking about who was where now.

We stopped in Bear Creek and saw our house. It had been added on to and looked well-kept. The garage was still standing, but was leaning over. The small chicken house was still there and a large lawn surrounded the house. We later spoke to the man who was living there, who owned a store in Dawson, and gave him the history of the house. We visited Margie Fry and her aunt Miss Boutilier. On the way back to Whitehorse, we camped at North Fork, a beautiful place. The power plant has not been there for some time. The north fork of the Klondike was still a pretty blue river.

In 1986, during Expo '86, Brian and Carol Campion, and their children, Cara and Colin, came to Vancouver and stayed with me while they went to Expo. In August, Brian surprised me with a ticket to Whitehorse. We spent a week on Tagish Lake, along with Ches, in their cruiser, camping and fishing. Brian laughed at my fishing gear but I caught some nice lake trout which he filleted. It was a fun trip.

My daughters, Susan and Hillary, and I flew to Whitehorse in 1992. Brian and Carol and their children were on a flying holiday, so we were able to borrow Brian's camper. We camped at North Fork, visited Bear

After a storm on Lake Laberge, 1978

Hootalinqua, 1978

Marjorie and Greg at Sunnydale, 1983

Stevenson house, Bear Creek, 1989

Church at Snag, 1992

Marjorie by her parents' grave marker in Mayo, 1999

Johnny and Gladys Hoggan's cabin
on the island, Bear Creek, 2010

Dad's garage in Bear Creek, 2010

Tailing pile reflected in a dredge pond, Bear Creek, 2011

Creek where Susan was amused to find a picture of Bobbie and me and our parents in the museum! This was open for only a few years probably because it was decided that the Bear Creek camp was an environmental hazard site. The camp is still closed. We stayed one night in Dawson, visiting Diamond Tooth Gertie's where John MacDonald, an old friend a year older than me, joined us after winning at the slot machine on which Susan had just given up. John and I had great fun talking about our past and the connections between our families, a connection that was significant for John. On his first trucking job, driving for the army, about 1954, he stopped to fuel up at Marsh Lake, Mile 883 on the Alaska Highway. John had filled the truck with the wrong fuel—diesel instead of gas, or vice-versa. Dad told him not to worry and cleaned the fuel system for him. When John retired in 1999, he was Field Mechanic Superintendent for the Yukon.

The next day we went across the Yukon River and over the Sixty Mile, otherwise known as 'Top of the World' highway, overnighting at Chicken, Alaska. We stayed the next night with a friend of Hillary's who was the Canadian Customs Officer on the Yukon–Alaska border. There we met a friend of his who told us the story of a "cute couple" who were originally from Dawson City and were on a bus tour. They had been at the gay nineties event and one of the dance-hall girls went into the audience, sitting on some of the men's laps. One of the men she chose was the husband of the cute couple. The wife was very embarrassed by it all. It turned out he was talking about Evy and Clary Craig and I could just imagine the expression of horror and embarrassment on Evy's face! We went to Snag, where my uncle Johnny supervised the building of the airstrip in 1943. There is little left there.

In 1995, when she was seventy-nine, Marjorie made her last trip down the Yukon River, Whitehorse to Dawson City in a small boat. Then in 1997, my mother and I returned to Whitehorse and went on to Mayo. I drove up from Whitehorse and Mum flew up with Brian Campion. The town had changed: it was alive, busy, and very different from our previous visit. The cemetery had been completely cleaned up, so much so that I had trouble finding Ned's grave—in my mind, it was in a corner. It was in fact in about the middle with a Yukon Order of Pioneers (YOOP) painted headboard. The gravestone was in Mayo, but it was decided that it should be placed on a concrete base, so it would have to be done at another time. We went to Dawson, where we visited Yvonne Burian, whose house on Stewart Island had gone into the Yukon River that spring. After we returned to Whitehorse, I drove down to Teslin. On the way back to Whitehorse, I decided to go down the Canol Road for a few miles as I like the terrain and had been there once with the army surveyors. It was May and, as I was turning around to head back, the front of the car sank down to the axle in mud. It was a front-wheel drive, so there I was scooping mud out from under the wheels as best I could and putting rocks under the wheels in the hope that I could eventually get out. There was little traffic on the road, but I was not terribly worried as I knew that Brian would get in his plane and come looking for me if I didn't return when expected. Then a highway truck appeared, and much to my shock did not stop until I shouted and waved at it. This was another rude awakening as to how the Yukon had changed. Not stopping when someone was in obvious trouble—unheard of! I'm sure my father and Ches Campion were turning over in their Whitehorse graves. The men were not much help but at least they had a chain and after I told them how to attach it to the car, they, or their truck, pulled me out.

I stopped at the lodge at Johnson's Crossing on my way back to Whitehorse. It had recently been sold by Ellen Porsild Davignon. I was talking to a man who was working there for the summer. It turned out that he was the brother of Don Sheridan whom I knew when he was a wrangler on one of the survey crews at Brooks Brook. Don had drowned that long-ago summer while taking the horses across the Ross River.

+ ✦ +

My mother's last trip to the Yukon was to place the gravestone on her father Ned's grave in Mayo, a project that she first thought of in 1989. Although it took 10 years from idea to completion—it was of great importance to her.

Marjorie—In July 1999, Brian Campion phoned me and asked if I was coming up this summer. I said no, couldn't afford it. He answered that he was sending me a ticket, first-class, leaving on August 6th and returning August 22nd.

We were going to Mayo to place the headstone on my father's grave. Pat Cummings, an old friend from Brooks Brook, joined us just out of Mayo. We stopped at the cemetery by the flight strip where Brian measured Dad's headstone. I knelt down on Dad's grave and said, "Dad, your Pup is here again," and shed a few tears of course. Tomorrow, Brian will make a cement base for the headstone. Mayo looks different from when we were there two years ago, new houses, etc. Then we went to the hotel where Jo and I had drinks and dinner, stayed the night, then came out to Elsa two years ago.

I find it incredible that here we are at Elsa where my brothers George and Greg worked some 70 years ago. Brian has 'connections' so got us V.I.P. housing above the mine (now closed down). Marvelous view of the valley and the road to Keno. We had 'happy hour' snacks and drinks and went to bed about eleven, Pat sleeping in her camper with her dog Pearl.

We drove around the old mine sites and Keno Hill the next day. It was not like I expected it to be—though I don't know what I did expect. The mining museum was most interesting. There was a picture of Nora, her Dad, and her brother John—Nora Ross, later Hare, was born and raised in the area. We went up some high, high mountains, spectacular scenery.

Joann—With her 1999 trip to Mayo to honour her parents, Marjorie rounded out 100 years of the family's life in the Yukon. I found this verse, which she wrote, in her papers:

Requiem

When I am gone,
Do not place my ashes
In a vase on a shelf,
Behind a survivor's clothes,

That are stored for winter.
My winters and summers
Have all come and gone.
All that remains of me
Should float free
On the river of my childhood,
Perhaps to wash up on a sandbar
Where I once ran barefoot,
A happy Yukon child.
Or perhaps to lodge
In a pile of driftwood
And there, perchance join
The bones of my Mother,
Washed from her resting
By the rushing water
And surging ice cakes
Of a spring river break-up.

Marjorie died May 22, 2009. In July 2010, eleven family members took her ashes back to the Yukon. We put some of her ashes in the Yukon River near Sunnydale where she was born and some in the Stewart River. A plaque on my father's grave in Whitehorse in memory of our mother reads:

In Memory of Marjorie,
née Hoggan,
Born in Dawson, 1916.
Died Outside, 2009.

We put some of her ashes on the grave. Many of my generation return their parents' ashes to the Yukon where they were born, or where they lived for a long time and where their hearts remained.

HOGGAN GENEALOGY

In order to keep this chart simple and easy to read, Ned and Kate's children, grandchildren, and great-grandchildren born in the North are depicted in italicized type. There are now many descendants, most living in British Columbia and Washington State.

John Edward ('Ned') Hoggan m. Catherine ('Kate') Posetti

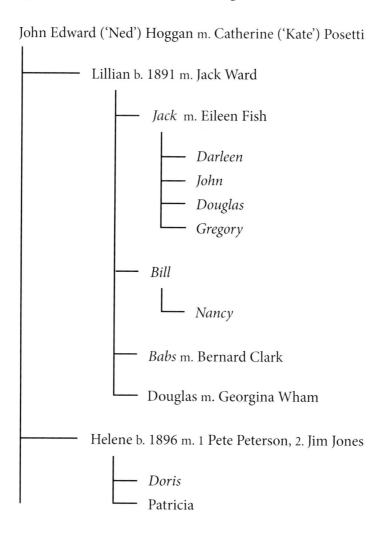

Lillian b. 1891 m. Jack Ward

Jack m. Eileen Fish

Darleen
John
Douglas
Gregory

Bill

Nancy

Babs m. Bernard Clark

Douglas m. Georgina Wham

Helene b. 1896 m. 1 Pete Peterson, 2. Jim Jones

Doris
Patricia

Dorothy b. 1900 m. H. Headon

    Paul

    Dorothy

John b. 1903 m. Gladys Gaundroue

    Peggy m. Gordon Tubman

        Maribeth

        Skipper

        Heather

        Dawn

    Frank m. Jean Gilbert

George b. 1906 m. Margaret Cruikshank

    Georgina

Florrie b. 1908 m. J. Crowe

Greg b. 1911 m. Romana Sorensen

Marjorie b. 1917 m. J. Stevenson

    Joann

    Roberta

GLOSSARY OF YUKON TERMS

Break-up   When the ice went out and the rivers were opened for navigation.

Cat trains   Goods were moved from Whitehorse to Mayo and Dawson by horses and sleighs in early days, and later the sleighs were pulled by Caterpillar tractors. There were heated Cat barns where the men and Cats spent the nights.

City   Many of the settlements were given the 'city' title with surveys done and streets laid out as was done at Stewart Island. This was in the hope that they would become true cities. Most were not big enough to be called a village. Most no longer exist.

Daylight   In Dawson City, there was close to 24 hours of sunlight in June and July. In winter, there were very few hours of light. In December, there were three or four hours of light and some twilight mid-day.

Dredge   Most of the gold mining around Dawson was done by very large floating dredges. They had a long boom with large 'buckets' attached which scooped up the gravel, sorted it, and discarded larger rocks into long tailing piles. A sorting system within the dredge then shook what was left and the gold, being heavy, fell through the screens and was collected. It was sent to the gold room in Bear Creek where it was further sorted, cleaned, and made into gold bricks. Dredges were very noisy.

Needle Ice	When the ice begins to thaw, it melts from the surface and drains downward which causes the ice to take the shape of tightly packed needles.
Outside	Any place below the 60th parallel.
Permafrost	In the more northernly area of the Yukon, the ground was frozen from only a few inches below the surface. If there was water—sloughs, rivers, creeks, there would be less permafrost, as was the case around Bear Creek where the ground had been worked from the early 1900s.
Points	Before the ground can be mined, the topsoil, or cover, must be removed and the permafrost thawed. This was done using long hollow pipes forcing water into the ground.
Roadhouses	There were winter stage routes with roadhouses every 25 miles or so where travellers could stay and horses changed if necessary.
Steamboats	These were paddlewheel boats that were on the rivers from break-up to freeze-up, usually from late May to mid-October.
Wood camps	The engines on the steamboats were powered by wood. Camps along the rivers supplied the boats. Wood was cut summer and winter.
Wintering over	In winter, steamboats and barges were moved via logways and winches to a place of safety away from the full force of the spring break-up and high water.

INDEX

JOANN ROBERTSON is the granddaughter of a Yukon pioneer and riverboat pilot. Born in Dawson City, she spent the first ten years of her childhood in Bear Creek, the centre of gold production from the early 1900s to 1966. Later, she lived along the Alaska Highway and in Whitehorse. She has a degree in Sociology from Simon Fraser University in Burnaby, BC, and resides in Vancouver.